T0354475

It's *Business,* It's *Personal*

From Setting a Vision to Delivering it
Through Organizational Excellence

SAAD AMANULLAH KHAN

WESTBOW
P R E S S®
A DIVISION OF THOMAS NELSON
& ZONDERVAN

WestBow Press books may be ordered through booksellers or by contacting:

WestBow Press
A Division of Thomas Nelson & Zondervan
1663 Liberty Drive
Bloomington, IN 47403
www.westbowpress.com
1 (866) 928-1240

ISBN: 978-1-5127-1274-2 (sc)
ISBN: 978-1-5127-1275-9 (hc)
ISBN: 978-1-5127-1273-5 (e)

Library of Congress Control Number: 2015915157

Print information available on the last page.

WestBow Press rev. date: 11/18/2015

Contents

Dedication

To my late father
Air Commodore (Retd.) M. Amanullah Khan (1931-2003)

Who I am today is all because of you;
my father, my mentor, my role model, my guide.
You taught me to base my life on strong values and to
never compromise them, despite consequences.

and

To my dear children, Sarah and Ameen,
I hope you find this book inspiring and that it helps
you to achieve your goals in life and become successful
human beings and positive contributors to our society.

Acknowledgement

Special thank you to my dear friend Berenike Ullmann, who despite a grueling schedule, found the time to proof-read my manuscript and give me detailed and quality feedback and suggestions. Also special thanks to all P&G managers who supported me and provided encouragement.

In particular I would like to thank and specially appreciate my dearest wife Ismaa whose support, backing and advice, not to mention multiple proof-readings and a grueling content edit (which we both survived), has made this book possible.

Also special thanks to IAL Saatchi & Saatchi team Imtisal Abbasi, Faisal Raza, Sarwat Azeem and Zeeshan Hussain, who helped me in multiple ways, getting it proof-read, helping with the artwork and for designing the amazing cover for my book.

Finally, I would like to thank Sofia Hameedullah of Alamut Consulting for her timely help in fixing my book's graphics.

Foreword

I welcome this initiative taken by Saad Amanullah Khan to provide guidance to entrepreneurs for sustainable enterprises. He is sharing his rich experience on soft skills, vision and strategy.

There is a special and intricate relationship between making business plans that help deliver your vision and having organizational excellence embedded in the organization's DNA which then catalyzes its delivery. Saad's analogy of using 'Masterpiece' in the field of art as an illustration to show the vital relationship between 'your plans' and 'organizational excellence' is fitting and apt.

The future of Pakistan lies in the hands of its youth and the army of entrepreneurs who will walk the talk by using their unique insights to create value. Saad touches all the critical areas that any entrepreneur or business owner needs to be effective. He has used his insights from working for nearly three decades in global organizations to write this book, which I believe, will inspire the reader and contribute to successful economic activity. Here we have a good example of a successful business leader helping create new leadership.

Syed Babar Ali
Pro-Chancellor Lahore University of Management Sciences (LUMS)

Endorsement

"It's Business, It's Personal is an appropriate reminder that building a successful and sustainable business depends on many interdependent factors, not just one latest 'flavor of the month' practice. Saad also reminds us of the vital importance of foundational values and principles guiding an organization. The book goes beyond the theory of business success but also provides very practical 'how to' guidance."

Werner Geissler,
Vice Chairman of Global Operations, Procter & Gamble (2007 – 2014)

"Mr. Saad brilliantly demonstrates the need for consumer centric purpose as a basis for enduring business success. Equally important is his conviction that good organizational practice is rooted in a strong value system. Equipped with 28 years of hard earned business experience at Procter & Gamble, the author goes beyond lofty principles, and provides time honored advice on how to turn a vision into a winning in-market execution."

Peter Corijn,
Vice President for the Regional Business Unit of Gillette, Procter & Gamble (2005 – 2013)

"I was proud to have worked with Saad and found him an effective leader, a most honest and dependable associate. A person I would like to work with in any assignment."

Fouad Kraytem,
President Middle East Africa and General Export (MEAGE),
Procter & Gamble (1988 – 2000)

"Saad has captured a treasure trove of insights from his long career at P&G. Insights that contributed to the outstanding success of the subsidiaries he was an important part of. It is almost criminal that non-P&Gers are offered the opportunity to read and learn from this book!"

Philippe Bovay,
Vice President/General Manager, Procter & Gamble Pakistan
(1996 – 2000)

"Excellent synopsis of the entire business exercise of vision setting and its associated processes. Saad captures in tremendous detail the entire process and goes into great depth on how to drive organizational excellence without which the vision would be powerless. The key to executing this process with excellence is what I call BOF i.e. "Brutal Obsession with Fundamentals."

Al Rajwani,
Vice President Arabian Peninsula and Pakistan (AP&P),
Procter & Gamble (2004 – 2015)

Preface

The idea to write this book came right after I appeared as a guest speaker at a seminar on 'Vision & Strategies' at the Marketing Association of Pakistan (MAP), Lahore Chapter. Post seminar I was bombarded with questions by a number of participants to recommend a book, which covered what I had basically just presented. Amazingly I could not think of any! Everything I have learned is from my professional as well as personal experience of nearly three decades of working for P&G and Gillette and from exploring business books and research articles.

There are many books written on vision and as well as on strategies, but I have not yet come across a single book which not only guides its reader to come up with a vision, teaches how to identify strategies but also gives insights on how to drive 'organizational excellence'. 'It's Business, It's Personal' covers the A to Z of 'direction setting' all the way through to 'organizational excellence', without which any vision or business plan is powerless.

This book is divided into two parts and each compliments the other. The following analogy explains the tightly woven relationship between the two parts of the book. For any painting to be classified as a masterpiece, two elements need to be present. The basic outline or sketch of the painting, this I call the 'direction setting' process. The color and shades in the painting is what I refer to as 'organizational excellence'. Without either, the painting will not look or feel the best and will definitely not win against competition and be considered a 'Masterpiece'.

The outline and sketch of the painting makes up Part I of this book and is all about 'direction setting'. Part II is focused on 'organizational excellence', which as I mentioned before make up the colors and shades in 'direction setting' and gives it life.

Direction Setting <u>without</u> Organizational Excellence

Direction Setting <u>with</u> Organizational Excellence

PART I is all about 'direction setting'. It starts with the concept of dreamers or visionaries, how they operate and impact the world we live in. The 'direction setting' process formally starts with having a mission or as we say reason to exist. This is followed up with a discussion on vision and goals, why are they important, how they are created and how can we make them impactful. Then comes the critical part of defining strategies and tactics; strategies are the action needed to deliver your vision—how does one go about creating strategy, why are they important, what is the difference between strategy and tactics, etc. All this discussion is intermingled with real life examples to help internalize the learning.

This is followed by the concept of measures and the importance of tracking your vision and strategies. A key aspect of deployment of your vision and strategies is examined in detail as well as watchouts and pitfalls that you may fall prey to as you work toward delivering your vision. Final discussions in this 'direction setting' Part I section are on executional excellence and celebrating success, two critical factors which are necessary to make sure quality and motivation of the teams remain intact throughout the process.

PART II is all about 'organizational excellence' which helps bring vision and strategies to life. In this section, we start by introducing organizational or corporate culture and the vital role it plays in driving behavior and attitudes, as well as in setting the 'smell of the place'. This discussion is followed by another important concept, which acts as the foundation of any culture, the notion of values; how to implement them, how to bring them to life, including examples from renowned companies as well as real life examples.

Other topics reviewed in this section include discussion on leadership, trust as well as some key insights from Jim Collins book *Good to Great* applied to individual performances and leadership. Particular chapters have been dedicated on how to raise the bar of your personal performance, striving to be the best and the role experiences, intuition and gut feelings play in making you effective. Final chapter of Part II is on embracing change where the theory and its pitfalls are discussed in detail including four case studies which helps to understand how different companies managed change and how that impacted their sustainability and operational excellence.

By incorporating both 'direction setting' and 'organizational excellence' you create a masterpiece. Together they create a combination that is lethal and acts as a formidable weapon in today's highly competitive business environment. Nothing substantial can ever be delivered if either one of them is missing.

PART I

POWER OF VISION AND STRATEGIES TO HELP TURNAROUND BUSINESSES

Introduction: Part I

Vision and Strategies

I approached the writing of this book with a view to make it as simple and business friendly as possible. I have explained each and every aspect in detail, from conceiving a vision and setting goals, to executing strategies, and finally to tracking the results. On the concept of 'direction setting' I have tried to educate, guide and explain various concepts related to vision and strategies in detail and complemented them with practical real-life examples from the business context.

I have been personally involved in the vision setting and strategy deployment processes in globally renowned companies such as Procter & Gamble and Gillette, and this gives me the knowledge and experience to explain it to you in such elaborate detail. This handbook includes specific examples on how to address local issues and innuendos in the business environment of Pakistan, a volatile market by any standard, but the learning imparted is applicable anywhere in the world.

It is interesting to note that for the last seventeen years I have been invited as a guest speaker at one of the top business schools in Pakistan, Institute of Business administration (IBA), in their final year MBA Capstone course of Corporate Strategy and BBA

Capstone course of Management Policy, to expose the students to the practical side of the theory that is being taught. Topics I cover include the effect of corporate culture, how 'direction setting' theory is applied, value-based/value drivers, business ethics, corporate social responsibility, real life examples on corporate vision setting, identifying strategies, converting action step into work plans, implementing the right culture, driving value-driven leadership behavior and finally celebrating success, are all included in my presentation. Also included is a section on how one can help drive 'organizational excellence', a key ingredient in delivering on the vision. I call this session "What makes P&G Tick?"

I hope you will find this book beneficial in helping you convert your dreams into reality and making a marked difference in how your business and personal lives progress.

Saad Amanullah Khan
June 22nd, 2012

Chapter 1 – Dreamers

"Nothing happens unless first a dream."
~ Carl Sandburg (1878–1967),
Writer and Editor

There have been many dreamers or what we call visionaries during our lifetime, and many before our time. These people had the ability to see opportunities and ideas that were not there— things that to a common person were utterly impossible. They made the impossible possible! To me, these dreamers are an inspiration for what can be achieved or what is possible if we apply our minds to a goal. These dreamers were nothing more than normal, everyday people, but the difference was that they had a passion and an obsession to change things for the better. Jonathan Swift (1667–1745) very aptly elucidated this feeling in his quote, "Vision is the art of seeing things invisible."

To help you understand the concept of dreamers, let me share with you the stories of a few famous dreamers who have inspired and changed the world forever. To fully realize the significance of these dreamers' achievements, try to transport yourself to their time and era and then imagine the boldness of their vision and the monumental challenge that lay ahead.

"Never doubt that a small group of thoughtful,
committed citizens can change the world.

Indeed, it's the only thing that ever has."
~ Margaret Mead (1901–1978),
American Cultural Anthropologist

1 A. Martin Luther King Jr.

Martin Luther King Jr. was born on January 15, 1929, in Atlanta, Georgia. He was a clergyman, an activist, and a prominent leader of the African-American fight to secure civil rights. Even today he is referred to as a human-rights icon. King took on the cause of civil rights early in his career, and he is well known for delivering the "I Have a Dream" speech in 1963. In this speech, he shared his vision of what he saw as the culmination of the civil rights movement and established himself as one of the greatest orators in US history.[1]

To me, King's dream was delivered on January 20, 2009, when Barack Hussein Obama II was sworn in as the forty-fourth president of the United States. Recall that when King made his historic speech on August 28, 1963, Barack Obama was only two years and twenty-four days old, and it took forty-five years for Martin Luther King's dream to be realized. Sitting today, imagine 1963 in your mind, especially in the South; there was open discrimination, and black people could not sit in the same bus or go to the same school as white people. In fact, they could not even drink from the same water fountain. Who would have thought that one-day a black person would hold the most prestigious job in the country! What King achieved as a visionary was to inspire multiple generations to practically *see* a just and fair future for themselves and their children. In his famous speech, King painted the picture in such minute detail that it inspired and started the most ambitious civil rights movement in the history of the United States of America.

"Change your thoughts and you change the world."
~ Harold R. McAlindon,
Management Speaker and Writer

What Did the Dreamer Do?

First, King looked at the predicament blacks were stuck in; they faced bigotry, lack of civil rights, inequality, and blatant discrimination. In this existing paradigm he envisioned a fair future for them. He realized that nothing was going to change without a struggle and a concentrated effort on a massive scale.

Using this insight and his knowledge as a clergyman, he went on to paint a picture for his fellow activists, friends, and for the public in general of the true equality of humans in front of God. First he helped the people, both black and white, to see what it meant to have all people treated equally. Secondly, King was a role model for his beliefs and he fought passionately for them—in fact, he was assassinated for these very beliefs on April 4, 1968.

King started on this mission at a very early age. He led the Montgomery Bus Boycott movement in 1955 and was arrested; the situation got so tense that white radicals bombed his house. He did not give up until the United States District Court ruled to end racial segregation on all Montgomery public buses on February 1, 1956. King later founded the Southern Christian Leadership Conference in 1957, serving as its first president. Again, he led from the front, leading his people in the March on Washington Movement in 1963, where he made his "I Have a Dream" speech and changed the entire face of the civil rights movement forever.

> **Vital Tip 1:** Dreamers are not always able to deliver their vision. Though the dreamers start the process of envisioning and direction setting, in many of the cases depending upon the complexity or challenges involved, they may not see the culmination of their dreams during their lifetime. But they do set the ball rolling, create inspired followers, provide guidance, set examples, and personally see their hard work progress in the right direction.

"The world needs dreamers and the world needs doers.
But above all, the world needs dreamers who do."
~ Sarah Ban Breathnach (b. 1962),
Inspirational Writer and Author of *Simple Abundance*

1 B. John F. Kennedy

John Fitzgerald "Jack" Kennedy was born on May 29, 1917, in Brookline, Massachusetts. Jack was the second son in a prominent Boston political family, and he was often referred to by his initials JFK. He went on to become the thirty-fifth president of the United States of America, the first and only Catholic president, and also the only US president to have won the Pulitzer Prize. He served from 1961 until his assassination in 1963.

Of the many incidents during his presidency, which included the early events of the Vietnam War, the Cuban Missile Crisis, the Bay of Pigs Invasion, the building of the Berlin Wall, the African American Civil Rights Movement led by Martin Luther King Jr., the one I would like to share with you is the Space Race. JFK vividly saw the future of the Space Race and shared it openly and with firm deadlines with the citizens of his country.

The USSR had taken the lead back-to-back on two occasions, and this had left the United States way behind in its wake. On October 4, 1957, the USSR launched the first manmade satellite into space, *Sputnik I*, which orbited the earth for the first time. A little over three years later, on April 12, 1961, a Soviet cosmonaut, Yuri Gagarin, became the first human to go into space and the first human to orbit the Earth. These two events hit the United States like a ton of bricks, as the Soviet Union clearly proved that they were years ahead in space technology.

Kennedy shared a dream with his nation, in which he announced the goal of landing a man on the moon. In a joint session of congress on May 25, 1961, he stated,[2]

> "First, I believe that this nation should commit itself to achieving the goal, before this decade is out, of landing a man on the moon and returning him back safely to the Earth. No single space project in this period will be more impressive to mankind or more important for the long-range exploration of space; and none will be so difficult or expensive to accomplish. We propose to accelerate the development of the appropriate lunar spacecraft. We propose to develop alternate liquid and solid fuel boosters, much larger than any now being developed, until certain, which is superior. We propose additional funds for engine development and for unmanned explorations—explorations which are particularly important for one purpose which this nation will never overlook: the survival of the man who first makes this daring flight. But in a very real sense, it will not be one man going to the moon—if we make this judgment affirmatively; it will be an entire nation. For all of us must work to put him there."

Kennedy stated his dream in no uncertain terms on multiple occasions. In a speech at Rice University on September 12, 1962, he again reiterated: "... and no nation which expects to be the leader of other nations can expect to stay behind in this race for space." ... "We choose to go to the moon in this decade and do the other things, not because they are easy, but because they are hard...".[3] The Apollo Program cost around US \$20 billion at that time; the equivalent of \$100 billion in today's money.[4]

Kennedy's vision guided NASA's human space-flight program from the beginning. Mercury, Gemini, and Apollo missions were designed with this objective in mind. On July 20, 1969, almost six years after JFK's death, Project Apollo's goal was achieved when astronaut Neil Armstrong, commander of Apollo 11, became the first human being to step on the moon.

What Did the Dreamer Do?

JFK painted the picture with clear milestones and expectations. He also helped drive the strategy, i.e., he went to Congress and broke down the funding barrier. In fact, the bill was so astronomical that initially JFK urged cooperation between the Soviet Union and America to help share the cost. JFK specifically recommended that Apollo be switched to "a joint expedition to the moon", Khrushchev decline.[5] JFK continued to lead from the front to break down barriers and to give a vision to the scientific community as well as set milestones to plan their strategy. Execution was impeccable, as the dream was realized just six months before the decade was over—as per JFK's dream. But sadly, he was not there to see it come true.

"All the wonders you seek are within yourself."
~ Sir Thomas Browne (1605–1682),
Physician and Essayist

1 C. Allama Iqbal

Closer to my home, Pakistan, Allama Iqbal was quite a visionary himself. Sir Muhammad Iqbal, widely known as Allama Iqbal was born on November 9, 1877, in Sialkot, India (now Pakistan). Iqbal was a lawyer by profession, and he was also an Urdu and Persian poet, a philosopher, and a politician.

It was Iqbal's vision of an independent Muslim state in India that inspired Quaid-e-Azam Muhammad Ali Jinnah to work for the creation of Pakistan. Iqbal was a prominent leader of the All India Muslim League and was the first politician to articulate what would later be known as the Two-Nation Theory, that Muslims are a distinct nation and thus deserve political independence from other religions and communities of India.

Iqbal encouraged the creation of a separate Muslim nation in his presidential address to the All-India Muslim League in 1930,[6] "I would like to see the Punjab, North-West Frontier Provinces, Sind and Baluchistan amalgamated into a single State. Self-government within the British Empire or without the British Empire, the formation of the consolidated North-West Indian Muslim State appears to be the final destiny of the Muslims, at least of the North-West India."

Although it was Iqbal who came up with the vision of Pakistan, he was well aware that he could not deliver this vision without outside help. Iqbal realized that he needed a strong committed leader to deliver this dream, for which he chose Muhammad Ali Jinnah. Iqbal was extremely impressed with Jinnah's strong abilities and track record as a lawyer and his unwavering and incorruptible character. Iqbal firmly believed that Jinnah was the only leader capable of drawing Indian Muslims to the Muslim League and maintaining party unity before the British and the Congress Party.

He went on to build a strong, personal correspondence with Jinnah, and was instrumental in Jinnah's return to India from his self-imposed exile in London to take charge of the Muslim League. He had found a genuine leader in Quaid-e-Azam Muhammad Ali Jinnah who was destined to lead the Indian branch of the Muslims to their goal of freedom. Iqbal wrote to him frequently to make sure he understood his vision and that it was close to Jinnah's own internal purpose. Allama Iqbal stated,[7] "I know you are a busy man but I do hope you won't mind my writing to you often, as you are the only Muslim in India today to whom the community has a right to look up for safe guidance through the storm which is coming to North-West India and, perhaps, to the whole of India."

"Do not follow where the path may lead.
Go instead where there is no path and leave a trail."
~ Harold R. McAlindon,
Management Speaker and Writer

Iqbal worked closely with Muhammad Ali Jinnah and guided his thought process to realize that without a separate formal state for Muslims, there was no future for them in India. Just ten months before his death, Allama Iqbal on June 21, 1937, again elucidated to Jinnah in a letter, his vision of a separate Muslim state,[8] "A separate federation of Muslim Provinces, reformed on the lines I have suggested above, is the only course by which we can secure a peaceful India and save Muslims from the domination of Non-Muslims. Why should not the Muslims of North-West India and Bengal be considered as nations entitled to self-determination just as other nations in India and outside India are."

Sixteen years and ten months later, Quaid-e-Azam was to deliver this vision in an incredible, focused and challenging fight for independence against both the Hindu majority and the British rulers, creating the nation of Pakistan.

"Dreams in life may seem impossible. They are not.
Impossible dreams are achieved one goal at a time."
~ Herman Cain (b. 1945),
Chairman of Godfather's Pizza

What did the Dreamer do?

Imagine the time when Allama Iqbal envisioned a separate Muslim state, India had been a single and united country with a fusion of Hindu's and Muslim's for centuries. Un-awed by the immense majority of Hindu's or the power held by the British, Iqbal utilized his vast knowledge of law, philosophy, politics, history, religion and economics to develop a strategy to safeguard the interests of the Indian Muslims in post-British India. Iqbal then painted the picture in minute detail, defining the borders of the new nation, the concept of self-government, etc.

To deliver his dream he identified a leader, Jinnah, and worked very closely with him, first to convince him of the rationality of his dream and then to inspire him to take this leadership and pursue the dream. Speaking about the political future of Muslims in India, Iqbal said,[9] "There is only one way out. Muslims should strengthen Jinnah's hands. They should join the Muslim League. Indian question, as is now being solved, can be countered by our united front against both the Hindus and the English. Without it, our demands are not going to be accepted." and "The united front can be formed under the leadership of the Muslim League. And the Muslim League can succeed only on account of Jinnah. Now none but Jinnah is capable of leading the Muslims."

1 D. Unique Visionary

There is another unique class of dreamers who do not fit any of the types stated earlier but this narrative would not be complete without their inclusion. These are the dreamers who came before their time. They dreamt the future, but the knowledge base, the technology and the level of advancement at that time was too primitive for their ideas to take shape. But their dreams were not ludicrous or absurd; these ideas would come to life as and when human civilization was ready. I am talking about one such visionary who is no other then the legendary Leonardo da Vinci.

"To Dream is to see beyond the horizon and to know that
we are capable of anything our hearts desire."
~ Anonymous

Leonardo da Vinci: In my eyes one of the most famous dreamer or visionary is Leonardo da Vinci. He was born on April 15, 1452, in Vinci, Italy and died at an age of sixty-seven. During his life he unleashed his genius by envisioning things that would not be invented for another 500 years and leaving a trail of inventions, drawings, paintings and articles which will continue to mesmerize intellectuals for eternity.

Leonardo was a scientist, inventor, mathematician, painter, sculptor, anatomist, botanist, architect, musician, engineer and a writer. A name used for such persons is polymath: A person whose expertise fills a significant number of subject areas. Leonardo is known for his unquenchable curiosity, which is only equaled by his power of invention. He is clearly rated as one of the greatest painters of all times and most definitely the most talented and gifted person who ever lived. Two of his paintings *Mona Lisa* and *The Last Supper* are world renowned and two of the most reproduced paintings in the world.

Leonardo is admired for his technological ingenuity. He conceptualized a helicopter[10], a parachute (flying machines had not been invented yet), an armored tank, a calculator, the double hull for ship safety and he also outlined a rudimentary theory of plate tectonics. Relatively few of his designs were constructed or were even feasible during his lifetime, but some of his smaller inventions, such as an automated bobbin winder and a machine for testing the tensile strength of wire, entered the world of manufacturing unheralded. As a scientist, he greatly advanced the state of knowledge in the fields of anatomy, civil engineering, optics, and hydrodynamics.

A person, who can see beyond his time whether it is a concept, a machine or even a theory, is known as a dreamer or a visionary. The dream could be about a business idea or about changing the existing reality; people like Steve Jobs, Mustafa Kemal Atatürk, and Syed Babar Ali are famous visionaries. Another aspect of a dreamer is that he must be able to paint the picture of his dream in order to help visualize and enroll the people around him. The dreamer has to show the way and help lay down the strategy for delivering the vision.

"It's never too late to be who you might have been."
~ Mary Anne Evans (1819–1880),
English Novelist (Known by the pen name George Eliot)

1 E. How to Make Dreams Come True

To bring a vision to life, the following sequence is extremely important:

✓ First there has to be a *dreamer*.
✓ The dreamer sets the *vision* and the ultimate *goal* or goals.
✓ The dreamer literally *paints the picture* of the future and enrolls his or her followers.
✓ The dreamer *sows the seeds* of his/her vision.
✓ The dreamer is also instrumental in the initial thinking and the *strategy* development needed for the delivery for the *vision*.
✓ Finally, they start the process by inspiring people, providing guidance and kick-starting the delivery.

To me a vision or a dream can be stated in two ways, i.e. in words and in numbers. Words are used to explain the concept behind the vision or to help 'paint the picture of the future'. For example a company wants to enter the Pakistan market and become the leading manufacturer and distributor of fruit juices. The vision would be something like "We want to be the largest fresh fruit juice manufacturer and distributor in Pakistan."

Having said this, the reality is that you are starting from naught, a new entrant and there are many existing fresh fruit juice companies in Pakistan. Based on which strategy you follow, i.e. what type of juices you introduce, do you do third party or have your own fruit farms, your packaging format, distribution options and channels, your pricing strategy, promotion tactics, etc. all of it will decide how quickly you will gain volume and share in the market.

Goals are all about numbers. Numbers will play a critical role when it comes to milestones and in tracking progress versus the overall vision. To agree on milestones for your team, you will have to carry out a detailed business modeling exercise, taking into account the competition and their reaction, consumer preferences, government policies, economic risk, cost of doing business, inflation, etc., and come up with a model which will predict how fast you will gain market leadership.

For simplicity's sake let's say you get market leadership nine years from the date of your launch as you have formidable competition. Hence the target year to achieve your vision will be year nine. However, there are a lot of stages in the middle, which you will have to lock-in as milestones and these will help you to track progress towards your vision. To me numbers are a critical part of setting your vision; they should be data based and deep rooted on solid market-tested assumptions.

"Any company that cannot imagine the
future won't be around to enjoy it."
~ Gary Hamel (b. 1954),
American Management Expert and Founder of Strategos

Chapter 2 – Mission Statement

2 A. What is a Mission Statement?

A mission statement is a short concisely written statement defining the purpose of a company or an organization. It is an essential part of direction setting and is literally the foundation on which the company will be built. It helps in guiding the organization, providing an overall direction, spelling out larger-than-life goals and guiding decision-making at all levels of management. It is critical that employees must believe in the mission for it to work. Do note that some companies, e.g. P&G, (Procter & Gamble), refer to the mission statement as the Statement of Purpose. For a mission statement to be effective it should ideally contain the following:

1. Overall purpose of the company's existence.
2. Organization's primary stakeholders, customers and the community they function in.
3. Responsibility of the management towards the stakeholders.
4. Socially meaningful objectives with measurable criteria.
5. Product and services offered by the organization.

"Great minds have purposes, others have wishes."
~ Washington Irving (1783–1859),
American Author, Essayist, Biographer and Historian

> **Vital Tip 2**: It is important that when preparing the mission statement one must do the following three steps:
> 1. Get full involvement of all employees in defining it.
> 2. It should be simple, concise and made up of a few select sentences.
> 3. It should be made public and broadly circulated.

Let me share with you some original one-liner mission statements of some globally renowned companies.

P&G - Improve the lives of the world's consumers.[11]
Gillette - The Best a Man can Get.[12]
3M - To solve unsolved problems innovatively.[13]
Walt Disney – We create happiness.[13]
Merck – To preserve and improve human life.[13]
Mary Kay Cosmetics - To give unlimited opportunity to women.[13]

These one-line statements are each supported by values and in some cases a set of principles that establishes the performance standards and drives organizational decision-making. We will talk more about values later in this handbook.

> "It is not enough to make progress; we must
> make it in the right direction.
> If we are facing in the right direction, all
> we have to do is to keep walking."
> ~ Buddhist Proverb

2 B. Key Attributes of a Mission Statement

The true intent of a mission statement is that it should be the *first* consideration of any employee when he is evaluating a business decision (strategic or any other kind). For example in the case of P&G, an employee while launching a new product, planning a promotion, or designing an advertisement campaign, in fact in everything that he or she does, must always keep in mind the mission statement, i.e. whether "their action will improve the lives of the world's consumers?" If not, then the intended action is not in line with the company's mission or purpose and that activity should not be pursued. Mission statements are extensively used in strategic planning and in deciding the *future direction* of a company.

If decisions are made contrary to a company's mission statement then there is a high probability that the company will not be able to deliver their goals, as company resources will be invested in a non-aligned direction. Mission statements bring focus into everything we do.

Vital Tip 3: If an organization decides to define its vision statement before the mission statement, then one must ask the following questions: What is the purpose behind the vision? Why does the vision exist? The purpose of a company is in fact your mission statement. Ideally the mission statement should be aligned and agreed upon before defining your vision.

Let's take another example to further absorb the concept of a mission statement.

Google – To organize the world's information and make it universally accessible and useful.[14]

The founders of Google, Larry Page and Sergey Brin, developed a revolutionary new algorithm to search information online, interestingly it had taken birth earlier in a Stanford University dorm-room. This algorithm was significantly faster than anything on the web at that point in time and returned relevant results in a fraction of a second. Using this state-of-the-art algorithm, Google quickly became recognized as the worlds' largest and most effective search engine. Hence the mission of Google is in line with their core competency and their technical know-how is best in class. The World Most Valuable Brands as per Forbes for 2015, Google was ranked at number three in value; others being Apple at number one and Microsoft at number two.

An interesting factoid for your mental neurons ☺: What's a Google? "Googol" is the mathematical term for a 1 followed by 100 zeros.[15]

> "Life without a mission is a tremendous omission."
> ~ Anonymous

2 C. How a Mission Statement Evolves over Time?

Many believe that mission statements should remain intact over time while being grand in scale, socially meaningful and measurable. However in certain unique circumstances, due to major shifts in demographics or advancement in technology, they may have to change to continue to be meaningful. Let me share with you some classic examples of how mission statements, which were truly grand in scale in history, evolved over time.

Ford Motor Company
   ✓ In early 1900s – Ford will democratize the automobile.[16]
   ✓ Today – We are a global family with a proud heritage passionately committed to providing personal mobility for people around the world.[17]

Sony Corporation
   ✓ In early 1950s – Become the company most known for changing the worldwide poor-quality image of Japanese products.[16]
   ✓ Today – To be a company that inspires and fulfills your curiosity.[18]

Boeing

- ✓ In 1950s – Become the dominant player in commercial aircraft and bring the world into the jet age.[16]
- ✓ Today – People working together as one global company for aerospace leadership.[19]

Walmart

- ✓ In 1990s – Become a $125 billion company by the year 2000.[16]
- ✓ Today – Saving people money so they can live better.[20]

Do note how a mission statement changes over time. Usually it should remain the same for decades, which in most cases it does. But one must accept the eternal secret of survival, which is to embrace change rather than having change forced on us. Hence we as a company and as individuals must always remain in touch with our changing environment. We must truly understand our customers, our market dynamics and define our mission, vision and strategies accordingly. We must also make sure that our mission is thriving, relevant, and must touch everyone's passion at a deep and emotional level.

Let us review some of these examples in more detail where companies changed their mission statements as a result of a major advancement in technology or a paradigm shift in market dynamics or consumer behavior.

Ford's mission has changed from the early 1900s when the automobile was a new phenomenon and the single most important objective was to 'democratize' the automobile, i.e. to make it common and available to everyone. Now they have moved on to a much higher purpose which is a great deal closer to what they do best which is to make the ride for their customers comfortable and enjoyable. As per their current mission statement they are focusing on two aspects, i.e. (a) targeting customers globally and, (b) providing personal mobility to people with a passion.

"I do not believe you can do today's job with yesterday's methods and be in business tomorrow."
~ Nelson Jackson (1872–1955),
First person to drive across USA in an automobile

Sony is a classic example of how the mission changed over time. In the 50s Japanese products were just reaching the global markets and had a serious stigma associated with them of being poor quality cheap imitations. Sony's mission in the 50s was to be the company that would change the global quality image of Japanese products. Today, that mission is no longer valid as Japanese products are some of the most advanced in design and contain high-tech technology. Hence the change in their mission, which is now on a much higher level in providing an inspiration to their customers, using innovation and state-of-the-art technology.

The change in **Walmart's** mission is driven more by their outlook towards 'what is important' rather than a change in market dynamics. In the 90s Walmart was single-mindedly focused on becoming the largest company that ever existed in the US (i.e. reach a $125 billion turnover), but now has realized that there is a deeper meaning to running a company than to be just big in size. Now they are focusing on improving the lifestyle standards of their customers, which is a higher purpose and much more motivating for the organization as well as for individuals. That does not mean that Walmart does not want to grow ($486 billion consolidated fiscal 2015 revenue), but their current purpose or mission is focused on something much closer to their heart, which clearly drives more passionate behavior.

"Decide carefully, exactly what you want in life,
then work like mad to make sure you get it!"
~ Hector Crawford (1913–1991),
Australian TV and Radio Producer

At the end I would like to share with you two classic examples of a comprehensive mission statement or statement of purpose in which the mission, the overall strategy they plan to follow to achieve their mission, and the final underlying benefit, are all embedded within the same mission statement. Such types of mission statements are unique, i.e. they are complete and make the life of employees and their managers clearer and confusion free.

Westin Hotels & Resorts

"In order to realize our vision, our mission must be to exceed the expectations of our customers, whom we define as guests, partners, and fellow employees [Mission]. We will accomplish this by committing to our shared values and by achieving the highest levels of customer satisfaction, with extraordinary emphasis on the creation of value [Strategy]. In this way we will ensure that our profit, quality and growth goals are met [Benefit]."[21]

Procter & Gamble

"We will provide branded products and services of superior quality and value [Strategy] that improves the lives of the world's consumers [Mission]. As a result, consumers will reward us with leadership sales, profit, and value creation, allowing our people, our shareholders, and the communities in which we live and work to prosper [Benefit]"[22]

To note, in case of P&G, they call this the statement of purpose and when sharing their mission broadly, P&G, sometimes uses the embedded mission statement on its own, which is to "improve the lives of the world's consumers."

2 D. How to Write a Mission Statement?

When preparing a mission statement you must make sure it is succinct and crisp; your audience needs to read it only once in order to grasp the direction the company or organization is committed on pursuing. It should incorporate the company's products, services, company values, activities and other socially responsible but meaningful measures.

In preparing it, one must try to involve the organization and make sure employees can understand the order of priorities to make proper strategic decisions. Finally make sure it includes some or all of the items given below:

1. Overall purpose of the company's existence.
2. Value system of the organization.
3. Stakeholders we interact with.
4. Desired public image.
5. Strategic focus of the company.
6. Description of our products and services.
7. Potential for growth and profitability.
8. Priority of activities for survival.

Remember if not properly developed or adopted, a mission statement is mere words. One must remember that what is critical are not the words in your mission statement but how they were put together, the process through which the mission statement was created and embraced. That is what will get your entire organization aligned across departments and geographies and will allow you to deploy proper and crisp strategies to your front-line employees.

·············-----━━ ━━-----··············

Chapter 3 – Vision Setting

3 A. Why is Vision Imperative?

"Where there is no vision, the people perish."
~ Bible (Proverbs 29:18 KJV)

The quote above comes from an ultimate source and could not be more direct or blunt, vision is essential for our survival and for our continued existence as societies, individuals and companies. Having a long-term direction is critical for supporting and improving quality of life at every level.

As business leaders the most important job is for you to provide vision or a sense of destination to your organization. This direction or destination must be in-sync with your purpose or mission and will act as guidance for all future business planning processes. If you plan your business without any defined and agreed destination, there is no guarantee where you will end up. Stephen R. Covey very aptly conveys this message in his book, *The 7 Habits of Highly Effective People* by saying "If the ladder is not leaning against the right wall, every step we take just gets us to the wrong place faster."

"The greatest tragedy in life is people
who have sight, but no vision."
~ Helen Keller (1880–1968),
Educator and Writer was both deaf and blind

Power of a Vision: I will share an experiment carried out to prove the true power of vision setting. Before sharing the said experiment let me ask you a question. How many of you have a vision of what you would like to be ten years from now? You can answer this question by giving any of the following three answers:

- ✓ I have never thought of it?
- ✓ I have a fair idea of what it would include but have not written it down. ☺
- ✓ I have written down what I want to be ten years from now. ☆

The same question was put to a class of business school graduates from one of the most prestigious business schools in America, Harvard University in Boston. The University was founded in 1636 by the colonial Massachusetts legislature and today is the oldest, most prestigious and the richest institution of higher learning in the United States with a total endowment of $36.4 billion and an amazing track record of creating 47 Nobel Laureates, 32 heads of state, and 48 Pulitzer Prize winners (2014).[23]

The answer about the true power of having a vision will mesmerize you. A survey was carried out ten years after a class graduated, when all of them were well settled in their jobs in prominent companies or had their own businesses. 83% of the class answered that they had no specific goals at the time of graduation. 14% said they had specific goals but had not written them down. The final 3% stated that, 'Yes we had specific goals and we had written them down at the time of our graduation'. The results are an eye opener: Those with specific written goals were earning **ten times** more than those with no goals at the time of their graduation.

Why was it so? Because every decision, every action they took was focused towards delivering their vision and its associated goals, i.e. it was written clearly in black and white. This emphasizes the true value of setting a vision and goals. The same fact is also true for companies. Every company must have a clearly written vision or direction to move towards and in doing so enhances their ability to perform at a higher level and deliver far better results. Hence the best way to predict your future is to create it by imagining the end in mind, preserving it by writing it down and then working towards delivering it.

A few things are clear from the example above:

✓ One must have a *vision* – be it an individual, a company or an organization.
✓ It must be *written down* – that would make it crisp and accessible to all.
✓ It should be done as *early as possible* in an individual's or a company's life.

"I always wanted to be somebody,
but I see now I should have been more specific."
~ Lily Tomlin (b. 1939),
American Actress, Comedian, Writer and Producer

Why does writing down your vision make such a huge difference?

Writing down your vision has two distinct advantages. First, you will appreciate the fact that writing anything always makes it very clear. By writing it down in black and white, you will have to be extremely clear-cut and explicit. Second, once written you can always revisit it, even after decades you can read exactly what your vision is. It is hence preserved for life.

To me the reason is clear, if an individual or an organization has a vision of what they want to achieve in the long run and it is in black and white and crystal clear to everyone in the organization, then all decisions that they make, every plan or move that the individual or company initiates, they do it always keeping the vision in view.

Vision should provide the direction for all planning and strategy development for growth. Bringing consistency and single-minded focus on the long-term goals, selective decision-making and choiceful strategies will inevitably deliver the vision. All other activities, strategies or decisions that will take you away from the vision, should not be pursued.

Vital Tip 4: Is having a vision more important than strategy?
One of the pitfalls many individuals and managers fall into is to have a bias towards action, i.e. without first aligning on a vision they start making decisions on driving their ambition and business. Vision and strategy are both important but there is a clear priority between them; vision always comes *first!*

If you have a clear vision, then the strategies you come up with are focused and sustainable. If you do not have a clear vision, then creating strategies is very much like shooting from the hip, they will most probably deliver immediate results but will not create value or be sustainable in the long run.

"The problem is never how to get new,
innovative thoughts into your mind,
but how to get old ones out."
~ Dee Ward Hock (b. 1929),
Founder of the Visa credit card

3 B. Vision in Action!

Let me share a famous historical example, which clearly highlights the important relationship between vision and strategy:

How many of you know how NCR was created and what these initials stand for?

To answer this question let me share with you an actual story that took place some 125 years ago. Story starts in 1887 in Daytona, a small town in the US Midwest; it's the same town where sixteen years later the Wright Brothers will make global history by building the world's first engine-powered aircraft and flying it successfully. A café/saloon owner James Ritter received a patent on a mechanical cash register that he had designed. Ritter created a company to hold the patent and sell the cash registers to merchants in his area. Unfortunately Ritter was barely able to sell a hundred cash registers over a five-year period.

One fine day another merchant by the name of John Henry Patterson offered him $6,500 for the patent and his company. Ritter and the business community in Daytona felt that "Paterson was a sucker who had fallen off a turnip truck" – a typical comment for a loser during those days. But there was something that John Patterson had which was missing from James Ritter and the other businessmen in Daytona; John had a vision while Ritter only had a strategy. He had clearly envisioned the immense possibilities of this exceptional invention. Before John died in 1922 he had sold over 22 million registers.[24]

Peterson's company became one of the most influential sales and marketing firms in the world. He named his company National Cash Register, or NCR for short. According to one author, one out of every six CEO's had received their initial training from NCR including Thomas J. Watson Sr., the first IBM CEO hired externally in 1914 and who led the three decades of IBM's golden age starting in 1950. It should be clear from this example what a difference a good vision can make.

> "Imagination is more important than knowledge."
> ~ Albert Einstein (1879–1955),
> Theoretical Physicist and Nobel Prize Winner

3 C. My Personal Example of Vision in Action.

P&G announced on Jan 28, 2005 the largest acquisition in its history, by agreeing to buy Gillette in a $57 billion deal that combined some of the world's most famous brands. P&G was already the largest US consumer goods company and according to billionaire investor Warren Buffett[25] (who owned 9% of Gillette, which was the largest single shareholding at that time) "This merger is going to create the greatest consumer products company in the world." To conclude the merger, wherever Gillette was wholly owned by Gillette USA, their back-office and businesses were merged into that country's P&G subsidiary. In Pakistan, Gillette was a joint venture while P&G Pakistan was a wholly owned subsidiary of P&G, hence they could not be merged due to their unique legal structures and continued to function independently.

On March 1, 2007, more than two years after this announcement, I was asked to take over as CEO of Gillette Pakistan. Gillette in Pakistan had suffered significantly since the global purchase of Gillette by P&G in 2005. Due to the lack of a merger in Pakistan and without a clear message on how the Gillette acquisition would be handled as it pertained to people, jobs and future business direction, nearly fifty percent of the organization had left the company by the time I took over. Such important roles such as the CEO, Finance Manager, Brand Manager, HR Manager, IT Manager, etc. were left empty as the respective managers decided to pursue other options.

The business heritage I acquired was not very impressive – growth rates were depressing, 0% growth rate for six years pre acquisition and turnover at a flat average of $9 million. On market penetration Gillette was serving only 25% of the shops as compared to what P&G Pakistan covered at that point in time. Availability of stocks was poor due to low international focus, high global demand, and tight supply and later I was to learn that due to this lack of focus Gillette products in certain months would be totally out-of-stock for weeks.

In-store displays were old and rusting and no solid display solution existed for High Frequency Stores, which accounted for the majority of our customer base. Despite being a reputed global brand with outstanding performance, the shopkeepers/trade was very upset and disillusioned due to lack of business focus and management support, and chronic supply issues during the two years of transition.

As I walked into my new role it was quite clear that things were not ideal, but I was not yet fully aware of the extent to which the situation had deteriorated. I took a deep breath and started to assess the situation. I had one-to-one meetings with all existing Gillette employees, made extensive trade visits to identify opportunities and issues, looked at the competition and our pricing in the market, discussed supply with my customer service department and charted the entire process flow from placement of orders to the actual supply to the customers.

Frankly the situation could not have been worse for me. This was my first stint as a Chief Executive Officer of a reputed multinational company. As is my natural instinct, I looked at the positive side (I believe that there is always a positive side to every situation) and finally came to the conclusion that things were not that bad as the situation provided me with a great career opportunity, "If I turned around the business, I would be heralded as a hero and if not, that was okay too as I had inherited a business which was already in a total mess. ☺"

After gathering all the relevant data, my initial gut feeling was a strong bias towards action and to immediately start fixing things, to focus on the lowest hanging fruit and to start giving out orders. But my experience had taught me that this would not be the most effective way to fix things, I had to have a vision before I started defining my strategies. The first thing I did was to sit back, unwind, focus on facts, envision the future, look at the possibilities and then decided to come up with a vision.

> "Vision without action is a daydream. Action without vision is a nightmare."
> ~ Japanese Proverb

At that stage I did not worry about how to fix things but single-mindedly focused on "How I want the company, Gillette Pakistan to look five years from now?" and also "How I want the company culture to look and feel like?" My entire focus was to come up with a crystal clear vision that would inspire the organization and bring a step-change in their motivation and hence drive disproportionate business growth.

I had learned though my twenty years in P&G that if you immediately started focusing on the strategy (How to fix?), it will inhibit your ability to think on what is possible (What can we achieve?). If I fell into this trap, I knew I would not be able to stretch my imagination on how big or how high I could take the company. What we needed at that time was a vision that was daunting as well as convincing so that it would inspire my organization to work towards achieving it.

I knew that if the vision was not compelling, then it would fail to enroll and excite the organization. If I was only a strategist and not a visionary, then my thought process would have followed the following route: "The situation is very grim, hence I should urgently fix all the key problems we are facing. I know what the critical problems are. I need to make sure we as a company do not bleed; we should try to improve our cash-flow to stay afloat, fix stock supply issues and try to grow beyond the $9 million sales barrier where we have been stuck since 2001."

You will agree that this kind of plan would not have been compelling or inspirational and no one would have felt excited about it. Using this vision I would never have been able to retain or motivate any of my existing employees and it would be near to impossible to attract much needed high-caliber new recruits to Gillette. In addition, such a plan would not have compelled the top management at our corporate headquarters to assign additional resources and funding to Gillette Pakistan.

"If you don't have a vision for the future,
then your future is threatened to be a repeat of the past."
~ A. R. Bernard (b. 1953),
Clergyman

The real struggle is between having a bias towards action versus sitting back and first creating a vision. That is the paradigm which many people get stuck in and they never question or pursue the 'what is possible?' route. Such people never ask how can we do more but remain at the level of how do I fix this? John C. Maxwell in his book "*Put Your Dreams to the Test*" very aptly states, "The problem is that people get stuck on the how. They don't see how they could accomplish more, so they throttle back their vision, convinced that they must be realistic. And, what they expect becomes their new reality"[26]. This is simply faith applied negatively.

In Gillette, I took the liberty of envisioning what the future would look like and created a very compelling and daunting dream for the Gillette Pakistan organization. To me if my dream excited me, then I was sure that it would excite my team!

I wanted Gillette to grow disproportionally and not incrementally that is why I named my vision, **Mission Dugna Tigna** (*Dugna* is double and *Tigna* is triple in Urdu). I did not want my team to think in increments, which would have taken us decades to grow to a respectable size; I wanted them to think of doubling (200% plus

growth) or tripling (300% plus growth) the business. As the vision I had created was very simple and in the local Urdu language, hence it was widely accepted by all, including my field sales force and all my external partners. I also wanted an impactful graphical representation or a logo to bring the vision to life (see picture). It had to be simple, literal and be able to communicate the spirit of my vision.

Once I had painted the picture of my dream in my mind and knew the overall goals in broad terms, I wanted my team to own it and to pursue it with passion. I organized an offsite and called it *Thinking BIG*. This historic day in the history of Gillette happened on July 18, 2007. I invited experts in various technical fields from our regional HQ to increase the capability level of my young team (50% were new to Gillette). I made sure I had a cross section of specialists from all disciplines, people expert in brand equity building, financial analysis, market research, consumer understanding, sales experts, distributor professionals, media, direct marketing, external relations, supply chain, information technology, etc.

I took all of them and locked them away in the Arabian Sea Resort just outside Karachi for three days. To jolt them out of the current reality I started my session in a very creative and provocative manner. Let me help you relive that inaugural session in 2007:

- ✓ I dimmed the lights; turned on nice eastern music, tabla and sitar and had incense burning.
- ✓ I told them to relax, to sit back and let their minds roam free, to dream on and to imagine what is possible.
- ✓ Then I told them: "Let me show you a vision of tomorrow, ☺, imagine you are in the future and looking back at Gillette Pakistan on March 19, 2013."
- ✓ I then transported my team to precisely five years and nine months into the future through a creative presentation, and asked them to visualize the journey.

✓ As I explained the dream of Gillette in the presentation, I intermittently showed them inspirational pictures of nature, scenery, achievements, and success – to help create an upbeat mood in the conference room.

✓ I listed for them the awards Gillette Pakistan had accumulated during this period ranging from the fastest growing subsidiary in the division to winning seven regional brand awards.

✓ I told them that this year we would touch $35 million in sales.

✓ How did we achieve these results? By launching Mission Dugna Tigna back in 2007, which I called the "Golden Year of Gillette."

✓ Later I shared with them key achievements and breakthrough ideas which we had implemented, by category, starting with Blades & Razors (B&R), then Braun, Personal Care products, Oral B and finally Duracell.

✓ Then I reminded them that they were still in my dream ☺.

✓ I gave them a wake-up call, switched on the lights, turned off the music and informed them that today was in fact July 18, 2007 and not March 19, 2013. Bringing them back to the present.

✓ Then I introduced them our vision, to **Mission Dugna Tigna,** which was to *"Grow Gillette Disproportionally".*

✓ I shared my Dugna and Tigna plans per category, painted out in broad strokes.

✓ I spent disproportionate time on *where* I saw us in five years and minimal time laying down the *how* part, i.e. what were the specific strategies to deliver the vision.

✓ I wanted the team to think up and brainstorm the strategies and build on my vision.

✓ I wanted them all to own this vision and then to deliver it.

✓ I reminded them that we have the next three days to brainstorm, make choices and come up with the key building blocks for Mission Dugna Tigna.

- ✓ I also told them not to look at limitations; let me be the one to say what is possible and what is not; they should just brainstorm and come up with a host of ideas to grow the company disproportionally.
- ✓ I promised that if they faced any barriers, I would break them down.
- ✓ I requested them to help me convert *my* dream into *their* dream.

"Great leaders speak about the future with such clarity,
it is as if they are talking about the past."
~ Simon Sinek (b. 1973),
Author focused on Inspirational Leadership

Results of the session were amazing! I had the complete attention of all my team players and the partners present, eyes were sparkling, minds were racing, ideas were flowing, they all felt energized, excited and ready to start the journey to deliver my 'dream', which was soon to become 'our' dream and 'our' company's vision. To be honest this was one of the most exhilarating experiences of my life. When anyone would ask me, "How in the world will we accomplish these outlandish growth rates?" I would just smile and say, "I'm not sure how, but I am confident it is going to happen. We will deliver it together. Just watch and see."

What is essential in such a situation is having *stretch mentality*. I wanted my people and organization to move away from incremental mentality

and start thinking of disproportional growth. You will notice that most businesses have a tendency to grow incrementally in nature. Reason for that is because many do a quick assessment on how the economy is doing, how is competition growing and then agree on a deliverable growth rate, e.g. 7%, and then say "that looks about right."

Going for stretch mentality or stretch goals is difficult for many, it requires taking risks. Everyone is programmed in taking the path of least resistance and the ability to incorporate stretch in any culture is very difficult. I knew from experience that to deliver stretch goals you had to start with the *end in mind* and then work backwards to figure out how to deliver them, and that is exactly what we did.

To me delivering stretch goals was not a linear progression but more of an exponential journey. Like they say "It is most difficult to make your first million" and for Gillette it was paramount that we take off our incremental thinking cap and put on the stretch mentality hat and set a foundation of stretch mentality from day one.

We spent the rest of the two days going category by category, brand by brand, distribution channel by distribution channel, socio-economic class by socio-economic class – we locked down strategies for each, making tough choices and bold decisions. We walked away with a document, which had four core strategies on where we planned to play. We had another four on how we planned to win in these areas. Each of the eight strategies had sub-strategies by department, i.e. what will finance do, what role will markets research play, etc.

"The rung of a ladder was never meant to rest upon,
but only to hold a man's foot long enough to enable
him to put the other somewhat higher."
~ Thomas Henry Huxley (1825–1895),
English Biologist

I am proud to share with you that in the first year we posted a +22% growth rate and four out of our five categories delivered the Mission Dugna Tigna goals. In a very short time we invented some revolutionary solutions for displays in the trade. We increased distribution by 300% in just the first nine months; this included an aggressive Modern Retail (MR) program in which we upgraded our displays in Modern Retail Stores and had them designed, fabricated and installed in just three months. For the top High Frequency Stores (HFS), which runs into tens of thousands, we conceptualized, designed, fabricated and installed a customized Hotspot (a metal frame right behind the cash counter, a prime spot for impulse purchases). I am proud to say that this entire process was completed in just seven months and the design was so revolutionary that the Vice Chairman of Global Operations Werner Geissler appreciated the idea as best in class execution and a great example for global reapplication.

For fixing the supply issue I personally visited Geneva and met with the Gillette Global Customer Service team and enrolled them into my vision. After this trip, Pakistan did not face any serious stock-out issues despite global supply constraints and our market got due importance and was supplied its aggressive forecast on time. All organizational gaps were filled in the first eight months of my taking over and I slashed 50% of my stock-keeping units to reduce complexity thus lowering the investment tied in working capital and reducing the portfolio significantly for my sales team to improve their sales call productivity. To fix so many things in such a short period was clearly driven by a strong commitment from each team member to the vision that we had all affirmed to deliver.

> **Vital Tip 5:** Once a vision has been delivered, it is important to set a new vision so that steady growth continues to take place. I always told my team to dream, and if at some point in time you find out that you can achieve it, then it is no longer a dream: Dream again.

"If you can imagine it, you can achieve it.
If you can dream it, you can become it."
~ William Arthur Ward (1921–1994),
Writer of Inspirational Maxims

In a matter of just twelve to twenty four months, my highly energized and committed team of laser focused managers delivered a slew of initiatives that helped to accelerate growth and build the equity and image of Gillette Blades & Razors among Pakistani consumers. With all the efforts made by my team I am not surprised that after years of flat sales, we delivered an impressive +22% growth on sales revenue in our very first twelve months. To me this entire exercise was a true testament of the power of vision setting and approaching business issues with the right attitude and with the right spirits. In the next few years we took Gillette Pakistan to become the fastest growing Blade & Razor subsidiary in entire Central Eastern European and Middle East Africa (CEEMEA) on multiple occasions.

"The secret of business is to know something
that nobody else knows."
~ Aristotle Onassis (1906–1975),
Greek Shipping Magnate

To be fair we did not deliver these outstanding results just because we had a great business strategy, we delivered them because we had a clear vision of where we wanted to be and it was owned not only by my entire local organization but also vertically by our Regional Vice President, Al Rajwani based in Dubai and the Gillette Global Business Unit Chief Peter Corijn based in Geneva. Just like I was breaking down barriers in Pakistan, Al and Peter were doing the same on a regional basis.

Our vision had been clearly defined, work-plans of all team members where aligned and they were all in one direction, driven by the contagious *to be the best* spirit and owned by everyone up and down the company's hierarchy. That is where it all started and that is where you must start if you want to change reality. If you are not happy with where you are now, you have to sit back, decide what you want, create a daunting vision and pursue it with conviction and passion.

Food for Thought:

A Gillette Pakistan Fact

In September 2012, the CEEMEA (Central Eastern Europe and Middle East Africa) division's Gillette Global Business Unit (GBU) headquartered in Geneva gave Gillette Pakistan the fastest growing Blade & Razor business award. This was the third straight year Gillette Pakistan won this elite award.

To me this was a clear validation that setting a daunting vision coupled with an inspired organization does pay huge dividends in the long run.

Other Global Examples of Vision Setting: Let me share a few other examples of famous visionaries of our time and what incredible feats they were able to accomplish.

1. <u>Thomas Edison</u>: His vision enabled a first grade drop-out to receive more patents then anyone in history, including those for recording sound, movies, generating electricity, and, of course, the electric light bulb.
2. <u>Helen Keller</u>: Her vision took a woman who lost her hearing and sight after her second birthday and transformed her from a bitter, hateful child into one of the most inspirational writers and speakers of the twentieth century.
3. <u>Ray Kroc</u>: His vision empowered a fifty two year old salesman of milkshake machines to quit his job and create

the most successful restaurant franchise system in the world – McDonald's ☺.

4. <u>John D. Rockefeller</u>: His vision literally turned a bookkeeper making ten cents an hour into the richest and most powerful man in the world.

5. <u>Steve Job and Steven Wozniak</u>: Their vision enabled two college dropouts to turn a hole-in-the-wall start-up software company into one of the most highly valued companies in the world.

3 D. How did I Come Up With a Vision?

Identifying an appropriate and winning vision is a very meticulous and well thought out process. It requires introspective reflection of one's deeper ambitions and goals. One needs to be very sure of their purpose in life, what legacy one wants to leave behind as well as the long-term benefits of the vision. The vision should be in sync with the mission in life as well as the value system. Vision is the lifeblood and the fuel that drives any plan to fruition.

To come up with a vision, one needs to be abundantly aware of the issues, the ground realities as well as what their mental picture of the future looks like. One needs to find a peaceful place, clear the mind and totally devote oneself to converting this mental picture into a list of words or numbers so that they can share the vision broadly. To help you in conceiving and implementing a vision, I have listed some key steps from my own experience that can help you do a quality job in bringing your own vision to life.

1. Go off to a place that inspires you; lock yourself away for a day or more.
2. Make sure you go prepared, i.e. with your laptop, pad, pen and some light music to create the right ambiance.
3. Make sure you do not get interrupted, turn off your cell phone and tell your secretary not to disturb you. Ideally,

if possible, do it offsite without any disturbances and constraints.

4. Get inspiration! As pre-reading I would suggest you read the book *The Richest Man Who Ever Lived – King Solomon's Secret of Success, Wealth and Happiness* by Steven K. Scott. It is an incredibly inspiring book based on proverbs of King Solomon giving a detailed roadmap for successful living today. He very aptly explains how we can all derive success in life.

5. Start by evaluating the current reality. You need a baseline from which you will build your vision. You need to be brutally honest about the current reality as that will act as the foundation for your vision.

6. Next you start by imagining what you want the future to look like. Create an actual painting or an image of the future in your mind with full details. While creating your vision make sure you do not use past trends or challenges on the ground as constraints, think BIG.

7. Jot down the various aspects on a piece of paper and make it as detailed as possible as you will have to explain it later to your team. Make sure you write all these details in the present tense as if all of what you have imagined is already happening. That way it is easier to sell and makes it much more believable.

8. Write down key milestones to deliver the vision; goals are vision milestones. These are goals and are very specific as regard to timing and value.

9. Make sure your vision is overwhelming and daunting. If the vision is not inspirational or exciting, it will be very difficult to get the organization enrolled to deliver it.

10. Further steps needed to keep the vision alive:
    a. Identify broad strategies on how you plan to deliver the goals.
    b. Call a companywide meeting and share your vision and strategies in broad strokes with everyone who

will be required to bring this vision to life. Makes sure you include external partners as well.

c. Keep the vision alive, walk the talk, share it in every company meeting, reward people who keep the vision active and above all have faith in your ability and your team.

d. You must always keep hope alive and stand steadfast behind your vision despite obstacles.

Vital Tip 6: In order to create a vision, you have two options:

1. The option discussed above, which I used to create an overall vision for my Gillette challenge.
2. An alternate option is to take your entire lead team off-site and do all the steps stated above but with your lead team and come up with an exciting and daunting vision.

In option two, you must lead from the front and also make sure that not just you, but all the lead team members come with an open mind; only think of the end and at this stage do not focus on how you will deliver that vision. That will come later.

"A leader is a dealer in hope."
~ Napoleon Bonaparte (1769–1821),
French General and Emperor

My personal experience is that delivering any daunting vision is extremely tough on ones intellect, mind and patience. There will be a time when the vision will look utterly impossible and you will feel like lowering it to make sure you bring it to a level where it can be delivered; if this happens it is no more a vision but a mere task. True inspirational leadership is where you never compromise the vision but work towards *raising the reality* to match your vision.

To me the ultimate power of any leader is to keep *hope* alive, and not get demoralized and disheartened due to setbacks. The true test of leadership is during difficult times, anyone can handle good times but only a tough leader can grab success out of a difficult situation. I remember less than a year after we set our formidable vision in July 2007 the world was hit by the 2008 financial crisis, which manifested as a liquidity crisis the world over. For the first time in more than half a century the global GDP (Gross Domestic Product) growth rate fell into the negative in 2009 at minus 2%. All businesses struggled and so did the Pakistan economy and businesses.

Our overall sales, like all other businesses in Pakistan, were lower than a year ago. At this stage my employees questioned me, "Our plan was to double or triple our business, we have negative growth in 2008, how will we ever deliver Mission Dugna Tigna?" My reply was firm and full of confidence that our vision is not a one or two-year vision but is for the next five years and beyond. One year's drop means that we have to do double the work in the coming years. My confidence was contagious and everyone kept their spirit high and continued to focus on finding breakthrough ideas for growth. The very next year we delivered disproportional growth, highest in the region and have not stopped since.

If we take hold of a powerful vision, pump it up with a lot of hope and mix the two thoroughly, it would certainly create an explosive combination. To me *hope acts like fuel* for the vision and helps to give it speed and momentum even under difficult situations. Prerequisite to all this is that we must have a strong value based culture, a strong capable team and strong inspirational leadership at every level to help drive us towards the vision.

> "The first task of a leader is to keep hope alive."
> ~ Joe D. Batten (b. 1962),
> Motivational Speaker and Consultant

Vital Tip 7: There are three visioning principles given by renowned Professor C. K. Prahalad[27], who was my MBA professor and taught me Strategic Studies at The University of Michigan's Ross Business School back in 1986, these are:

- ✓ Aspiration (vision) must always exceed present resources. In other words, the vision must be a big stretch, and it need not be obvious how it will be attained.
- ✓ The vision must not be an extrapolation from the past. Rather, the process of progressing towards the vision must be a process of discovery, of "folding in the future" which means we should set targets and work backwards to achieve the same.
- ✓ Adoption of 'best practices' will not help to realize a vision that is not an extrapolation of the past. Rather, there must be innovation, and development of best practices.

3 E. Reward for Keeping the Vision Alive

As they say *"You get what you reward."* People are programmed to deliver what will eventually get rewarded and recognized. Hence it is essential that you constantly keep an eye for behaviors and results that are in line with the company's vision and for employees who show a high level of passion and commitment in delivering it.

Rewarding and encouraging people should be consistent and frequent. People should be able to see how they can gain company-wide recognition by living the vision. In Gillette, I incorporated the Mission Dugna Tigna Award which had the logo embossed on an expensive table watch. This award was given once a year based on an employee's performance that was clearly over and above everyone's expectations and on projects and actions that were consistent with Gillette's vision.

Vital Tip 8: One needs to keep the vision alive at all times. The vision should be part of every major meeting, every discussion and should be shared openly within the organization. Vision is not something for the CEO to keep locked away or only for the leadership team or for the Board of Directors to use in their internal discussions. It has to be deployed, employees need to be enrolled and bought into the dream, each and every member of the company should know, "How they can contribute in their daily work towards the agreed company goals?"

Vision can be set at all levels of the organization, departments, the production line at the local plant etc. all can have their own vision's. The *key* is that these departmental visions should be fully aligned and congruent with the overall company vision. In fact it is ideal if they add up to the organizational vision, thus ensuring that tracking gaps versus the company vision will become easier and accountability will be transparent.

"Believe me, the reward is not so great without the struggle."
~ Wilma Rudolph (1940–1994),
American Olympian Athlete

Vital Tip 9: Companies and individuals, who set visions <u>without</u> full alignment of all concerned departments and especially top management, are at a risk of failure. Remember vision setting should be driven top-down else it may not be effective. Lack of proper modeling and analysis before broadly sharing the vision is another sure way of failure. Vision should be stretch but achievable, in-line with the overall capability and within the competence of the employees. Employees need to be convinced that based on the investment plan, organization capability, aligned strategies and leadership passion and guidance, and by pushing their capabilities to the limit, they can achieve the vision.

Your job as head of the organization is to show them the path based on rough conceptual building blocks to help achieve the vision. The path you define may have gaps, may be based on a number of major yet realistic assumptions but it must be intellectually stimulating to inspire them to own and pursue it.

Chapter 4 – Goal Setting

4 A. Why Goals?

Goals are vision's milestones!

Once you have defined your vision, the next step is to give this vision a form, a shape, a structure, and an outline. Goals help in making the vision clearer and well defined. If your dream is a picture, then the goals will be the outline of the picture and the vision will be the color that you fill in to give your dream a life. The more vibrant the colors, the more challenging the dream!

From a business context, vision is the text that you use to describe the dream, and goals are the dimensions that help describe the vision's size, shape, and timing. Diana Scharf-Hunt, author and time management guru defines "Goals are dreams with deadlines" which is a creative way of defining goals as the culmination or fulfillment of a dream or a vision. Always remember that the people who you plan to lead would like to know where they are heading.

Vital Tip 10: A possible drawback of goal setting, highlighted by some experts is that implicit learning may be inhibited. Reason given is that by setting specific goals you end up encouraging single-minded focus on an outcome without openness to exploration, understanding or growth.

To address this, it is important to set challenging goals which require out-of-the-box thinking and looking for non-conventional solutions. In research it has been shown that specific and challenging goals lead to higher performance than easy or no goals.

"Your life is controlled by your thoughts.
Your thoughts are controlled by your goals."
~ Earl Nightingale (1921–1989),
American Motivational Speaker and Author

Goal setting has been used for driving achievement since the early 1800s. In the early 1900s Napoleon Hill an American author, who was one of the earliest producers of the modern genre of personal-success literature, conducted extensive studies into the lives of more than 400 of the world's leading business men and published his findings in several works, the most popular being *The Laws of Success* and *Think and Grow Rich.*

Hill studied the characteristics of these achievers and wrote *Laws of Success*, a set of fifteen laws, which can be applied by anybody to achieve success. *Think and Grow Rich* condenses these laws further and provides the reader with thirteen principles in the form of a philosophy of personal achievement. His one key finding was that goals drive human behavior and the ability to do the impossible. All successful leaders have very clear, transparent and challenging goals. According to Hill his success as an author was driven by goals in one form or another.[28]

"There is one quality which one must possess to
win, and that is definiteness of purpose,
the knowledge of what one wants, and a
burning desire to possess it."
~ Napoleon Hill (1883–1970),
American Author

There is constant research being carried out across the world on the impact of goals on performance by studying athletes, celebrities, entrepreneurs, CEO's, etc. Some key insights from these researches reveal that in order for goals to help increase performance, they must be difficult and as specific as possible.

1. Goals that are easily attained tend to correlate with lower performance versus the much higher performance attained by setting goals that are difficult to attain.
2. A vague goal does not enhance performance. For example a goal such as 'increase distribution disproportionally' will not enhance performance, as the specifics are not clear. Goals can become more specific by quantifying them and making them time-bound such as by demanding 'doubling distribution in twelve months' or '20% increase in market share by July 2016.'

"It's a dream until you write it down, and then it's a goal."
~ Anonymous

In business, goal setting encourages participants to put in substantial effort. In a business environment each employee has a clearly defined work plan but managers cannot be always present to drive motivation or keep track of an employee's work on a constant basis. Goals therefore act as a self-regulating mechanism to help employees prioritize their tasks.

Goals that are considered to be difficult tend to increase performance more than goals that are not. In the study titled "The study of work motivation in the 20th century" the researcher identified four ways that goals setting can impact outcome, they are,[29]

1. **Choice:** Goals narrow attention and direct efforts to goal-relevant activities, and away from perceived undesirable and goal-irrelevant actions.

2. **Effort:** Goals can lead to more effort; for example, if one typically produces 4 widgets an hour, and has the goal of producing 6, one may work more intensely towards the goal than one would otherwise.
3. **Persistence:** Someone becomes more likely to work through setbacks if pursuing a goal.
4. **Cognition:** Goals can lead individuals to develop and change their behavior.

"A goal without a plan is just a wish."

~ Anonymous

Vital Tip 11: One key pitfall of goal setting occurs if goals are not properly assigned and are not pursued across the organization. Conflicts can arise where the goal of a manager is not aligned with the goals of the organization. This lack of alignment will directly impact the performance of both the manager and the organization. In such situations the manager will be more focused on delivering his goals and the organizational goals will suffer.

That is why it is extremely important that both the vision and its associated goals are deployed across the organization and each and every employee's work plan reflects alignment with these goals. In addition, the work plans must be reviewed periodically to make sure they always remain in alignment with overall goals, thus keeping all conflicts out of the system.

---

4 B. Golden Tip on Goal Setting

"Nothing happens, no forward steps are taken until a goal is established."
~ David J. Schwartz (1927–1987),
American Motivational Writer, Author of *The Magic of Thinking Big*

SMART goals are used to make sure that the goals you assign to your vision are effective, aligned and drive performance-enhancing behavior. To achieve that you need to make sure that each goal meets the SMART criteria.[30]

Goals have to be:

✓ S = **Specific**
✓ M = **Measurable**
✓ A = **Attainable**
✓ R = **Realistic**
✓ T = **Timely**

Specific: The goals should be crystal clear, crisp, simple and easy to understand. Being specific will help to focus efforts properly and to clearly define what we are trying to achieve. It is important that you put it down on paper. This will help make it real, tangible and difficult to ignore. Once the goals are defined, the next step will be to define strategies, which will answer the following questions: "What are we trying to achieve?" "Why is it important to achieve this goal?" and "How will we achieve these goals?"

"What's the use of running if you are not on the right road."
~ German Proverb

Measurable: Like they say "If you can't measure it, you can't control it." Hence do make sure you always set goals that are measurable. Goals that you set are in fact a measure of the success of the overall task. If you deliver all of them you have achieved your objective. Goals can be broken down into multiple milestones and you can have several checkpoints along the way to track progress. It is important to celebrate the completion of each milestone to make the team feel energized and excited as they move towards delivering the overall vision.

"If you want it, measure it. If you can't measure it, forget it."
~ Peter Drucker (1909–2005),
Writer and Management Consultant

Attainable: When we set goals we should make sure that they are a stretch but are still attainable. Building stretch mentality for your goals is important in order to make your team think of achieving something impressive and something to be proud of. While setting such goals one must take into account the team's ability, capability and skills as well as the financial capacity of the company. If you set goals, which are beyond the reach of your team, you will demoralize them and they will not be able to function at their peak performance levels.

Vital Tip 12: Goals are defined to drive single-minded focus on delivering the vision and not just to identify an end point. Goals should act as inspiration and not as limits to what can be achieved. Like they say, "Set goals, not limits."

"Either do not attempt at all, or go through with it."
~ Publius Ovidius Naso (43 BC–AD 17/18),
Roman Poet

Realistic: The plan and strategy should be sensible and doable. Goals should not be easy, but should still be within the scope of the team's capability and skills. The work plan should fit within the overall vision and should require the team to stretch their skills in order to achieve it. And make sure that the goal should not be such a stretch that they break their backs. Hope is an essential ingredient of delivering any vision, hence realistic goals help drive a team's best behavior. Unrealistic goals erode hope and instead of motivating the team, dishearten and quash motivation.

"The pessimist complains about the wind;
the optimist expects it to change; the realist adjusts the sails."
~ William Arthur Ward (1921–1994),
Writer

Timely: It is important to assign clear timelines to all the goal milestones, as without a deadline there is no urgency to deliver projects on time. Always remember that by aligning on timelines up front you create a heightened sense of urgency and achievement in the mind of the employees. The organization must be clear on the timeline to deliver their projects, that way employees have a clear target to work towards. If you don't set proper timelines, then most likely the project will never get done or get delayed so much that its true benefit will be lost.

Vital Tip 13: To achieve success we must write down the goals. Just agreeing on goals and not writing them down, you face the risk of confusion and misalignment on what the goal is in the future. If you recall, in the Harvard graduate  survey given in the vision chapter, the real impact of setting a vision took place only when the graduate had written down their goals. The same fact is also true for companies; the goals should be written and shared broadly within the company for full alignment.

"Strategy is the art of making use of time and space.
I am less chary of the latter than the former;
space we can recover, time never."
~ Napoleon Bonaparte (1769–1821),
French General and Emperor

4 C. Top 10 Reason for not Delivering your Goals:

Majority of people feel that there is a clear correlation between setting goals and attaining a better life, but you will be shocked to know that approximately 80 percent of people never set goals for themselves. As per Douglas Varmeeren in his study "Why People Fail to Achieve Their Goals", he states an even more shocking statistic, where 20 percent of the people who do set goals for themselves, roughly 70 percent fail to achieve their goals; a mere 6 percent of people who set goals for themselves ever deliver.

As per Varmeeren research, there are two categories, i.e. "be" goals and "do" goals—who do you want to be or what do you want to achieve? In addition, within each category, there are four areas of goals: wealth, health, relationships, and self-fulfillment. To have a fulfilling and successful life, you need to set both "being" and "doing" goals for each of the four areas.

Before venturing further it is important to share the top ten reasons why people fail to achieve their goals. As per Varmeeren they are,[31]

1. **Fear of success and/or failure:** Some people are afraid they will fail, or even worse, they may actually succeed. Such people lack belief in themselves and in their potential. In their mind, if they fail, everyone will think negatively of them. And if they succeed, people will be envious and think negatively of them. So it becomes a lose-lose situation no matter how they look at it.

2. **Lack of understanding about the goal-setting process:** Many people mistakenly believe that goal setting simply means putting a goal on paper, setting a date for completion, marking off checkpoints as they occur, and then starting all over again. Such a mentality hinders people from success, as setting a goal is really about changing yourself for the long-term. Goals aren't short-term, quick-fix things.

3. **Lack of commitment to the goal:** Even though people state they want to achieve a certain goal, in truth, they're really not committed to it. Because of this lack of commitment, they don't give the act of goal attainment their full effort.

4. **Inactivity:** After setting a goal, writing down dates, and setting checkpoints, some people stop. They never actually take that first step needed to progress toward their goal.

5. **Analysis paralysis:** Many people let questions and doubts paralyze them. They believe they can't start on a goal until they have all the answers to every "what if" scenario. However, no matter how long and hard you prepare, you will never have all the answers to the questions you ask.

6. **Lack of a real destination:** People often begin setting goals without a solid destination of who they want to become or what they ultimately want to achieve. But if you don't have a destination in mind, then you'll never know which road to take to get where you want to go. Your destination needs to be clear – something you can visualize and describe to others.

7. **Failing to plan:** While many people understand the formula of goal setting, they don't have a plan for goal attainment that's personalized to them and their experiences. In other words, they neglect the gifts they possess which can help them attain the goal, as well as the people they know who may be able to help them.

8. **Having too many goals:** Some people have too many goals and not enough focus. It's like they're standing in front of a dart-board with three targets in mind. Hitting just one target is difficult enough; hitting three targets simultaneously with one dart is impossible. You need to realize that you have only so much time and energy. Therefore, chose the goal that will give you the highest ROE (Return On Effort).

9. **Feeling unworthy of the end result:** Some people really don't believe they're worthy of attaining the goal. As such, they self-sabotage themselves. Perhaps they suddenly walk away from the key contact who will help them with their goal, or they neglect to do a critical activity that will enable them to achieve their goal.

10. **Lack of motivation to change:** Finally, many people are simply satisfied with what they have and where they are in life. As such, they don't explore what else is available or what greater things they could achieve.

4 D. Big Hairy Audacious Goals (BHAG)

The first time I heard of BHAG I got goose bumps all over my body! This extraordinary concept was introduced to me during a Pampers business review meeting while I was posted in Saudi Arabia by Harald Einsmann, who during the mid 90's was Executive Vice President and President of P&G's Europe, Middle East and Africa business. BHAG (pronounced BEE-hag) as a concept was first proposed by James Collins and Jerry Porras in their 1996 article entitled "Building Your Company's Vision".[32]

They refer to BHAG as a form of vision statement " ...an audacious 10-to-30-year goal to progress towards an envisioned future." Collins and Porras further expanded and stated, "A true BHAG is clear and compelling, serves as unifying focal point of effort, and acts as a clear catalyst for team spirit. It has a clear finish line, so the organization can know when it has achieved the goal; people like to shoot for finish lines." Collins has also used the BHAG concept in his book, *Built to Last.*

> "In between goals is the thing called life,
> that has to be lived and enjoyed."
> ~ Sid Caesar (1992–2014),
> American Actor and Writer

Big Hairy Audacious Goals

To me BHAG is a special kind of stretch goal, stretched even further. It is always good to call a spade a spade i.e. if it is a crazy, giant and challenging goal – then give it a name that suits it. By calling it a Big Hairy Audacious Goal you are in fact giving it a life, a shape and a form. People know that this is not a normal run-of-the-mill sort of goal, but a huge challenge and your team will automatically treat it as such. The only reason for me to share the BHAG concept here is that in many cultures and environments it works extremely well and inspires the right kind of behavior and attitudes. So use BHAG where you feel appropriate. Let me share some inspirational BHAG's used by famous companies,[32]

- **SpaceX**: Enable human exploration and settlement of Mars.
- **Microsoft**: A computer on every desk and in every home.
- **Facebook**: To make the world more open and connected.
- **SolarAid**: To eradicate the kerosene lamp from Africa by 2020.
- **Amazon.com**: To be Earth's most customer-centric company.
- **AIESEC**: Engage and develop every young person in the world.

"The starting point of all achievement is desire.
Keep this constantly in mind.
Weak desires bring weak results,
just as a small amount of fire makes a small amount of heat."
~ Napoleon Hill (1883–1970),
American Author

••••-------- ----------••••

Chapter 5 – Strategy Development

5 A. What are Strategies?

There is a famous Japanese proverb "Vision without action is a daydream. Action without vision is a nightmare." This quotation clearly highlights the strong relationship between vision and strategy. Setting the vision is just the first ten yards of a hundred-yard dash it ensures you start your race in the right direction and with the right momentum. Majority of the race will be spent in finding ways of delivering this vision, i.e. identifying and deploying the right strategies to the teams. Strategies are the actions that need to be pursued in order to move towards the agreed vision. Strategy is the "means to an end," to achieve your end, which is your vision.

What are strategies? **A Strategy is a plan of action designed to achieve a particular goal**.

The word strategy has military connotations, because it is derived from the Greek word *stratēgia* (art of troop leader; office of general, command). Strategy is different from tactics. In military terms, tactics is concerned with the conduct of an engagement while strategy is concerned with how different engagements are linked. In other words, how a battle is fought is a matter of tactics: The terms that it is fought on and whether it should be fought at all is a matter of strategy.[33]

Let me now define how someone in the consumer goods industry would define strategy:

> **Strategy** is a <u>conscious set of choices</u>, which define how you intend to beat competition on a <u>sustainable basis</u>, in meeting consumer needs.

Two things should immediately be obvious from this definition:

I.   Strategy is a set of choices.
II. Strategy should be winnable and sustainable.

5 B. Strategy is a set of Choices – Where Do We Play Choices?

In the book *The Game-Changer* by A. G. Lafley (Chairman of the Board, President, and Chief Executive Officer of P&G, originally retired in 2010, he rejoined the Company in May 2013 and again retired in Nov 2015 after streamlining its strategy) and Ram Charan, they describe strategy as: "Strategy is about choices – about deciding which business or businesses a company should be in and not be in." It is also as Peter Drucker said, "The most fundamental choice every company must make." It's a question that demands a continuous, strategic assessment of the company and its core capabilities, and the industry in which a company competes or could compete."

As mentioned before, making choices is the most critical decision that every company must take at some stage. If you take your team and brainstorm the various actions that need to be taken to deliver the vision, I am sure you will come up with a laundry list of ideas. You cannot put all these ideas into action, due to constraints. These constraints can include the capacity of your teams, financial resources at your disposal, systems potential or organizational capabilities, to name a few. You will have to make choices and select a few hard-hitting strategies that will make the biggest difference in achieving your dreams while operating within the financial and resource constraints.

One way to make these choices is to define where you want to play or which areas you want to focus your activities on (i.e. region, category, channels, tiers, etc.) in order to achieve your vision. Jim Collins while researching for his book *Good to Great* discovered that "Greatness is not a function of circumstance. Greatness, it turns out, is largely a matter of conscious choice and discipline."

> "Emphasize everything and you emphasize nothing."
> ~ Herschel Gordon Lewis (b. 1929),
> American Filmmaker

Let me explain this concept using an example: In Gillette, one of our key product categories is called Blades & Razors (B&R) category. This category is made up of the following three types:

1. Systems   (Top Tier)   includes ProGlide, Fusion, Mach 3, Sensor Excel, etc.
2. Disposables (Mid Tier)   includes Blue III, Blue II, Blue II Plus, Gillette 2, etc.
3. Double Edge (Low Tier)   includes 7 O'clock blades.

If we are to define strategies to build the business we must first decide 'Where do we want to focus?' Do we focus our energies on growing all three categories or just one? To decide whether we should focus on one or more categories, one has to answer the following questions:

1. What is the size of the prize? How big are these categories? What is their future potential?
2. Which category does R&D support? Which have future upgrades in the pipeline?

3. Which of these categories is profitable, considering markets dynamic such as affordability, competitive pricing, government regulations, customs duty, taxes etc.?

In addition to the above questions, you also need to decide and make the following choices:

1. Which socio-economic classes (SEC) you want to focus on, i.e. SEC A, B, C, D or E? (Socio Economic Classification involves classifying / categorizing people in a given nation based on their education and the occupation of the household's chief earner where A is the highest and E being the lowest).
2. What product line within the category should you market? In Systems should you market all the product lines or just the high-end Systems such as ProGlide and Fusion?
3. Which geography would you like to focus on, top ten towns, urban or rural?
4. Which trade channels would you like to focus on, i.e. Global Customers (GC), Modern Retail (MR), High Frequency Stores (HFS) or Wholesale?
5. What consumer awareness activities should you pursue, i.e. media, billboards, direct to consumer activities, promotions, sampling, etc.?

Properly answering all these questions is critical in defining correct and effective strategies or what I call "*choiceful and impactful strategies.*" To answer these queries you need to do some serious market research, gain insights into consumer habits and practices, investigate trade channel potential, understand government policies, as well as find out more about your company's up-stream research and development plans for that category.

Once you have figured out the size of the prize of each category, you should pick the ones that deliver the highest long term potential, both on the top line growth (sales revenues) as well as the bottom line margins (profits).

"Cherish your freedom of choice."

~ Chick Corea (b. 1941),
American Jazz Pianist and Composer

Once all the tough choices have been made, using data based logic and comprehensive financial scrutiny, we are ready to articulate our strategies. We must at this stage write down in black and white a clear strategy in words, i.e. where in the B&R category we want to play as a company? Clarity is extremely essential as all departmental action plans, as well as individuals work plans will flow from these choices.

Let me share with you a fictitious scenario to make a point: Based on market and financial data, we can make the following where-do-we-play choices: "We plan to compete in the Systems segment only. We will disproportionally focus on SEC A & B urban consumers only and drive Best in Class distribution and visibility in Global Customers and Modern Retail channels only. We will market only three product lines, i.e. Mach 3, Fusion and ProGlide."

One can see from the above strategy statement that clear choices have been made, such as:

a. We are not going to play in the Disposables and Double Edge categories.
b. We are not going to play in the rural areas or among SEC C, D & E across Pakistan.
c. We are not focusing to disproportionally penetrate the HFS and Wholesale trade channels.
d. We are not marketing product lines in top end such as Sensor Excel, Vector and M3 Power.

Such clear and crisp choices will help make the development and deployment of action plans more focused and effective as well as allow management to efficiently allocate the finite resources and cash of the company to the agreed plans.

"Look at your choices; pick the best one,
then go to work with all your heart."
~ Pat Riley (b. 1945),
American NBA player and coach

5 C. Strategy should be Winnable and Sustainable – How Do We Win Choices?

The strategies you have created based on the choices you have made when you defined 'where do we play?' should be winnable on a sustainable basis. These strategies should be robust enough to continue into the future while delivering the key objectives of your vision. One key ingredient of winning is to make sure that the strategy is built around and should utilize a company's core competencies.

Core competencies are the main strengths or strategic advantages of any business house. They are a combination of the pooled knowledge, experiences and technical capabilities that allows a company to win over its competitors on a sustainable basis.

Food for Thought:

Core Competency

Core competency is a concept in management theory that was first proposed in 1990 by C. K. Prahalad and Gary Hamel, two business authors, when they published their article titled "The Core Competence of the Corporation." They defined core competency as a key strength that a business sees as being central to the way the company or its employees operate. In the view of the authors, for it to be a core competency, it must fulfill the following three key criteria,[34]

1. Competitors must not be able to easily imitate that strength.
2. The company must continue to reuse this strength in its services and product launches and hence provides potential access to a wide variety of markets.
3. The strength must make a significant contribution to the full satisfaction of the consumer's final experience.

Core competencies can take various forms, ranging from a strong technical skill, in-depth knowledge of a relevant subject matter, a unique product innovation, an inimitable manufacturing process, or a durable in-depth relationship with customers and suppliers.

P&G 'core competencies' or as they are sometimes called 'core strengths' include factors such as,[11]

1. Consumer Understanding: Uncovers the unarticulated needs of consumers,
2. Innovation: Translates consumer desires into new products,
3. Brand-Building: P&G brands are among the world's best know household names,
4. Go-to-Market Capability: Reaches the retailers and consumers at the right place and time,
5. Scale: Drives efficiency and consumer value.

Any product strategy in P&G and now Gillette, which incorporates any one or a combination of these core competencies, has a sure-fire chance of winning. Do note that the aforementioned competencies matter most for any player in the consumer goods industry and yet they may wary from industry to industry.

Another integral aspect of a good strategy is that it should be able to stand the test of time; it should not be designed to win in the short run only. Hence the choices we make must ensure that we win in the market place. To win one must keep in sight the following four factors:

1. Must make sure we fully utilize our core competencies or core strengths.
2. Have the right resources, funding, and systems in place.
3. Have the right organization in place to deliver these strategies.
4. Have the right winning culture in the organization.

If we miss any one of these factors, the chances are high that we may not have a winning or sustainable strategy.

> **Vital Tip 14:** When we are making choices on where-to-play and how-do-we-win, one factor should not change and that is our value system, without which nothing we do will be sustainable. Our core values should always remain constant while our strategies may get modified over time, in line with the changes in demographics or the competitive environment.

Let me explain this with three bold examples:

1. Pringles, an innovative product designed by P&G and launched for the first time in the United States in October 1968, and distributed internationally in 1975, did well in its first decade of launch. P&G, based on consumer feedback and complaints on existing potato chips being broken, greasy and stale, with air in the bags, had created the perfect potato chip, which addressed all these issues. In the late 70's and early 80's Pringles started facing an uncertain future as its sales stagnated and it seemed that Pringles might have to be shelved.

A small group of passionate P&G managers who were also die-hard Pringle lovers took over the project and refused to accept that this product was a failure. They believed this was a winning and innovative product that met all the needs of the potato chips consumer, but they also realized that somehow the communication to the consumer was off-track and the focus very myopic. They went back to the basics, looked at its prime prospects, the equity of the brand in the minds of the consumers as well as its promotional and advertising campaigns. They reviewed its key operational and marketing challenges and checked them vis-à-vis P&G core competencies.

They came up with some key insights. Pringles was spot on when it came to 'Innovation', 'Go-to-market Capability' and on 'Scale'. However, on the other two, i.e. 'Consumer Understanding' and 'Branding-Building' it left a lot to be desired. The huge unmet opportunity, the youth, had not been penetrated. In addition, the current model, which was in place since Pringles initial launch, was much too focused on ladies and as a formal party snacks. It was not being portrayed as a snack on the run for the youth of today.

It was sad to see this outage, as P&G prides itself in knowing and understanding its consumer. The team redesigned the packaging, and redid the marketing and promotional programs. In early 80's, the company launched the Pringle Jingle, whose lyrics were "Once you taste the flavor ("It's a deep-fried taste!"), then you get the fever ("With a crispy crunch!"), then you've got the fever for the flavor of a Pringle!" Starting in early 90's (and continuing to today), Pringles advertises its products by comparing them to bagged chips, which they viewed as greasy and broken.

The results were amazing. Pringles quickly went on to become a new member of the Billion Dollar Club among the P&G portfolio of brands. Its acceptance among teenagers and craving by the youth reached a crescendo, when in a survey done with Japanese teenagers, the number one answer to the question "If this was your last day on earth what one brand would you like to eat?" was no other than Pringles ☺. (Fact: On Feb 15, 2012 P&G sold Pringles to Kellogg Company for $2.7bn which helped boost Kellogg's standing to world number two in the savory snack market).

2. Let's assume that as part of the where do we play choices we decide that our distribution strategy is to cover the entire country, i.e. both urban and rural Pakistan. Of course Go-to-Market Capability is one of our core competencies but having made this choice, you also need to review the how-do-we-win checklist. The basic question you need to answer is whether this strategy is sustainable? This requires an evaluation of our funding, resources and infrastructure capability. The reality on the ground is that our distributor has presence only in the top fifty towns or roughly 30% of the population of Pakistan. Going to rural areas will require us to serve the balance of the population (additional 70%), which entails an exponential increase in sales force resources, a much more complex supply system and a huge increase in infrastructure such as warehousing, branches, vans and IT equipment.

So when we carry out this how-do-we-win analysis, we will come to realize that although we may have the knowledge and expertise in the area of distribution, we are not ready for this level of expansion or investment and that it would require a step-change in funding and resources to implement this strategy. This would force us to review our where do we play choices so that they are in sync with our funding and resource potential.

3. One of the goals that every company drives is top line or sales revenue growth. In order to capture a bigger chunk of the market share, imagine a company, which slashes its prices by 50%. If initially our product was only affordable by SEC A and B consumers (which make up the top two tiers of Pakistan's population), with the steep price decrease we will suddenly be able to penetrate a much bigger chunk of the population by becoming affordable also to the low income SEC C and possibly SEC D+ consumers. SEC E, which is the lowest socio-economic class, will still remain beyond the scope due to affordability. We have with one bold action added nearly 40% more consumers who will realize that this is now affordable and within there reach.

The company will clearly meet their top line growth objectives, but is this strategy sustainable? Not at all! As we will immediately start bleeding as soon as we slash the prices and will not be able to sustain these low prices for a long period. Now if we increase the prices again the sales revenue will plummet as our consumer base will be slashed by one third and you will totally confuse the consumer with your yo-yo action.

Always remember that the formation of every business strategy is a two-step process, first decide where-to-play and then how-do-we-win? Whatever choices you make, try to first make sure you fully utilize and build on the organization or company's core competencies and then make sure they are sustainable and long term in nature. As you create consumer loyalty, trust begins to take root and then it becomes critical that we continue to deliver products of high quality and a value proposition that the consumers can live with.

"There is nothing so useless as doing efficiently
that which should not be done at all."
~ Peter Drucker (1909–2005),
Writer and Management Consultant

5 D. Strategy Drives Action Plans

Once you have made your choices and agreed on a strategy, you can roll it out to your team, who will then work on identifying specific action plans, which will in turn make up each individual employees work-plan. In fact the end objective of this whole exercise should be that if anyone were to ask any employee, from any department the following question, "How does your work-plan link to the overall company's goals and strategies?" They should be able to clearly show the link to the company's specific goals and strategies, which their work directly impacts. That is when, one can say, vision and goals have successfully been deployed and the organization is fully enrolled.

"Do not wait for leaders; do it alone, person to person."
~ Mother Teresa (1910–1997),
Albanian Catholic Nun and Missionary

Sources of Growth: It is vital to know where the future growth is coming from and you must focus your resources and funding on the strategies which deliver the most benefit and overall growth. If you have a goal to reach, say $50 million in five years and that requires you to grow your sales revenue at a +20% annualized basis, it is essential that you know exactly where this +20% year-to-year growth is going to come from. Using the same example as used earlier on B&R let's say that growth comes from three strategies, namely:

1. Expanding distribution from x to y in Global Customers and from a to b in Modern Retail.

2. Increase awareness of Systems via media and direct-to-consumer activities.
3. Launching new and improved upgrades to further grow the Systems segment.

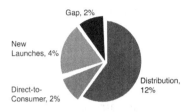

You now need to know how much each of these will contribute to business growth in the next five years. Let's assume that the growth you derive from strategy number one is +12% per annum, followed by +2% on strategy number two and +4% on strategy number three. A pie chart is an ideal way of capturing sources of growth as it emphasizes the importance of each strategy in achieving your goals.

Gap analysis vis-à-vis Goals or Measures: Once the strategies have been defined and you have carried out a detailed analysis to figure out the size of the prize for each of the identified strategies, you will then need to add them up and check versus the overall goals that you have shared with your teams (i.e. 20%). If the sum of all your strategies matches or is higher than the goals, then you are in a very strong position and are ready to go ahead with full steam on your strategies. From the above example you clearly know two things:

a. You will not reach your vision in time as the cumulative total of your current strategies only delivers growth of +18% annualized and not the 20% needed.
b. Distribution is the most critical of all strategies, as it alone will deliver 60% of the total goal.
c. You have a gap of 2% growth which you need plug!

To do this you need to go back to your drawing board and come up with more ideas of generating top-line growth and using these new ideas help plug the 2% gap. While thinking of top-line growth, one has to be very careful not to take our eyes off the bottom line. Any proposition to deliver growth should be sustainable and profitable for the business in the long run.

> "However beautiful the strategy,
> you should occasionally look at the results."
> ~ Winston Churchill (1874–1965),
> British Politician and UK Prime Minister

To me *gap analysis* is like a gyroscope of an airplane, it keeps you on track to reach your goals. As in the example above, you have a gap of 2% versus your stated growth goals. In this case, you should still deploy your strategies to the organization, but inform your teams of the existing gap. You will then need to relook your set of strategies, either give each of them a further top spin to plug the gap, or re-evaluate other ideas that were gathered in the earlier brainstorming session to deliver your vision. Pick one, which delivers a growth of at least 2% over the next five years.

Vital Tip 15:

1. It would be ideal if you identify growth ideas that add up to more than your target. In that case if any unexpected event happens, such as strong competitive reaction, major devaluation, change in government policy, etc., you will have a buffer and still be able to deliver the target growth rate.

2. Gap analysis of our goals or measures should be an on-going activity as external factors or competitive reactions are very dynamic, additional gaps may appear and they will have to be monitored and plugged. When facing major challenges and capability issues, the size of the prize of each strategy should drive prioritization of which strategies you and your teams should be focusing on.

"The tragedy in life doesn't lie in not reaching your goal.
The tragedy lies in having no goal to reach."
~ Benjamin Mays (1894–1984),
American Minister, Educator, Scholar and Social Activist

5 E. Have Faith in your Strategy

Once a strategy has been developed and deployed, it is critical that one must have strong faith in it and not get disheartened or discouraged if the initial results do not start flowing in as expected. Remember that defining a strategy, testing and deploying it is a long and tedious task. It involves having detailed discussions, inputs and feedback from the entire team, in depth analysis etc. Based on the data and market experience, you create a booklet (detailed launch plan), which contains volume, sales turnover, financials, marketing investment, promotions, discounts, profit, etc. for the next five years. You may even have goals and targets for each of the fiscal's quarters. Hence it is vital that you and your team have strong belief in your work and an unwavering faith that the agreed strategy will deliver.

What sometimes happens is that when the initial results are discouraging, many inexperienced managers react by saying "Oh no! This strategy is no good, it is not working!" What you should be doing at the first indication when results are off track is to go back to the drawing board and check out each and every assumption and figure out the reason for the poor results. The last thing you should be doing is damaging your team's faith in the strategy and in turn hurting the team spirit. Giving up too early on one's strategy is clearly one of the key reasons why so many companies and initiatives fail. Thomas Edison the famous American inventor summed this up very aptly when he said "Many of life's failures are people who did not realize how close they were to success when they gave up."

"Success consists of going from failure to failure without loss of enthusiasm."
~ Winston Churchill (1874–1965), British Politician and UK Prime Minister

Having faith in your work, your ideas and your analysis is one of the most critical virtues, which will attract success. Your ideas must hold water; they must be able to withstand critical examination and should be based on strong tested assumptions. If all these factors are true, then you must focus on finding the reasons behind the deviation and strike back with new learning's and analysis. There are scores of assumptions and all of them must be perfectly executed in order to keep the project on track. From my experience, the key reasons for an initiative to fail are:

1. Lack of proper tracking or systems to help rectify any deviation from the agreed plans.
2. Not following key assumptions, e.g. not taking agreed price-ups, not making marketing expenditures in-line with the booklet or just poor execution at various stages.
3. Distribution gains not in line with expectations. Many times we are too bullish in how quickly we will gain distribution and consequently expose volume build up.
4. Inadequate consumer trials. This is a critical indicator and is dependent on many factors including media, pricing, packaging, distribution, etc. and each aspect has to be on track.
5. Not having a strong advertisement copy on-air that would drive trial and awareness. Remember that a poor or below average copy will require the same investment but will deliver poor results.
6. Unexpected external shocks such as sudden currency devaluation, supply issues from the plants, law and order (in Pakistan) and how well you react to these will define success.

"Nearly every person who develops an idea
works at it up to the point where it looks
impossible, and then gets discouraged.
That's not the place to become discouraged."
~ Thomas A. Edison (1847–1931),
American Inventor, Scientist and Businessman

Nobody is suggesting on having blind faith in ones strategy. In order to deliver on all success factors it is important to have a check-list of items that must be tracked and analyzed like a hawk during the first few years of the initiative. In fact during the first twelve months, I would suggest you do it monthly and then on a quarterly basis. These will include items such as:

1. Are we spending in line with the agreed plan in the booklet?
2. Are distribution gains on track? This should be done by trade channel and geographies.
3. Is our pricing strategy in line with the booklet plan?
4. Are the volume gains, stock-in-trade and consumer off-take in line with the plans?
5. Is awareness and trial build-up on the new initiative in line with objectives?
6. Are the resources deployed on the project in line with agreed budgets?
7. Is the financial progress in line with booklet objectives, i.e. profit, sales revenue, etc.?

One aspect that is often overlooked while planning an initiative is not taking into account and in most cases under estimating the reaction by your competitor. You must realize that if you launch something new in the market, competition will not sit around and watch you take away their market share. They will fight you tooth and nail for every share point. Never try to get into a price war especially when your pricing is not sustainable; never fight on disproportional marketing spending if you cannot afford to do so. The key is to focus on building your brand equity, as in that case the consumer will buy your product for its equity and for believing that it will provide a superior consumer experience.

The best way to anticipate and predict competitive reaction is to put yourself in the competitors shoes and see how you would react if your competition had launched such a product or such an initiative. There is no better option to fight competition than to be prepared.

> "Perseverance is a great element of success.
> If you only knock long enough and loud enough at
> the gate, you are sure to wake up somebody."
> ~ Henry Wadsworth Longfellow (1807–1882),
> American Poet and Professor

Vital Tip 16: I still remember a comment made by the CISCO chief at a global P&G seminar in Cincinnati many years ago. He asked the following questions: "At what stage in an initiatives product life cycle, should one think of changing ones strategy?" When I think of his answer to  this question, even today, I am amazed at the insight built into the reply. He said "When you are most successful" this is because according to the 'Product Life Cycle' you reach peak performance when you are most successful (maturity) and if you continue to follow the same strategies, your performance will drop as competition or even customers will become more knowledgeable and demanding.

Hence, the best time to change your strategy is when your idea has reached its peak. This way your business growth will not drop into a trough but you will move from peak to peak. Bottom-line is that if you are not fast, flexible and responsive, you will never win the race. Always be in-touch with your environment, competition and the market conditions and know when your initiative has reached its maturity stage.

5 F. Power of a Good Strategy

Here is a real-life story on the 'Power of a Good Strategy.' Once in a management training session in Geneva, I met a fascinating athlete who in his life had won many 100 and 200 meters gold medals for his country. Let's call him Mr. X. He told us a story, which very aptly highlights the impact of a well researched and well executed strategy.

Mr. X told us that as a kid he loved to race although he picked up track and field later in life when a coach saw him running and saw his potential. He took part in local events as well as junior championships on a regional basis. His problem was that he was not consistent. Sometimes he would come first but on many occasions he would rank second, third or even lower. He kept training and running with passion but he could never win races with consistency. This finally changed when he met his current coach who was very impressed with his physique, his passion and his natural flair to run fast.

The coach asked him "What is your strategy when you run a race?" Mr. X was a bit taken aback with the question and said "I put in the last ounce of my energy in every race and the only strategy I follows is to run as fast as I can." The coach again asked, "I understand that, but do you follow any specific strategy?" This time Mr. X was stumped and said, "No there is no specific strategy but to run as fast as I can."

The coach told him that you need a strategy to win any race. By strategy he meant how to best utilize his finite energy and stamina while running the race. The coach further explained that for a 200-meter race, you start full throttle from the blocks and immediately take the lead, this will demoralize your competitors. Maintain the lead for the first twenty-five meters. As it's a long race, after twenty-five meters you continue to run fast but try to conserve energy, benefitting from your momentum and not accelerating at this stage. This you do for the next seventy-five meters. Once you have covered hundred meters, you should again move into your higher gear and start to accelerate and build up your speed for the next fifty meters. Once past the 150 mark, you accelerate and speed up like hell and use up every last ounce of your energy.

Mr. X told us that he listened in amazement, as he had never thought that you could break up a race into portions and have a different strategy for each portion with regard to speed, utilization of energy and stamina. His coach also gave him a similar breakup for the 100-meter race. Mr. X started to practice with this in mind and after a few months he would automatically change gears at pre-aligned milestones and he started to win races with consistency. He then went on to win major tournaments including the European Championship, the World Championship and the Olympics.

My recollection of the coach's detailed strategy may not be exact, but the key point I am trying to make is that for every activity you need a strategy. With a good, well thought out strategy you can outdo competition on a sustainable basis. If your strategy is not delivering the required results, you must take a step back and revisit it. In short, a good strategy makes all the difference between winning and losing.

"There is always a better strategy than the one you have;
you just haven't thought of it yet."
~ Sir Brian Pitman (1932–2010),
Banker

Food for Thought:

The Cobra Effect

Majority of strategies make perfect sense to their planner but unfortunately many still do fail. What the planners have failed to do is act as devil advocates and review all possibilities and reactions under which this strategy can survive in the real world where competitors or the public could be much more creative and cunning. Let me share an excellent example of a strategy, which looked great on face value but they went terribly wrong and failed miserably.

Cobra Effect: During the British rule in colonial India the British government was very concerned about the number of venomous cobra snakes found in Delhi. To solve this rampant infestation the government offered a bounty to anyone who killed a cobra and brought its dead body. This strategy initially worked perfectly as a large number of cobras were killed for the reward. Where the strategy failed miserably was when some enterprising individuals started to breed cobras. Eventually the British government had no option but to scrap the program, causing cobra breeders to set their worthless snakes free. As a result of this strategy the wild cobra population increased exponentially which continues to impact India even today.

This is a great example of where an apparent solution to a problem made the situation even worse. The cobra effect occurs when an attempted solution to a problem actually makes the problem worse and today this term is used to explain causes of incorrect stimulation in economy and politics.

5 G. Strategy vs. Tactic

It is important to understand the difference between strategy and tactic, as both are needed for delivering your vision. There is a widespread misconception that strategy and tactics are one and the same, which is absolutely untrue. Let's start with the definition for each:

Origin and Definition of Strategy[32]
Etymology: This word is derived from the Greek word *Strategos*, which again is derived from two words: *Stratus* meaning army and *Ago* meaning leading. Strategos was initially used for a military commander during the age of Athenian Democracy ~ 500 BC.

Origin and Definition of Tactics[35]
Etymology: This word is derived from New Latin *Tactica*, from Greek *Taktike*, fit for arranging, from *tassein* to arrange. It is the art of organizing military or naval forces for battle and maneuvering them in battle. It refers to any mode or procedure for gaining advantage or success—a plan, procedure, or expedient for promoting a desired end or result.

As stated in Wikipedia: Strategy is distinct from tactics. In military terms, tactics is concerned with the conduct of an engagement while strategy is concerned with how different engagements are linked.

> "Do not repeat the tactics which have gained you one victory,
> but let your methods be regulated by the
> infinite variety of circumstances."
> ~ Sun Tzu (544–496 BC),
> Chinese Military General, Strategist and Philosopher

Business Perspective: Jeremiah Josey, Business Consultant and a member of Mensa International explains it very well when he states in one of his presentations,[36]

- Strategy is the What, Where, Why and the 'Big Picture' while
- Tactics is the How, Tasks, Activities or as we say the 'Devil is in the detail'.

To succeed in any activity, initiative or action you need to have both, strategy and tactics. Without a proper strategy, tactics will fail and without proper tactics, strategy will fail. Jeremiah further elucidates that 'the order' is, first comes talking and then comes action, that is:

- Applying strategy without tactics is all talk but no action; nothing actually gets done (too much strategy).
- Implementing tactics without strategy is like 'the blind leading the blind'. It is when someone is too busy cutting down the tree to stop and sharpen the saw or see where the tree will finally fall, i.e. ready, fire and then aim! (too many tactics).

People are generally fearful of commitment, a trait learnt when one is younger, (don't make mistakes!), this leads to too much strategy, too much talking and nothing actually gets done. On the other hand people are also fearful of being accused of not being productive, another mannerism learned when one is young, (you must look busy to be successful!), which leads to lots of tactics, doing a lot but nothing is properly planned and the wrong things get done.

To top it off, according to Jeremiah these two personality types do not tend to mix well, specifically:

- To a tactician, strategists appear non-committal, airy-fairy, light headed, and fanciful.

- To a strategist, tacticians appear hard headed, dogmatic, aggressive and single minded.

In another interesting comparison to help understand the differences, Jeremiah states:

- Not making a commitment for fear of making mistakes increases strategy and decreases tactics – nothing gets done.
- Fear of not looking busy decreases strategy and increases tactics – wrong things get done.

"Strategy without tactics is the slowest route to victory.
Tactics without strategy is the noise before defeat."
~ Sun Tzu (544–496 BC),
Chinese Military General, Strategist and Philosopher

Strategists don't understand tacticians and tacticians don't understand strategists. It is the balance between the two that is critical; each project or activity has its own balance point. Some projects require lots of strategy and fewer tactics and some require very little strategy and lots of tactics. Some require an equal mix. Experience is really what tells us in what proportion each is required. The key is to recognize the importance of the balance between strategy and tactics and this can only be done if one focuses on the output and measures performance closely.

If the same strategy is applied in different environments, the tactics can vary significantly depending on demographics or changes in technology. A strategy, which grew business fifty years ago, may still apply today. However, due to technological changes, demographic and economic changes, yesterday's tactics will definitely not work today and will have to conform to the new environment. Simplest way to remember the difference between strategy and tactic is that they require different focus.

Strategy looks at the big picture or the forest, while tactics focus on individual trees.

> "All men can see these tactics whereby I conquer,
> but what none can see is the strategy out
> of which victory is evolved."
> ~ Sun Tzu (544–496 BC),
> Chinese Military General, Strategist and Philosopher

When you are leading an organization you set a *vision* with its associated *goals*. Next you lay down your *strategies* to help deliver your vision. To help drive your strategies you have to figure out the right *tactics*. Many of us overlook the difference between the two. Strategy in this case is the overall game plan that will help deliver the goals, while tactics are the tools that you will use to fulfill your strategy. So in simpler words strategy is your *plan* while the tactics are the *execution* of these strategies.

In a military context in World War II the German's used a strategy, which they called *Blitzkrieg* (German strategy of concentrating all military power and barging into enemy territory with lightening speed generally attributed to German Panzer division commander General Heinz Guderian). While the tactic in this case was the actual combat, managing logistics, etc. Let me substantiate with a business example:

Vision: To be the largest fruit juice company in Pakistan.

Goals: Achieve market leadership in the fresh fruit juice segment.

Be known as the largest exporter of packaged fruit juices.

Strategy: Convince consumers that your fruit juices are the purest and freshest juices available in the market for both high-end and low-end consumers.

Tactics	Sample fruit juices in all Global Customers stores.
	Have best in class distribution in High Frequency Stores.
	Advertise heavily on TV, cable and FM radios stations.
	Make sure all high-end hotels use our fruit juices in their hotels.
	Get endorsements from celebrities.

5 H. Path to Success: A Summary

We have completed the first portion of this handbook and have learned what a mission is and what it means to have a vision. We know how to define them and how to implement them. The pyramid summarizes the first five chapters of this handbook. Summary of the process is:

1. Define the purpose for which the company has been established, basically your company's mission in life and its reason to exist.

2. Next you must carefully set a vision that is in line with your mission. This defines where you want to be in five to ten years: The vision should be crisp, clear and inspirational for the organization. Your job will be to literally paint a picture of your vision so that you excite and energize your organization in such a way that they want to deliver it. Come up with an inspirational name for your vision, which helps to keep it alive, use this name in all your communications to make it a part of everyday business discussions and decision-making.

3. The numbers that help you define your vision are called goals. Goals should most certainly be stretch, which means that at this point in time you and your team are not clear on exactly how you will deliver them. Goals must be achievable but not unrealistic so as not to demoralize the organization. Your goals also need to follow the SMART principle. Remember the clearer, more specific and relevant your goals are, the better you will be able to drive behavior towards impactful and focused activities. People by design work more intensely and put in more effort when goals are well defined.

4. Next come the most time consuming and mentally challenging work, that of defining the various strategies to help deliver your vision. Here you need to test your strategies against two fundamental questions:
    a. Where do you want to play as a company, i.e. what product lines, what channels, what geographies, etc.
    b. How do you intend to win? Are you utilizing your company's core competencies to achieve your goals, are you strategies sustainable, do you have the right resources and capabilities to deliver the choices.

5. If all of your strategies pass this test, than you are ready to list down and identify the key tactics, or the actual tasks and activities to execute your strategies. Tactics are the devil in the detail and are the critical action steps to bring your strategies to life.

As the diagram aptly portrays, all of this is done in an environment of trust, where company values are followed to the letter. And finally, the foundation of your success rests on your ability to deliver executional excellence, meaning immaculate planning, perfect in-market execution and flawless implementation of tactics.

The remainder of this section of the handbook (Part I) is focused on how to deploy these strategies and tactics, how you set their respective measures, how they are tracked, how to achieve executional excellence and finally some key watch-outs which if not focused on could significantly hurt your entire vision setting process.

••••••━━━ ━━━━━••••

Chapter 6 – Setting Measures and Tracking Them

6 A. What are Measures?

"Measures are for strategies as goals are for vision."
~ Saad Amanullah Khan

Measures are strategy's goals and act as a barometer of whether the strategy is effective in delivering the overall expected growth, profitability or consumer benefit. It has been very aptly stated by Peter Drucker, "If you want it, measure it. If you can't measure it, forget it."

If you want people to focus on a specific strategy, then you must be able to measure the results that are delivered by it, else having a strategy without measurability is as good as not having one at all. Measurability also helps in guiding and monitoring the strategy, hence measures should be created or calculated from authentic data with due care. Employees need to be very clear on what the measures stand for, only then will their actions and decisions impact the strategy in the intended manner.

"It's no use saying, 'We are doing our best.'
You have got to succeed in doing what is necessary."
~ Winston Churchill (1874–1965),
British Politician and UK Prime Minister

6 B. The SMART Concept

Measures, just like goals, should follow the SMART concept, i.e. they should be **S**pecific, **M**easureable, **A**ttainable, **R**ealistic and **T**imely. Defining measures should be done very carefully as they will not only help drive the delivery of the strategy but also the motivation of the team. Missing out on any of the SMART factors will reduce the success of a specific strategy.

All five SMART factors are important but two, to me stand out. First is **Timely**, i.e. delivering the strategy on time. As Charles De Gaulle said "You have to be fast on your feet and adaptive or else a strategy is useless." Let me emphasize timeliness with an example. One distribution strategy could be to win with all Global Customers (GC). GC's such as Metro, Makro and Hyperstar (Carrefour's local name) were entering Pakistan in 2006 in a big way. Hence, it was important that we gain the first mover advantage and negotiate a strong placement at the time of the opening at all new GC stores. But if one is not focusing on timeliness then one may just miss the boat as most GC's sign yearly contracts with their customers. If you miss this cycle, you will have to wait a whole year before you can register your products or your company with that GC. Hence timeliness is a critical factor.

> "Until you value yourself, you won't value your time.
> Until you value your time, you will not do anything with it."
> ~ M. Scott Peck (1936–2005),
> American Psychiatrist and Best-Selling Author

The other is **Measurable**, i.e. we must have the tools to properly track and conclusively measure the outcome of a specific strategy. When I took over Gillette we did not have any retail audit or market share data. Hence setting a measure of market share at that point in time would not have been advisable as we would be unable to measure the impact of any changes in market shares. Therefore, all the measures I set were those that could be calculated, tracked and accurately audited.

Selecting the right measures is a tough job and requires in-depth knowledge of the business. One should not have measures where all you do is compare performance versus the previous year's plans or budgets. The pitfall of measuring your performance in this manner is that you may feel very happy with the internal growth you are delivering but versus competition you may not be doing so well, they may be growing much faster.

So do include some measures that are externally focused and help evaluate performance of your managers and organization vis-à-vis the external world. Being externally focused is a key P&G principle and utilizing this principle will always give you unbiased feedback on your company's true performance.

> **Vital Tip 17:** Make sure that the measures you have deployed are well understood by everyone. That is the key reason why following the SMART concept is so important. If you miss any one of the SMART factors, you may end up deploying your strategy and have half the organization confused and misdirected on how to measure its success, thus impacting the effectiveness of the strategy.

6 C. Balanced Scorecard and Top 10's

I am a firm believer in the power of Scorecarding. One of the reasons for the success of top rated companies is that these companies actively use the concept of Scorecarding and also focus on the Top 10's, two simple but very powerful priority setting tools.

> "What gets measured gets done. What
> gets rewarded gets repeated."
> ~ John Schnatter (b. 1961),
> Founder of Papa Johns

Scorecard: The roots of using scorecards to measure performance dates back to the 50's when General Electric started using it in their projects. Another example of using a scorecard comes from French process engineers (who created the *tableau de bord* – literally meaning a 'dashboard'), which they used in the early part of the 20th century. Art Schneiderman who worked for Analog Devices, a mid-sized semi-conductor company, carried out the first use of the Balanced Scorecard in 1987.[37] Today the scorecard is a standard reporting tool used to track company progress versus its strategies. It captures and tracks all key business performance measures and makes progress transparent and available at all levels and all departments.

Harvard professor Dr. Robert S. Kaplan and others carried out an early application of this concept in a Nolan-Norton Institute study group. Kaplan and Norton's first book, *The Balanced Scorecard* remains the most comprehensive and popular book on this topic, but it lacked guidance on how to develop strategies. Their second book *Strategy-Focused Organization* added another dimension, i.e. Strategy Map. This new book has gained considerable popularity and following, and is used by many commercial companies, governments and non-profit organizations in helping provide a visual way to develop business strategies.

The scorecard that worked effectively for me at Gillette was the simple one-pager that tracked all key measures. Gillette scorecard was made up of a simple table (see a portion recreated below) and the following columns and rows:

- Column 1 contains all of our agreed strategies and their respective measures.
- Columns 2 to 13 are the twelve months of the fiscal year.
- Columns 14 to 18 show the four quarters of the fiscal year and total fiscal year.
- Column 19 is the target for each measure that we should deliver by the end of the fiscal.

Column 1	2	3	4

GILLETTE PAKISTAN LIMITED
COMPREHENSIVE SCORECARD

Row	FINANCIALS (all # in $'s)	Jul-09	Aug-09	Sep-09
1	Volume			
	Index vs. Year Ago			
2	Net Outside Sales			
	Index vs. Year Ago			
3	Total Delivered Cost			
4	Controllable Overheads			
5	Marketing Spending			
6	Gillette business in GC/MR			
	Index vs. P&G Split in Gc/MR			
7	# of Hotspots (Perfect Stores)			
8	Modern Retail Program			
9	Recievable Days			

The rows below the titles of the columns are driven by the question "What do we want to measure to help deliver our strategies?" Each of the measures tracked is closely tied to a specific strategy that we want to deliver as per our Mission Dugna Tigna game plan. As an example, Gillette played mainly in the premium segment and for this reason I wanted to win big in the high-end channels, i.e. Global Customer and Modern Trade. To drive this growth I set a strategy, which required us to double our share of business in these two channels vis-à-vis, other key Multinational Corporations (MNC's) share. If other MNC's did 10% business in GC and MR, I wanted Gillette split to be 20%. My scorecard clearly showed the Gillette split (measure 6 in the scorecard excerpt).

Another measure that was tracked was the Perfect Store Hotspot program (see chapter on Vision Setting) and Modern Retail Program, i.e. how many stores were added that met the success criteria of having a Hotspot behind the counter and a full portfolio displayed by the trade (measures 7 in scorecard excerpt). Similarly the balance of the scorecard covered all the other strategies via a measure that we could track and which would give us an indication whether we were on the right track and were making timely progress towards our vision.

Scorecarding is a powerful tool if used properly. Once you have the month-to-month trend as well as the goal of where on that specific measure you are (defining success), you have a very potent tool in your hands. You can use it in many ways, let me substantiate with a few examples:

1. You can look at the month-to-month and quarter-to-quarter trends.
2. Another effective way is to track past three months, six months or nine months historical rolling averages in order to help smoothen out the data and to help remove any spikes or noise. (See graphs below).
3. You can also add a column to project the 'actual to date' on a full fiscal year basis (pro-rata). This will allow you to project your measure to the end of the fiscal year and assess that if you were to continue delivering based on current growth trends, how will you end the fiscal year.

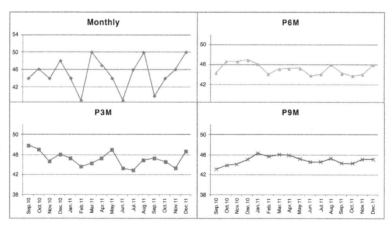

Remember to always com-plement your scorecards with line or bar graphs; they help you to visually see positive or negative trends that may be embedded in the data. To further augment the importance of delivering your goals or measures, superimpose a bold line on top of the graph showing goals or targets of a specific strategy, this would highlight the progress of monthly trends and whether they are driving towards the eventual goal or measure for your vision or strategy.

Vital Tip 18: One fact highlighted by Robert S. Kaplan and David P. Norton in their book *The Strategy-Focused Organization* is that even at senior management levels they found evidence where managers had difficulty understanding and selecting measures. To test their hypothesis they gave a list of thirty measures to a ten-person executive team and asked them to identify the ones that they felt should be on the Balanced Scorecard, only one measure, i.e. ROCE (Return of Capital Employed) appeared on all ten lists.

Hence it is important that while defining the measures, in depth discussion is carried out and measures are agreed on with the team's participation and alignment. Remember it is the team that will be required to deliver these goals and it's important that they buy in and understand the importance of the measures and how they are linked to the task.

Top 10's: Another tool that is very effective in driving result-oriented behavior is the effective use of Top 10's. The Top 10's is an outstanding tool to ensure that the entire organization is working in the same direction on agreed top priorities, with the proper focus to get things done faster, and is also a top motivation tool. I have personally found them to be very effective and utilize them a lot. My boss back in 1996, Vice President/General Manager Mr. Philippe Bovay first introduced me to the concept of Top 10's when he came to head P&G Pakistan and I was his CFO.

How it works: At the beginning of every quarter, each functional leader and team leader lists their Top 10 priorities, more than ten would result in insufficient focus to get the top things done quickly.

This Top 10 list is agreed on with the general manager and the management team, so that all are aware of what the organization is doing, and can ensure they provide enough support to projects that require multi-functional cooperation. At the beginning of each month the management team meets to review the progress on each project in the Top 10s, and break down barriers that may be hindering their completion. Once projects are completed they are crossed off the list, giving all those involved a strong sense of accomplishment, and thereby providing positive energy to tackle the next projects.

Management while prioritizing the Top 10s also takes into account the size of the prize of each initiative, as well as the importance of the project to the overall success of the company. This concept is very close to the Pareto Principle, also known as the 80-20 rule or the 'law of the vital few' that states that 80% of your sales come from 20% of your clients. This principle has been tested and comes true in nature, in human behavior and in our daily life. For you the implication is that 20% of your projects will deliver 80% of the growth and value creation.

Hence the Top 10's inherently help you focus on a few and most probably the top 20% of the projects in the company's pipeline. By driving your Top 10's through your teams and by bringing focus to these ten high value projects, you will automatically drive 80% of the growth towards your vision.

6 D. Performance Evaluation Scorecards

All of my work experience since I graduated from University of Michigan with an MBA in Finance has been with P&G and then Gillette, and they constantly use the scorecard very effectively not only in running their businesses but also in evaluating performances of its top leaders and general managers. Evaluation of all general managers used to be carried out every six months with what is called the GM Performance Scorecard. It is a succinct two-page document, which not only covers all the relevant financial and business performance measures but also includes equally important measures on the general manager's leadership and team-building abilities.[38]

Just like all employees, the GM also goes through a 360° review, i.e. their bosses obtain feedback and inputs from their lateral managers as well as from their direct reports. I have not come across many companies where the board or senior management obtains their GM's feedback from junior managers and if they do, in many cases no concrete action is taken based on the feedback. To me the 360° review is probably one of the most important factors when it comes to assessing the true nature of a senior manager's leadership, collaboration and team-building skills. Scorecarding is used very effectively to manage employee performance, their career planning as well as their development needs.

6 E. The Five Traps of Performance Measurement

An attention-grabbing article *"The Five Traps of Performance Measurement"* by Andrew Likierman in the October 2009 issue of *Harvard Business Review* takes a look at some key traps that managers face while measuring performance. Remember delivering on measures (that track all strategies and tactics) is the key to the success of delivering your vision. Hence tracking the right measures and rewarding managers for the right performance (that builds business sustainably) is essential for delivering any vision. As per Mr. Likierman the five traps are:

1. Measuring Against Yourself
2. Looking Backward
3. Putting Your Faith in Numbers
4. Gaming Your Metrics
5. Sticking to your Numbers too Long

Below are the explanations as per Likierman of the five traps as well as my personal inputs by incorporating relevant local and international examples:

1. **Measuring Against Yourself**

   In a majority of companies when they review their yearly results, what do you think makes up the bulk of the numbers? Most likely they would be comparisons of current results with an existing plan or budget. If that's the case, you're at grave risk of falling into the first trap of performance measurement: *Looking only at yourself or your own company.* You may be doing better than your plan, delivered your budgets, but are you beating competition? To measure how well you are doing, you need information about the benchmarks that matter most, the ones outside the organization. This will allow you to define competitive priorities and connect executive compensation to relative rather than absolute performance.

   The trouble is that comparisons with your competitors or feedback from your customers cannot be carried out easily in real time – which is precisely why so many companies fall back on measurement against current or previous year's plans and budgets. On this front you have to be creative but factual on how to find the relevant data or some proxy for them.

   A key example to support this trap used by Likierman is of a car rental company Enterprise. This company uses the Enterprise Service Quality Index to measure customers repeat purchase intentions. Each branch of the company telephones a random sample of customers and asks whether they will use Enterprise again. When the index goes up, the company gains market share, when it falls, customers are taking their businesses elsewhere. All Enterprise branches post results within two weeks and put them right next to charts showing profitability and overall growth versus last year. This index plays a key role in the branch employee's performance evaluations and in how well they did versus last year, as well as forecasting the future potential of that branch's profitability and growth.

Similarly, my brother Ali and I started a burger restaurant in 2012 by the name of Big Thick Burgerz (BTB), in Karachi, Pakistan. The idea came from my love of making burgers. For over twenty-five years I char grilled them at home for my family, friends and colleagues. I

made burger patties by hand mixing minced meat with various spices and exotic ingredients. The most popular burger on our menu, the *Most Wanted,* is my personally perfected recipe. ☺ In the first year of our operation, in order to keep our cost low, our business model was delivery only. We had a one-minded focus on performance, customer experience and acceptability of our unique offering of being the only char-grilled burger made over actual coals, just like the ones I made at home on my BBQ grill.

My brother had started an index, which was based on feedback received from all customers who had ordered from BTB a day before. We rated the response on a scale of 1 to 10 and the only acceptable scores were above eight, which reflected that the customer would order again. If any day we got a score of below eight, we felt that the customer will not order again and went into an overdrive to find the reasons why and asked the customers for help to find out which part of their experience (food, delivery, packaging, services, etc.) brought down the scores. Due to this focus, 95% of our scores today are above eight, and in 2013 we opened our first dine-in restaurant and have diversified beyond just delivery service. This index has played a key role in our success to-date, and drives our team performance evaluations as well.

"Performance is your reality. Forget everything else."
~ Harold S. Geneen (1910–1997)
American Businessmen and President of ITT

2. **Looking Backward**

The comparison in majority of executive performance assessments includes comparisons between this year and the last. If so, watch out for the second trap, which is *to focus only on the past*. Beating last year's numbers is not the only point; a performance measurement system needs to tell you whether the decisions made last year were correct and whether they are going to help you in the coming months and years. You need to look for measures that lead rather than lag the profits in your business. The catch here is to identify the quality of managerial decision-making; you need to look not only at what your manager has done but what he has not done!

Likierman share an excellent example where a major investment bank in Europe measured performance by the outcomes of deals they had turned down as well as by the outcomes of deals they had won. If the ones they have rejected turned out to be lemons, those rejections count as successes. This kind of analysis seems obvious once stated, but there is a persistent bias in all of us to focus on what we do over what we don't do. Good management is about making choices, so a decision not to do something should be analyzed as closely as a decision to do something. One of the most critical factors to look at is the decision that will drive the true ability of the company to succeed in the future.

3. **Putting Your Faith in Numbers**
Good or bad, the metrics in majority of your performance assessment packages all comes as numbers. The problem is that number-driven managers often end up producing reams of low quality data. Think about how companies collect feedback on service from their customers. It is well known to statisticians that if you want evaluation forms to tell the real story, the anonymity of the respondents must be protected. Yet, out of a desire to gather as much information as possible we routinely collect personal data and in many cases the employees who provide the service watch customers fill out their forms. Bad assessment has a tendency of mysteriously disappearing! Number driven companies also gravitate toward the most popular measures. The question of which measure is the right one gets lost.

"Dictum de Omni et Nullo. ... Out of Nothing, Nothing Comes."
~ Aristotle (384–322 BC),
Greek Philosopher, Student of Plato

Likierman elucidates with another example where an HR Manager undertakes to assign an ROI (Return on Investment) number to an executive training program. Typically, he or she would ask program participants to identify a benefit, assign a dollar value to it, and estimate the probability that the benefit comes from the program. So a benefit that works out to be $70,000 and has a 50% probability of being linked to the program means a benefit from the said program of $35,000. If the program cost $25,000, the net benefit is $10,000; the ROI will be 40%. Think for a minute, how on earth can the presumed casual link be justified?

Correct way to evaluate it would be that once the program has ended, you look beyond immediate knowledge gains but try to capture on-the-job benefit resulting from this knowledge.

HR should send evaluation forms at least six months after the training to the participant, which focuses on capturing any direct or indirect benefit resulting from the said training session. Another example is from a soft drinks company Britvic where the HR assesses its executive coaching program by tracking coachees for a year afterward, comparing their career trajectories with those of people who didn't get coached.

"A good decision is based on knowledge and not on numbers."
~ Plato (428–348 BC),
Classical Greek philosopher and Mathematician

4. **Gaming Your Metrics.**
What if the numbers or estimates you are seeing is manipulated? You have to be careful, when the amount of data is daunting and people show numbers selectively! There are two key reasons for this: a) Everyone wants to win and gain their yearly bonus. b) People are afraid of sharing bad news. So before you put faith in numbers make sure you have a high level of trust in the organization. Build an organization where employees voluntarily 'raise red flags' when things go wrong rather than hiding the facts, as that can be suicidal in the long run as by the time you learn of the problem, damage could be considerable. Spend quality time deciding on what the true measures should be and work out a system by which quality data is available which is transparent and actionable.

"Man is the only kind of varmint that sets his own trap, baits it, then steps in it."
~ John Steinbeck (1902–1968),
American Author and Pulitzer Prize Winner

There are many examples where due to higher tangible benefits or just to save their skins a number of prominent companies have cooked up and manipulated there accounting books to look good. The people involved range from as high as CFO's, CEO's and even the external auditors. Examples are from all over the world, such as: Enron (US 2001), WorldCom (US 2002), Satyam Computer Services (India 2009), Parmalat (Italy 2003), Royal Ahold (Netherland 2003), etc. You can't prevent people from gaming numbers, no matter how outstanding your organization. The moment you choose to manage by a metric, you invite your managers to manipulate it.

To avert manipulation it helps to diversify your metrics, because it's a lot harder to manipulate several of them at once. Add multiple measurement criteria for each strategy and makes sure the measures come from a variety of sources. You can also vary the boundaries of your measurement, by defining responsibility more narrowly or by broadening it. One way is to make individual performances get impacted by the entire team's performance.

Vital Tip 19: You should loosen the link between meeting budgets and performance; far too many bonuses are awarded on that basis. Managers can either pad their budgets to make them easier to deliver or pare them down too far to impress their bosses and in turn impact operations. Build controls and systems to be able to see beyond, as in real life managers who try to hide overspending are usually caught after the damage had already been done.

5. **Sticking to your Numbers too Long**

As the saying goes, you manage what you measure. Unfortunately, performance assessment systems seldom evolve as fast as businesses do. Smaller and growing companies are especially likely to fall into this trap. In the earliest stages, performance is all about survival, cash resources, and growth. Comparisons are to last week, last month, and last year. But as the business matures, the focus has to move to profit and the comparisons to competitors.

The key question is that while it is easy to spot the need to change after things have gone wrong, how can you evaluate your measures before they fail you? The answer is to constantly evaluate the measures you are using and compare them against the company's needs and challenges and also to make sure that the measures are as precise as possible. In my Gillette re-launch experience, the measures that were important in the first year were not that impactful once we had fixed the basics, we had to add and/or modify the measures to make sure the right strategies were being tracked and progress assessed.

When I took over in March 2007 things were in total disarray and we had to fix all the fundamentals. All measures in the first year were focused on things such as number of stores covered, number of perfect orders delivered, discontinuing unprofitable sizes, having the right people in the right jobs, etc. Once the fundamentals were fixed we had to move to other measures which focused on continuing the growth such as initiative success rates, forecast accuracy, non-performing inventory management, number of consumer claims, etc. If I had stuck to the same measures even for another year, our growth would have stagnated and taken us off the path of our vision, i.e. Mission Dugna Tigna

Another interesting case in point shared by Likierman in his article is regarding the credit-rating agencies like Moody's that provide AAA ratings to companies, and when many of them fall into trouble, these agencies come under attack. The agencies argue in their defense that lenders misunderstand what the rating mean. The AAA rating, they claim, is awarded on the basis of the borrowers' credit records, and it describes the likelihood of default under normal market conditions, it does not factor in what might happen in the event of a massive shock to the financial system. Reasonable as this explanation may be, it is of no consolation to those who thought they knew what the magic AAA rating represented.

Reason behind these five traps is that the people who are managing performance systems are generally not experts in performance measurements. Finance people are experts in tracking cash flows, budgets, profitability, etc., but they seldom have a grasp of how operating realities connect with performance and they are precisely the people who strive to reduce judgment to a single ROI number.

So take quality time out and work on measures in a cross-functional team format so that the experience of the entire lead-team is imbedded into the measures which can then be used to help drive company performance.

····························

Chapter 7 – Vision and Strategy Deployment

Identifying a vision and strategy is a critical and essential part of direction setting, but deploying it across the organization, making sure that each individual employee understands and embraces it with full commitment is what finally brings it to life. This is the most difficult and yet vital key to the success of any visioning attempt. I have heard and personally seen scores of examples where an organization has very passionately identified a compelling vision and the associated strategies but have failed miserably to deploy it. They have paid dearly in terms of time, effort and resources, all due to the lack of commitment and ownership shown for the vision and strategies by the organization.

In fact, some experts have given a lot of weight to deployment; James C. Collins and Jerry I. Porras[39] in a *Harvard Business Review* article titled *"Building Your Company's Vision"* have stated that "Building a visionary company requires 1% vision and 99% alignment."

To me the deployment process is made up of five distinct stages. They are:

A. Clear Vision and Crisp Strategies
B. Embracing the Change
C. Breaking Down Barriers

D.   Initiate Disciplined Tracking

E.   Keeping the Vision Alive

7 A. Clear Vision and Crisp Strategies

In the vision chapter under 'Power of Vision' I have made it amply clear that "if an individual or an organization has a vision of what they want to achieve in the long run and it is in black and white and crystal clear to everyone in the organization, then all decisions that they make, every plan or move that the individual or company initiates, they do it always keeping the vision in view." Any ambiguity in defining or owning the vision can have significant negative impact on the functioning of the organization. The only way you will win as a company is if, and only if, everyone in your organization understands the vision and are 110% aligned and working in the same direction. Nothing is worse than having an organization that is misaligned and everyone is working within his or her own silos heading towards different directions.

Let me explain this through my favorite sport, Formula 1 sports car racing. For a Formula 1 racing team to work efficiently the following aspects have to *function in perfect harmony:*

a)   Each of the 5000 separate components of a racing car, of which 1,500 are movable.[40]

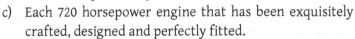

b)   Each of the 150 mechanics that are absolute experts in their areas of responsibility.

c)   Each 720 horsepower engine that has been exquisitely crafted, designed and perfectly fitted.

Then and only then will the F1 car win races and set world records. To give you a taste of the executional excellence of their strategy, take a look at the pit-stop statistics. The pit stop crew can change all four tires plus fill up the car with petrol in less than three seconds!

Similarly, for an organization to deliver disproportional results the vision has to be clear, inspirational and challenging. The organization needs to be totally aligned; teams empowered and well trained to deliver the vision. Everyone must know their roles and responsibilities in delivering the vision, which in our case is also about winning races, not on the F1 circuit but against competition and in the market place.

> "We need to advertise our goals to ourselves."
> ~ Steve Chandler,
> Motivational Speaker

Sticking to Agreed Strategies: Let me further substantiate this concept with a personal example. In the late 90's P&G Pakistan had rolled out its vision and had agreed on which categories we wanted to play in, and potato crisps (Pringles) was not one of them. As time passed, I suddenly noticed a huge influx of Pringles into Pakistan either smuggled or through regular trade, or as parallel imports. As it was one of my favorite brands and a very successful P&G global product, I wanted to add it to our portfolio in Pakistan.

I did some homework on its business potential, pricing and sourcing options and went to see my boss, the general manager, and suggested we add it to our business portfolio. My boss looked at me and asked "Is this within the scope of our where-do-we-play choices?" I said "No, but we can add it because at the time we made the choices we missed this opportunity." My boss replied "No discussion, we have made our choices and we will stick to them as we have already deployed them across the entire organization, allocated resources and they are focused on delivering each and every strategy. We will not question, change or add anything to our choices for at least a year." End of discussion!

As they say hindsight is 20/20, today when I look back at that meeting with my more experienced mind, I realize how right he was. Do quality work in defining your choices and once the choices have been made and aligned, then stick to them, have faith in them and you will eventually win. If you keep modifying or adding items to your strategy, you will confuse the organization and impact their ability to prioritize work and deliver the agreed strategies. Launching Pringles would have been a distraction at that point in time as resources and funding had already been deployed. That day, my more experienced boss taught me a very valuable lesson!

I hope you will appreciate this simple but important example that strategies have to be clear, crisp and choiceful so that they are clear to all employees. After deployment the focus should remain on delivering executional excellence and not on rattling the priorities and refocusing attention by adding new strategies. The entire organization must know, a) what needs to be accomplished, and b) what work needs to be avoided.

> "The hardest thing to learn in life is which
> bridge to cross and which to burn."
> ~ David Russell (b. 1958),
> American Film Director, Screenwriter and Producer

7 B. Embracing Change

To deliver disproportional results it is implicit that something different has to be done. If you keep doing the same thing, over and over again, you will inevitably get the same results. Hence, it is critical that for any organization to be successful, each and every individual must embrace change and accept challenges with full fervor, determination and commitment. The change could be internally generated, e.g. change in strategy or it could be imposed on the company externally (such as change in government policy, competition reaction, currency devaluation, etc.) either way we have to meet it head-on to succeed.

Each employee, each leader and each department must be ready to own and deliver the new strategy and embrace the new business reality. Otherwise, management will end up fighting push-backs, rejections and lack of commitment to the new vision, rather than having a well oiled fighting machine, as is the case with the Formula 1 teams, where every employee is focused and aligned on delivering the vision; winning the race

Everyone in the organization needs to be constantly ready to handle any kind of change; each and every member of the organization needs to be a change 'champion'. We all know that our business environment is constantly changing and the only way to succeed is if we as an organization are willing to accept and face the unrelenting changes that are imposed on us.

> "Change will not come if we wait for some
> other person or some other time.
> We are the ones we've been waiting for.
> We are the change that we seek."
> ~ Barack Obama (b. 1961),
> 44th US President

Some of the characteristics that we must instill in our employees in order to embrace change include: flexibility, adaptability, openness to suggestions, listening skills, and at all times remaining in touch with the latest development in their discipline and industry. Being out of touch is very much like not knowing what the latest fashion is, where the best restaurants are in the city or the most popular hangouts are during the evening.

In a *Harvard Business Review* article on *"Leadership in the New World"* the authors introduced three new concepts or models on how to handle change.[41] According to them in the new world, leadership will require new skills tailored to an environment of urgency, high stakes and uncertainty. The concepts that they introduced are:

1. Foster Adaptation: Helping people develop the *next practices* that will enable the organization to thrive in a new world, even as they continue with the best practices necessary for current success. A nice quote by Rudy Giuliani encapsulates this concept when he states, "Change is not a destination, just as hope is not a strategy."

2. Embrace Disequilibrium: Keeping people in a state that creates enough discomfort to induce change but not so much that they fight, flee or freeze. Dissatisfaction with the status quo is extremely important to make any organization responsive and ready for taking on new and varying challenges.

3. Generate Leadership: Giving people at all levels of the organization the opportunity to lead experiments that will help it adapt to changing times. Breed *Change Champions!*

> "It is not the strongest of the species that survives, nor the most intelligent that survives. It is the one that is most adaptable to change."
> ~ Charles Darwin (1809–1882),
> English Naturalist and Geologist

Change Champions and Dissatisfaction with the Status Quo:
For change to take place in any organization you need to make sure that you identify specific employees at every level of the organization who 'champion' the change program. You need to have these champions acting as catalysts that inspire others,

engage them and bring them on-board. Once the management can see that their organization has a healthy dissatisfaction with status quo, then that organization is bound to succeed.

Remember there is nothing wrong in disagreeing but in the end we must move forward as a team. Employee's must highlight their issues or disagreements, everyone must be given a chance to have a healthy and open discussion, but once the decision has been taken, then everyone must accept the decision with an open heart and full commitment. Continuing to have dissent in any form is a sure-fire way of extinguishing the flames of change.

7 C. Breaking Down Barriers

A critical part of vision and strategy deployment in addition to enrolling people into your vision and strategies is to empower them. But empowering an organization without enabling it will result in frustration and defeat. You need to make sure that assignment planning, right people in the right seats, proper and timely training is carried out in line with the new business reality. In addition, you also need to make sure that while you empower your organization, you also break down any barriers that may exist and which are not within their circle of influence or authority.

To me a key function of senior managers and specially the CEO of a company is not only to challenge their teams but to make sure that they have all the skills required as well as resources under their control to deliver that challenge. In case of any barriers, the CEO or leadership team must take onus of removing them. "Ninety percent of what we call 'management' consists of making it difficult for people to get things done" Peter Drucker.

This topic can be well explained using the example of implementing SAP ERP (Enterprise Resource Planning) in a company. Just challenging your organization to implement it without looking at all the existing barriers will result in a major disaster, a waste of company money and resources. SAP is not just a financial accounting system; it is a complete ERP tool and needs full support from all departments ranging from information technology, finance, customer service, plant operations, and sales organization. One needs to temporarily increase enrollment by hiring temps as the two systems will have to run parallel for a while (i.e. SAP and the existing accounting system).

Major augment in overheads should be planned and budgeted to handle increase in travel, training, extra staffing, system licenses, etc. If these issues are not addressed, the challenge to the organization is unfair and will result in de-motivation and frustration for all. I can count a number of examples in Pakistan where professional organizations have failed in their first attempt to implement SAP, only because their top management failed to address all the issues and these created barriers that botched the project.

> "Success comes from good judgment.
> Good judgment comes from experience.
> Experience comes from bad judgment."
> ~ Arthur Jones (1926–2007),
> Founder and Inventor of the Nautilus Exercise Machines

If anyone asks me "What were my core responsibilities as the CEO of Gillette Pakistan?" The top five tasks that would come immediately to my mind are:

1) Set a vision, roll it out and keep it alive – Always.
2) Set a system of tracking goals and measures and share them and their progress broadly.
3) Agree on key strategies and make sure they are executed with excellence.
4) Drive a culture of trust through a set of core values.

5) Help break down barriers so all my teams can function at peak performance and in turn deliver breakthrough results.

To me breaking down barriers is a leader's key responsibility and if you asked anyone in my company about this, you would only get one answer "We are supposed to deliver our work-plan on time and with quality. If we come across any barriers or hurdles we try to overcome them. However, if we realize that surmounting some of the barriers is not within our circle of influence, then we must go to our CEO for help. Saad has told us in very clear terms that if he ever finds out that despite our best efforts the project got delayed because of some barrier and that we did not go to him for help, he will not accept this delay as a valid reason."

This concept empowered my people and they delivered their very best performance with full dedication, as they knew I was always on their side and would immediately jump-in to help them out. I was always in touch with my team, my desk was amongst my team members and I had one-to-ones with each department head on a monthly basis, religiously. I was an integral member of the team and was equally concerned about them delivering the company strategies. I have intervened on countless occasions as sometimes pulling rank on other departments, outside agencies, distributors or suppliers does break down barriers and expedite problem resolution.

There are a few creative traditions, which if followed in companies will assist in circumventing creation of potential barriers. Like they say *prevention is better than cure*, using the same logic I am listing a few ideas that will help:

1. Enhance your team's capability.
2. Streamline systems and wean out non-value added work.
3. Role model the behavior you want everyone to follow.

4. Make simplification a way of life.
5. Not using multitasking as a way of doing your work.

The first four are pretty much self-explanatory, but let me explain the last one; on face value most of you will say that multitasking helps us manage multiple priorities. To many, this means the ability to do many things at the same time. The point I am trying to make is to be aware of the difference between *Multitasking* and *Chunking*.

Multitasking means to do multiple things *at the same time*. Examples include trying to type an urgent email or meet a person on an important issue while answering phone calls discussing a different issue, both concurrently. You will agree that this is not the most efficient or even fair way of accomplishing multiple tasks. Neither of the tasks will get done properly and the discussion with the person or the memo will not be of high quality, as your mind is not designed to concentrate on two things at the same time.

Chunking is to do multiple tasks one followed by another, *in sequence*. Taking the same example, if you are working on an important document and someone comes for an urgent discussion, move away from your computer and give the person your full attention. Similarly, turn your phone on silent or hand it over to your secretary so that you are not disturbed in the middle of an important meeting or discussion. This way you can listen and handle the issue with quality and when done, return to writing your memo.

> "The shortest way to do many things
> is to do one thing at a time."
> ~ Samuel Smiles (1812–1904),
> Scottish Author and Government Reformer

I personally have become a champion of chunking. People are amazed with my footprint and how I handle all my numerous commitments. Let me give you an idea. While being CEO of Gillette, I was also President of American Business Council, Executive Committee Member of Overseas Investors Chamber of Commerce and Industry, Chairman of Taxation, Corporate Social Responsibilities and Intellectual Property Committees, Chairman of Pakistan Innovation Foundation, Vice President of National Entrepreneurship Working Group, Board Member of South East Asia Leadership Academy and AIESEC. I sat on over a dozen advisory boards of NGO's, wrote bi-monthly articles in newspapers, wrote this book plus was an active member and later became the President of the Public Interest Law Association of Pakistan. I handle all these duties with total commitment and do not allow anything to fall through the crack as every day I chunk two-dozen different priorities and activities, back to back.

Always bear in mind that trying to do two tasks concurrently will hurt the quality of both, waste time and will be very frustrating to whoever is standing there and discussing an important issue with you. Remember it is also a mark of respect if you give people the proper regard for their time and problem. They will respect you in return.

Vital Tip 20: Imagine you want to discuss something important with your boss and he invites you to his office, but throughout the discussion he continues to focus on and read a memo or an email on his computer. He rarely looks at you, keeps grunting and nodding, answering phone calls and occasionally acknowledging you. You are quite sure that your boss is not following the discussion. You will feel quite humiliated and will not have much respect for your boss and his behavior. The decision in such meetings will not be optimal either. So it is important that you do not do multitasking and focus on one issue at a time, on the other hand handle as many different issues as you like throughout the day, back to back, but never concurrently.

7 D. Disciplined Tracking

There are two important concepts imbedded in this title, i.e. Discipline and Tracking. Let me take each one and explain their significance:

Discipline: It is one of the most important virtues, which has to be present in every person, organization or even a country, if it aspires to progress, develop and grow. If you look at any successful leader or an organization or a country, you will always see the presence of discipline in their culture. All companies have a culture, most companies have discipline, but very few companies have what we call a *Culture of Discipline.*

Jim Collin's in his book *Good to Great* found that all those companies that had achieved the status of *greatness* had what he called the culture of discipline. Jim goes on to explain, "When you have disciplined people, you don't need a hierarchy; when you have disciplined thought, you don't need bureaucracy; when you have disciplined action, you don't need excessive controls: And when you combine a culture of discipline with a culture of entrepreneurship you get, *"The magical alchemy of great performance."*

Tracking: Everyone must have heard the famous saying by Peter Drucker, "If you want it, measure it, if you can't measure it, forget it." This clearly describes the importance of being able to track your progress versus defined goals and measures. You need very strong discipline in carrying out this tracking exercise on a timely basis. Hence, once the vision and goals are defined, deployed and reflected in each department and employee work-plan, a clear transparent and open tracking system needs to be designed, deployed and shared with the organization. Tracking should be done for the overall goals of the company that flow from the vision as well as for each of the measures that helps us track the success of every strategy.

While tracking the results, if it emerges that we are not delivering as per the milestones, then we must go back to the assigned teams who own that strategy and request them to review their work plans and either top-up their existing strategies or focus on further improving their executional excellence in order to plug the gap. Ensuring this tracking is done diligently and in a timely manner will significantly enhance your ability to deliver your vision. I again draw on Winston Churchill's famous quote to emphasize my point, i.e. "However beautiful the strategy, you should occasionally look at the results."

7 E. Keeping the Vision Alive

All human minds have a certain time span for retaining key facts and their importance. Hence it is imperative that in order to keep any message alive, it must be repeated and refreshed in peoples mind periodically. Just like you air an advertisement on TV multiple times to raise awareness which leads to product recall and finally compels the consumer to buy the product, similarly for the success of vision setting, it is imperative that we keep the vision alive. To achieve this goal I would suggest the following steps:

a) Roll out the vision at the annual company function with everyone present. Always be available to answer any queries or questions that may arise and require clarity.

b) In your day-to-day work always try to link each and every business project to the vision. Make it abundantly clear that the vision is the foundation of everything we do or attempt to accomplish in the company.

c) Every recommendation must have a compulsory rationale on how this initiative supports and helps deliver the company vision.

d) As vision is long term, the company progress towards this long-term goal should be constantly reviewed and shared with the organization. I would suggest that in order to get the maximum enrollment and motivation from the organization, the results should be broadcast across the company through newsletters and company-wide meetings at least once a quarterly basis. Timely and frequent sharing is the key in this case.

e) A company-wide reward and recognition policy should be linked to the vision. Management must always highlight how the team's work benefits the company to move closer to their vision and overall goals.

"The greatest value in creating a plan is not the final document. It's the communication, prioritization, focus, clarity and learning that make the process worthwhile,"
~ Jim Horan (b. 1950),
Consultant, Author, Speaker and President of
The One Page Business Plan Company

••••---- ---- ---•••

Chapter 8 – Cautions and Watch Outs

Ideal way to share watch-outs is to start with a real life example and from that gain some critical learning's. Until 2012 my younger brother Ali Amanullah ran a Telenor franchise (mobile service provider with walk-in customer service as well as a distribution network) in Karachi, Pakistan. We were amongst the founding members of the Telenor family of franchises since early 2005 when Telenor first launched its operation in Pakistan. Getting a business started in a new industry is full of challenges and certainly not easy. We had to learn the ropes the hard way, by making mistakes!

> "Experience is simply the name we give our mistakes."
> ~ Oscar Wilde (1854–1900),
> Irish Writer, Poet, and Prominent Aesthete

As it was the first time we had started our own business, we were overtly aware of our lack of experience in this field. My brother had a full time job as the National Sales and Marketing Manager in Samsung Electronics, so we hired a very experienced and expensive person to head our franchise who we felt knew the cellular industry intimately. Based on blind faith (idiocy in hindsight) we set up the entire business model based on his inputs, i.e. commission structure, volume forecast, investments, etc. Unfortunately the business did not do so well. After the initial two months pipeline fill-up behind the launch, our business went downhill. Every time we asked for a reason for this lackluster performance he would tell us a cock and bull story, which we would reluctantly believe.

As our knowledge in the telecommunication industry was very superficial, we failed to see or check ground reality. In simple words we were not being brutal enough about the cause behind this month-to-month business slide and failed to penetrate the underlying reasons. The best decision we took was to ask the GM to leave just after five months and my brother took over the business full time. Everything suddenly became crystal clear as now we saw through many of the earlier reasons and excuses he gave for the softness in the business.

The most important lesson we learned was to face the brutal facts head-on, to roll up our sleeves and figure out the solution rather than stick our head in the sand and hope the problem would go away. We had finally stopped trying to see the problem from someone else's eyes or rational. The more hands-on we were, the more we penetrated the business, more we found and could finally make an honest assessment of our business health.

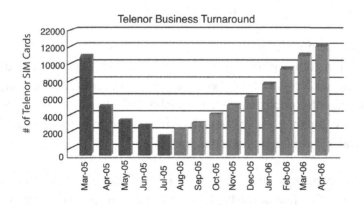

Ali turned our business around instantly. He looked at the ground reality, went to the trade, met with the retailers, talked to our sales reps and as you can see the business turned around from July onwards; our business rebounded and continued to do well from then on. Later when I look back at the early dismal period, I am struck by how we had brought the debacle on ourselves. From the very first month I had a feeling that something was amiss but seeing the immense confidence shown by our ex-GM, we clearly did not face reality, we took everything on face value and failed to questions the basic assumptions. From this experience I have learned six major lessons, namely:

A. Confront the Brutal Facts
B. Confidence vs. Competence Paradox
C. Have the Right People in the Right Seats on your Bus
D. Always Remain in-Touch with Reality
E. Benefit of a Virtuous Circle
F. How to Maximize Productivity

8 A. Confront the Brutal Facts

"There is no worse mistake in public leadership
than to hold out false hopes soon to be swept away."
~ Winston Churchill (1874–1965)
UK Prime Minister

I love the phrase 'confront the brutal facts' which I have taken from Jim Collins who is the author of some of the most insightful books on successful businesses such as *Good to Great*, *Built to Last*, and recently published *How the Mighty Fall*. He states that only those companies climb the ladder from good to great that face brutal facts upfront and act accordingly.

A classic example that comes to mind is of IBM post 1980. As you all know that IBM or the Big Blue has had an exceptional history of driving change in the information technology and revolutionizing the way companies and organizations work and operate. Although

IBM had a brilliant double-digit growth for over five decades (mid 30's to mid 80's) their future was not as hunky-dory as they had expected.

With the advent of Personal Computers (PC's), that ironically were first introduced by IBM themselves, resulted in a near disaster for the company. Introduction of PC's changed the entire computer industry landscape as:

a) It become more affordable for small and medium sized businesses to own one.

b) They dramatically undermined IBM's core mainframe business as the PC revolution placed computers directly in the hands of millions of users.

c) IBM's problem was further exasperated with the development of client/server application which linked many PC's together as well as with larger computers where data and applications resided. This totally transformed how the customers viewed, used and bought computer technology and it shook IBM to its very foundations.

Why did IBM miss out on the golden opportunity to own the PC market, just like it did by owning the mainframe computers market for decades? The answer to this question is closely linked with IBM's unprecedented decision to contract out PC components (both software and hardware) to third parties such as Microsoft and Intel. This was totally against its history of being vertically integrated but was done in an attempt to quickly gain a chunk of the PC market, hence IBM chose not to build proprietary operating systems and microprocessors although they had both the resources and the technical know how.

Ironically it was this fateful decision which marked the end of IBM's monopoly of the computer industry and paved the way for the creation of billions of dollars of market value outside IBM, in companies such as Microsoft, Intel, Compac, Dell and many others.

IBM failed to see or accept the brutal facts as reality unfolded right before their eyes. It led the change, but complacency settled in as they let go of their core competitive advantage as a technology leader in both software and hardware. They failed to see the signs as the market demographics changed.

They could have leveraged their might and their impressive research facilities to reverse the tide, but they did not confront the brutal facts until it was too late. Today competition and innovation in the computer industry has developed along segmented lines versus the past vertically integrated lines (which was IBM's core competency), and companies such as HP (printers), Compaq (PC's), Dell (PC's), Novel (networking), Seagate (disk drives), etc. evolved and prospered. This is a classic example of change happening while your management is not willing to confront the brutal facts of reality head-on or as they say sticking your heads in the sand while competition changes market dynamics and runs away with your competitive advantage.

Collins further goes on to qualify 'facing brutal facts' with what he calls 'unwavering resolve or faith in the end game'. Just facing brutal facts according to Collins is not enough, as it must be associated with an unwavering faith to be successful. He calls it "having unwavering faith amid the brutal facts." As an example if someone has a vision but is facing major challenges and the brutal reality is only doom and gloom, than according to Collins you must maintain an unwavering faith in your plans and your vision, and provide hope to the organization through your commitment as well as your steadfast support of the endgame. Collins substantiates this fact with an example from the Vietnam War, which he calls "The Stockdale Paradox".[45]

The Stockdale Paradox[42]: The name refers to Vice Admiral Jim Stockdale who was the highest-ranking United States military officer in the 'Hanoi Hilton' as the prisoner-of-war camp was known during the height of the Vietnam War. Tortured over twenty times during his eight-year captivity from 1965 to 1973, Stockdale lived out the war without any prisoner's rights, no set release date, and no certainty as to whether he would even survive to see his family again. He shouldered the burden of command and did everything in his power to increase the survival rates of prisoners while constantly fighting an internal war against his captors.

After his release, Stockdale became the first three-star officer in the history of the Navy to wear both aviator wings and the Congressional Medal of Honor. Collins once got an opportunity to meet the Admiral. However before the meeting he read the book *In Love and War* that was written by Stockdale and his wife Sybil, each writing-alternating chapters chronicling their experiences during those eight difficult years.

While reading the book Collins was deeply touched and felt quite depressed reading about the bleak and hopeless situation the Admiral was in, which was further compounded by the brutality of his captors. Suddenly Collins realized that he was sitting in his comfy room overlooking the beautiful Stanford campus on a beautiful Saturday afternoon and was getting depressed merely by reading the book. Imagine how Stockdale must have felt as he had no idea how the story would end; would he survive, or ever be reunited with his family? Collins thought that if he felt so depressed right now how on earth did Stockdale deal with it when he was actually there and did not know the end of the story?

When asked the same question, Stockdale replied, "I never lost faith in the end of the story. I never doubted not only that I would get out but also that I would prevail in the end and turn the experience into the defining event in my life, which, in retrospect, I would not trade." After a long silence Collins asked him, "Who did not make it out?" and to his surprise Stockdale replied "The optimists." "The optimists, I don't understand" said Collins on hearing this answer he was very confused considering what Stockdale has just said.

Stockdale continued "The optimists. Oh, they were the ones who said, 'We're going to be out by Christmas.' And Christmas would come, and Christmas would go. Then they'd say 'We're going to be out by Easter'. And Easter would come and Easter would go. And then Thanksgiving and then it would be Christmas again. And they died of a broken heart." Then he turned to Collins and said, "This is a very important lesson. You must never confuse faith that you will prevail in the end – which you can never afford to lose – with the discipline to confront the most brutal facts of your current reality, whatever they might be." Collins says that to this day, he carries a mental image of Stockdale admonishing the optimists: "We're not getting out by Christmas; deal with it!"

This interaction had a profound impact on Collins' and influenced his thought process. He realized that life is unfair – sometimes to our advantage, sometime to our disadvantage. We will all experience disappointments in our lives, setbacks for which there will be no reason, no one to blame it on. It could be a disease, loss of a loved one, an accident or it might be getting shot down over Vietnam and thrown into a POW camp for eight years. What separates people, Stockdale has taught us, is not the presence or absence of difficulty, but how we deal with the inevitable difficulties of life. In wrestling with life's challenges, the Stockdale Paradox (you must retain faith that you will prevail in the end and you must also confront the most brutal facts of your current reality) has proved powerful for coming back from difficulties not weakened, but stronger.

Looking at IBM with 'Stockdale Glasses' it becomes clear that IBM was either overconfident or an optimist when they launched the IBM PC as they had always owned and won in the computer industry, so they thought they would do well in this new venture as well. They failed to see the brutal facts of reality, due to which they fell and only after some major restructurings, spinning off several businesses and laying off thousands of employees, they are now again doing well. The lesson unfortunately has been learned the hard way.

Our experience with the start-up of our Telenor franchise had everything to do with this insight of Collins; we refused to confront the brutal facts and kept our head in the sand and continued to accept whatever reasons were presented to us by our ex-GM. We took the data he offered on face value, we accepted the logic he gave for our lackluster performance without deep diving and checking the reasoning ourselves and never truly visiting the market or talking to the traders or even other franchises to figure out why our franchise's performance was so poor. As they say, hindsight is 20/20, and now when we review that period we realize that our biggest fault was having an unwavering belief in the business but not confronting the brutal facts due to which we ended up paying a very high price.

The Stockdale Paradox example from my Personal Life: I read about the Stockdale Paradox just a few years back and was very encouraged to see that in my own personal and professional life I have been an active practitioner of it. As background, when I was posted back to Pakistan by P&G in early  1994, I went through a very difficult and messy divorce. From my first marriage I have two lovely, bright and loving children Sarah and Ameen. During my divorce my wife used our children as tools to get back at my family and me. To cut the long story short my children were illegally kept away from me for years without any rhyme or reason and against court orders. My wife concocted very serious allegations to buy time, to manipulate the court system, to flaunt court orders and used all her strong connections to prolong litigation. She used this delay to constantly brainwash my  children against their paternal family and me. She never could prove anything, her only objective was to isolate my children from me and to brainwash them to detest me and in this she succeeded.

"You don't know a woman till you've met her in court."
~ Norman Kingsley Mailer (1923–2007),
American Novelist, Journalist and Film Director

 Finally in 2009, fifteen years from the day it all started, my ex-wife lost all pending cases and her false allegations were thrown out of court. The children were requested by the judge to meet me but as expected they refused. Her plan had worked, frivolous cases and long drawn out delays due to litigation had given her and her family enough time to totally brainwash my children. This was a devastating and extremely disheartening experience for me. During this entire episode I was always brutally clear that things will not get normal anytime soon but I continued to have an unwavering belief that one day I will clear my name and meet my children.

This mindset kept me going through fifteen years of litigation and even today I am very pleased and satisfied on how well I dealt with depression and the hopelessness of the situation in a mature and productive manner. I did not let it destroy my life as they had hoped for and was able to bestow my love and care to other poor and needy children through my philanthropic work. I did not let the mental tension and emotional torture derail my career, in fact I rose from a mere Finance Manager of P&G Pakistan in 1994 to a Deputy General Manager of P&G and finally to the position of CEO of Gillette Pakistan, I got elected twice as the President of the American Business Council (ABC is the largest single country business chamber in Pakistan), became an Executive Committee member of the Overseas Investors Chamber of Commerce and Industry (largest foreign company chamber in Pakistan) plus served and continue to serve on the Advisory Boards of a dozen social enterprises/NGO's as well as founding five social/entrepreneurship organizations to date.

I am a human after all and I did waver and felt extremely depressed and hopeless, but a vital piece of advice from my late father always guided me; one must try his best, his ultimate best, in everything one does and then leave the rest to God (and not fret over what could have happened or what more I could have done). God will only help those who help themselves.

During this horrifying experience my faith was strengthened and I was able to split my personal tragedy from my professional life. This is one of the key outcomes of the Stockdale Paradox, I never raised my hope on a quick resolution to this very personal problem, I never raised my hope that I will meet my kids this summer or next Eid or on their birthdays, but I sincerely believed that one day I WILL meet them as long as I did nothing unethical or illegal and pursued the case with full honors and with high morals.

SPLIT MY ATTITUDE
PERSONAL TRAGEDY
PROFESSIONAL LIFE

I continue to have an unwavering belief that one day when my children have grown up and breakout of the shell created by my ex-wife and her immediate family, they will research, meet people who know me or those whose lives I have touched and will realize the true reality of this injustice. Finally, I believe that one day they both will come to me with open arms and genuine spirit; I miss them every day and love them very much.

Remember that for the Stockdale Paradox to work one has to have a very strong and unwavering belief from the depth of one's heart on the end result, while constantly being brutally aware of the current reality, else it will not work.

8 B. Confidence vs. Competence Paradox

"Experience tells you what to do; Confidence allows you to do it."
~ Stanley Roger Smith (b. 1946),
Former American Pro Tennis Player

First some definitions to set the basis (from Wikipedia):

- **Confidence** is generally described as a state of being certain that either a hypothesis or prediction is correct or that a chosen course of action is the best or most effective.

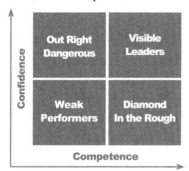

- **Competence** is a standardized requirement for an individual to properly perform a specific job.
- **Self-confidence** is having confidence in oneself.

Confidence and competence are two virtues, which if infused together create the groundwork for a visible and inspirational leader. If you look at the diagram it shows two axis one for confidence and another for competence, the further away you move along the two arrows, the higher is your confidence and/ or competence. If a person is strong on both aspects then they will be located in the top right corner quadrant, which is called Visible-Leaders, which is where all true leaders lie.

However, if the person has one strong aspect and one weak, then they will either be in the Out-Right-Dangerous quadrant (strong confidence and weak competence) or in the Diamond-in-the-Rough quadrant (weak confidence and strong competence). As clear from the name Out-Right-Dangerous is used for the person who has low competence but a high level of confidence, they act as if they are all-knowledgeable but in reality have low knowledge and skill levels thus are very dangerous. People follow them by their misplaced confidence only to realize later that they have no idea how to lead or deliver difficult challenges. On the other hand, individuals falling in the Diamond-in-the-Rough quadrant have true potential in becoming strong leaders if given the right opportunities such as proper grooming, training and competence building.

One of the key issues we faced with our Telenor GM during the first five months of the Telenor franchise start-up was that our GM fell in the top left quadrant, he displayed total confidence and know-all attitude but the reality was quite different. We, due to our ignorance, continued to follow his advice as he showed immense confidence and portrayed data in a selective and distorted manner. In such situations you can blame no one but yourself for the eventual outcome. Luckily we saw through his misplaced confidence and replaced him before irrevocable damage could be done.

> **Vital Tip 21:** Most of us interpret a confident manner as evidence of competence, and a hesitant manner as evidence of lesser competence. In today's society it is customary to value confidence and in doing so we automatically expect them to have knowledge and expertise, i.e. competence, which may not be true. So a word of caution, not all confident people have competence, check before you start to follow a person with confidence blindly.

Dunning-Kruger Effect[43]: Majority of us assume that confidence comes from competence and if you are unsure of yourself and hesitant, you have less competence and hence less skills and abilities. However there is strong evidence that states that confidence and competence are inversely correlated.

This phenomenon was discovered by the pioneering work of Justin Kruger and David Dunning, who working at Cornell in 1999 and is called the Dunning-Kruger effect. They performed experiments that yielded results consistent with these four principles:

1. Incompetent individuals, compared with their more competent peers, dramatically overestimate their ability and performance.
2. Incompetent individuals are less able than their more competent peers to recognize competence when they see it.
3. Incompetent individuals are less able than their more competent peers to gain insight into their true level of performance.
4. Incompetent individuals can gain insight about their shortcomings, but this comes by gaining competence.

Taken together, these four factors contribute to an inverse correlation between confidence and competence — exactly the opposite of what most of us assume. So beware of incompetent individuals, they are the *most* dangerous, as they feel very confident that they are indeed competent.

"If you have no confidence in self you are
twice defeated in the race of life.
With confidence you have won even before you have started."
~ Marcus Garvey (1887-1940),
Jamaican Political Leader, Publisher, Journalist

8 C. Do You Have the Right People in the Right Seats on your Bus?

The age old adage 'people are our most important assets' is only true if we have the right people on the bus (i.e. our business) and that these people are assigned to the right jobs, i.e. are in the right seats on the bus or business. Otherwise having mediocre resources, and placing them in the wrong seats, assigning a job that is not their core competency is a recipe for disaster.

The basic expectation from any good leader is to set a vision, identify its associated strategies and tactics and deploy them – wrong! Who makes the vision, strategies and tactics? The 'people' do that, it is made by the teams and by the involvement of the entire organization. Hence, the most important job and in fact the very first job undertaken by the leader is to find the right people to run the business and place them in the right jobs. Once that is accomplished, the leader must challenge the organization to come up with a daunting vision, followed by identifying strategies and tactics and finally focus on delivering it.

In the case of our Telenor franchise experience having the right people on the bus in the right seats was clearly missing. We had handed over the entire company into the hands of a person who was clearly not the right choice. And he was given full authority to decide the hiring in the organization as well as laying down its strategies, and developing company policies and procedures. Clearly not a smart decision on our part, but again if you do not make mistakes, you will never learn!

Once my brother Ali took over the responsibilities, the first thing he did was to decide that there will only be places in the Telenor bus for top rated sales people or people whose skill were critical for our daily functioning such as finance, accounting, customer service, sales, data entry, etc. Next he rolled out the company's values and key principles, based on which the business will be run. Once Ali had the right people on the bus and the values and principles rolled out, he then decided to give his full attention to the 'How' question. He and his team focused on how to turn around the business, recognizing opportunities, identifying niches and growing the business profitably. Based on this he came up with a vision and few choiceful strategies. These he deployed to the entire organization and the franchise continued to do well as long as we operated it.

8 D. Benefit for a Virtuous Circle

One thing we realized during our challenging experience at our Telenor franchise start-up phase was that in order to deliver good results, every link of the chain has to be strong, every member of the team has to be focused, fine-tuned, all working in the same direction and in doing so each team member and process must complement and support each other. That is how true synergy develops and grows and that is how organizations can deliver peak performances. It takes immense amount of planning, discipline and coordination to make this a reality. This phenomenon is most commonly known as the Virtuous Circle.

Let me give you a formal definition of the virtuous circle for clarity:

- A beneficial cycle of events or incidents, each having a positive effect on the next.[44]
- Self-propagating advantageous situation in which a successful solution leads to a more desired result or another success which generates still more desired results or successes in a chain, i.e. one after another. For example, compound interest earned on a deposit keeps on generating even greater amount of interest.[45]

If I take the example of leadership, one of the key objectives of a leader, as discussed earlier, is to set a vision, align a strategy that will help deliver the vision and distinctly change reality. Without any tangible change no leader will be successful. Also one of the key components of visioning is to identify the winning strategies to drive change.

Change does not happen by itself, but is driven by successful implementation of each strategy and properly tracking and measuring it at every step until eventually the vision is delivered. If this is done immaculately you will see a beneficial cycle of events or incidents where each has a positive effect on the next and this way the process gains momentum until the vision is delivered. This is a virtuous circle or virtuous cycle. Always try to create such a virtuous cycle in your business and your life.

> "In our view, successful reform is not an event.
> It is a sustainable process that will build on its
> own successes - a virtuous cycle of change."
> ~ Abdullah II (b. 1962),
> King of Jordan, Ascended the Throne on Feb 7, 1999

There is a downside to the virtuous cycle, which happens when the leader ignores alignment within his team, when strategies are not aligned with the vision and the leader continues to ignore negative feedback; it is then called a Vicious Cycle. I personally prefer to depict the vicious cycle with a diagram of a tornado which starts from the top, i.e. having vision and strategies but due to lack of alignment and harmony eventually drops down to zero or naught, is destructive and destroys company equity and value and much more.

Vision & Strategies

Naught

A classic and recent example of a vicious cycle was the US government's strategy in handling Hurricane Katrina, which many of you will agree was one of the worst episodes in US history mainly due a faulty strategy, delayed response and ignoring the early but apparent sign of vulnerability which unfortunately resulted in an unprecedented tragedy to many. On the other hand another example of nature's fury, the eruption of Mount Helena, was well handled, the area around it in the Washington State was evacuated, early warning announcements were made and rescue operations alerted, which resulted in a virtuous cycle with a minimum loss of life.

> **Vital Tip 22:** When tough times come in any company's life, one of the most inevitable realities is to conserve cash and drive cost cutting to improve profitability. However, when you do that, one thing you must keep in mind, never meddle with factors based on which you have built the company's equity and culture, or in short your core strengths. These could be your product development, sales force, systems, processes, investment in people, etc. If you do, then the company will not survive for long. The message is simple - Don't mess with your DNA - that is, don't mess with what makes you unique.

It is important to have your mission statement, your vision, your strategies and measures, all in-sync. Any slip-ups or lapses in this process may turn a great idea into a money-losing preposition. On the other hand having them all in full synchronization is the key to your success. Try to find and nurture the virtuous cycle in your circle of influence and see it work miracles.

8 E. Always Remain In-Touch with Reality

One of the biggest mistakes my brother and I made when we started our Telenor franchise in early 2005 was that we were not in-touch with reality. It was a totally new industry, new consumers, and new customers, all very different from what both of us had experienced before, it was even more critical for us to do in-depth research before venturing into the launch head-on. We were 'shooting with blindfolds on' during the first five months of the launch. Something we learnt through experience was that one must always remain in-touch, both internally and externally.

Internally in-touch means to know the systems and processes of our parent company, in this case Telenor, understand how decisions are made, what makes them tick, what should be the commission structure, what were Telenor Pakistan's vision, goals and strategies, etc. Partial blame has to be given to Telenor Pakistan, as at the time of launch they did not provide any proper systems or processes to franchises. Being externally in-touch means to understand your consumers, your customers, your competition and sometime even in-touch on a much broader scale, i.e. understand the country's economic outlook, investment policies, taxation regime, etc. In fact as we say in Gillette that you can never be too much in-touch!

"Things are not always as they seem; the
first appearance deceives many."
~ Phaedrus (c. 444 BC–393 BC),
Athenian Aristocrat Depicted in Plato's Dialogues

General Colin Powell a retired four-star general of the US Army, who has held positions of US Secretary of State, National Security Advisor, Commander in Chief US Army and finally retired as the US Armed Forces Chairman, Chief of Joint Staff is well known and is broadly admired for his leadership qualities and insights. Based on his many years of experience in leading troops he states in his *Leadership Primer*: "Never neglect details. When everyone's mind is dulled or distracted the leader must be doubly vigilant."

This is a true characteristic of a strong leader who must not be distracted by all the noise in the environment and is able to locate true insights hidden amidst all the data. Leaders have the innate ability of finding the needle in a haystack, a tough job but possible by a leader who is genuinely in-touch with reality.

The In-Touch Gap Analysis: Before proceeding further, let's first understand what 'in-touch' truly means. It means to actively listen in order to learn, to understand, to know what is happening around you, to know your competition and their strategies, to search for perspectives that are alien to you and to incorporate them into your strategy and tactics. Basically being in-touch does not require any money or investment, it is free and it helps you stay connected with reality, which you will agree is a good thing. Knowing something 'the way it really is' versus 'how you perceive it to be' is much better in the long run.

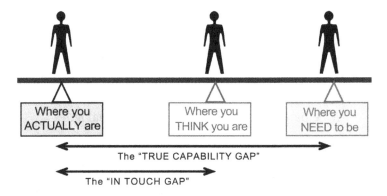

In a leadership course in P&G we do a survey of how you rate yourself on leadership skills such as envisioning the future, empowering your people, exciting them, helping them break down barriers, etc. The same survey is carried out among the key stakeholders including direct reports, peers and as well as the bosses. The smaller the gap between your leadership scores and the average of all others reflects how in-touch you are with reality regarding your leadership abilities. This is called the in-touch gap, i.e. this is the gap between where your leadership skills actually are (external survey) versus your perception of where you think your skills are (your personal survey).

The result of this in-touch survey can be a rude awakening to many as they finally realize that they are not as good in the eyes of others as they themselves perceive to be. Once the reality check is complete, one needs to then work towards closing the gap versus where you ideally would like to be, i.e. the True Capability Gap. Where you need to be, is a fixed place, which reflects the best in class ability on all key leadership skills. It is critical to plug this gap else your decisions, your strategies and your ability to deliver on your strategies and your credibility as a leader of your team is compromised.

How does one get In-Touch?

To be in-touch with reality, one is required to listen, observe, understand, and using this information stay informed and to identify key insights. It is critical to know your 'reality' by being curious, by going beyond the obvious and by always being in a learning mode. However in everything one does, one must keep an open mind, and proceed with a mindset of learning new facts, new insights, and new information. What one must not do is to go with preconceived notions of what one should be expecting to find; that negates the entire effort of being in-touch. People who have a closed mind, who are opinionated, who live in the past or who are not active listeners can rarely be in-touch with reality. So my advice is to go beyond the obvious and listen patiently.

Once you are in-touch both internally and externally, you will be able to deliver significantly better business and organizational results by incorporating insights into your plans and tactics. You will be less afraid of the unknown or of what is out there. Keep carrying out reality checks constantly and build them into your plans and you will rarely go wrong.

Not being in-touch with reality can have a catastrophic impact, you can lose your edge in the market (e.g. IBM) or you can even cease to exist (e.g. Polaroid, Pan Am, Woolworth, etc.). On the other hand being in-touch with reality can do wonders; you can corner the market, gain market leadership and be a winner (e.g. Intel, Apple, Caterpillar, etc.). Your intuition and gut feelings will also develop over time, the more you are in-touch the more aware you will be of your potential and limitations. So are you in-touch with reality?

"The important thing is to never stop questioning."
~ Albert Einstein (1879–1955),
Theoretical Physicist and Father of Modern Physics

> **Vital Tip 23:** Being in-touch to me is a way of life; it helps you not only in your professional life but also in your personal life. Are you in-touch with your family, their needs and desires, do you spend time talking and listening to them, if not then you are not in-touch and it could lead to problems later. It is strongly recommend that you carry out an 'In-Touch Gap' analysis with your close family and loved ones.

8 F. How to Maximize Productivity

Have you ever noticed how there is always never enough time at work, you always have more on your plate then you can possibly deliver? Every day I go to office, I have a to-do list of items to complete that day, but when I am leaving at the end of the day many of them are still there as new items have suddenly popped in, each request being positioned as extremely urgent. Interestingly even people, who have less work on their plates, seem to experience the same.

There is a famous adage, which goes by the name of Parkinson's Law, which states: "Work expands so as to fill the time available for its completion." As a result symptoms emerge such as staying late, neglecting lunch, missing deadlines, not being able to deliver quality work, etc. Unfortunately this is human nature. However, the same people if placed under pressure by setting deadlines or by prioritizing their work tend to cover more ground and deliver better results. Treating the day as 'free for all' without any plans or deadlines or expectations, will not be efficient or productive.

Following are some ideas on how to maximize your productivity at work:

a) **Have the Courage to say "NO"**: In order to succeed at work and to be able to deliver your best performance, you will need to make some serious changes. Top among them is to start having the courage to say no. A lot of leaders in today's corporate world lack this courage and feel if they say no to a project, it will be perceived negatively against them and their ability as a leader. Your ability to say no should be based on rational thinking it should be directly linked and in sync with the company's vision.

Bear in mind that you don't have all the time in the world plus resources are limited, both human as well as financial. By diverting these scarce resources towards non-critical projects you will undermine the company's trust in you and invariably end up delivering lower growth due to lack of proper support and resources.

b) **Prioritize your Work**: Prioritize your projects based on the size of the prize or in simpler words sort the projects using financial tools such as Net Present Value (NPV), Internal Rate of Return (IRR), or Payouts. Due to your inability to prioritize projects and focusing on projects that deliver a lower return on investment you will negatively impact the company's potential to grow and win in the marketplace. Like Stephen Covey very aptly states "The key is not to prioritize what's on your schedule, but to schedule your priorities."

c) **Set Targets with Clear Deadlines**: Another sure fire way of driving productivity is to set targets with clear deadlines for every project. Try to create a culture of urgency and assign clear success factors to each project. Research has proven that well defined and time driven goals or targets do lead to more effort by humans. People work more intensely in order to reach a goal.

d) **Sanction Projects In-Sync with Vision and Strategies:** Your key objective as a manager is to deliver the company's strategies in order to reach its vision. Hence, for every project that is suggested or approved a mandatory litmus test must be carried out to check whether it is synchronized with the company's mission and vision. This will make sure that every project that is ever pursued, or on which the company's limited resources are deployed are linked to the overall vision and hence will deliver high value to the company.

When I took over Gillette in early 2007, the situation on the ground was far from ideal. Opportunities to fix things were all around us. After our first off-site meeting where we set our vision of Mission Dugna Tigna, we also went through a detailed brainstorming session by category and by department. We came up with a laundry list of projects and ideas to grow Gillette, these all added up to more than a hundred. One reality, which no one can ignore, is that if we are to deliver peak performance we must work within our limited resources both on the people and financial front.

Do realize that you may be able to do more projects but by stretching every resource to its limit, the quality of execution will not be the same. In order to deliver quality execution we had to be choiceful and selective. If I had agreed to do all the projects identified, it would have led to serious trouble later on as a lot would have been done but none with quality, as people and other resources would be stretched beyond their capacity. The budget would have been all spent but we would have experienced very poor return on this investment due to mediocre execution.

The key question was whether all these were valid projects? Each owner of that specific project thought so. But in reality only a few of these projects were absolutely critical and totally aligned with our vision. By focusing on these few high return projects, we freed a lot of resources. Overall delivery of these selective projects due to ideal allocation of resources was of very high standards and that is what helped drive the early growth of Gillette Pakistan. Credit clearly goes to my young team for having the courage to say 'no' and to properly prioritize the project based on return on investment and the size of the prize. We delivered on our Mission Dugan Tigna targets that we had set for ourselves for the first five years and are well on the way to delivering our vision and goals even beyond this horizon.

To emphasize my point, P&G's entry into Pakistan is a classic case in point. P&G sells nearly 300 brands in various categories all over the world. When we started business back in 1991, we started by launching only two brands Head & Shoulders and Oil of Olay. The next brand we launched was the Vicks line extensions such as throat drops, inhalers and vaporub via local contract manufacturing in 1992. By early 1994, out of all these brands only Head & Shoulders was showing good growth potential.

Next high potential brands launched were Camay and Safeguard after purchasing a soap plant at Hub, Baluchistan in 1994. By 1998 we had only added Pantene and Ariel to our portfolio. We then made an important decision when we realized that the size of the prize of Vicks and Oil of Olay were not justifying the resources allocated against them, therefore we decided to discontinue Vicks Inhaler, Vicks Throat Drops as well as Oil of Olay creams. This was a tough management decision but now in hindsight a very prudent one. Resources working on these brands were redeployed on the two recent launches, i.e. Pantene and Ariel, and these two brands have delivered outstanding growth and share numbers.

Pertinent to note is that in the first seven years of P&G's existence in Pakistan they had a portfolio of only seven brands out of a potential of 300. The mega brand Pampers was not launched until 2000. During this period many people used to ask me: "P&G has so many famous brands like Pampers, Always, Fairy Liquid, Tide, Pringles, etc. why don't you launch them in Pakistan?" The answer was clear – we will be selective as we have limited resources and only those brands, which will show a significant size of the prize, will be launched. We need to deliver quality execution on large brands rather than sub-quality execution on many smaller brands.

I must emphasize that P&G management had the courage to say no in order to do justice to the brands that we were currently marketing. Bear in mind that during the first five years of P&G's entry into Pakistan we still had a relatively inexperienced and a young organization. Systems and processes where being developed and we were not mature enough or experienced enough to take on significantly large challenges. We could not give our teams more than they could chew, else it would have been a recipe for disaster.

In summary I would like to urge you to gain the courage to simply say no when confronted with a decision that is ahead of its time or for which you do not have the resources available. Always be true to your vision and its associated strategies. Also encourage the rest of the organization to do the same. Create a culture where every new idea or new project is evaluated on its own potential and its links to company strategies, if they don't fit, kill the idea. Be ruthless, as that will encourage your people to do the same. It is better to nip the problem in the bud rather than to face failure later on when it becomes a full blown serious problem.

"No one will improve your lot if you yourself do not."
~ Bertolt Brecht (1898–1956),
German Poet, Playwright, and Theatre Director

●●●●●▬▬▬ ▬▬▬▬●●●●

Chapter 9 – Executional Excellence

"Look at a day when you are supremely satisfied at the end.
It's not a day when you lounge around doing nothing:
it's when you've had everything to do and you've done it."
~ Margaret (Iron Lady) Thatcher (1925–2013),
Longest-Serving British Prime Minister

9 A. What is Executional Excellence?

To me execution is one of the most misinterpreted word or concept in the business world. If you ask any business leader or manager, you will get different answers. When I addressed this question to managers from various companies at a seminar, the most common answer I got was that "Execution is the final stage of any project and is the only one which the customer or consumer actually gets to see." That may be true, but in reality execution is embedded in every action or decision that is taken in the company. Execution is a set of behaviors that gives any organization its true competitive advantage.

To me execution is a complete discipline in itself. Execution is not a tactic or a strategy but the ability to do everything very well, with total quality and with excellence. For it to be present, it has to be entrenched in the company's culture, in the making of its vision, in the setting of its strategies and in its ability as an organization to remain in-touch with reality. Companies that are execution-oriented tend to accept and manage challenges, both internal and external, faster and with excellence. To achieve executional excellence the leadership team of the company must be hands-on and deeply involved in every aspect of the business, this responsibility must not be delegated for any reason; it's one of the most important jobs that leaders ever do.

How does one ingrain executional excellence into the DNA of its organization?

To me the sure fire way to achieve this goal is by role modeling. If you as a leader only spend time in defining the vision, and setting of its strategies and leave the rest to the organization to execute because you feel that is academic, you are totally off the mark. Leaders have to own execution at every stage, they have to guide, they have to help break down barriers and they have to set the gold standard for execution at every stage of the project. Many companies who have failed or lost out to competition are those who have lost their ability of driving quality execution within the organization.

Leaders have to *walk the talk* and not merely *talk the talk*. Leaders must practice what they preach and role model executional excellence personally rather than give it a lot of lip service. Lack of constant top management focus on execution is a sure-fire way of losing your competitiveness in the marketplace. Who do you think in the company has the most experience, who in the company has the most knowledge of past successes and failures, who has the ability and understanding to fix issues and break down barriers? It is the top management! And if they pass the execution baton off to their subordinates they are for sure short-circuiting the company's ability to deliver superior results and its ability to drive excellence.

> "Excellence isn't just doing things right, but
> rather doing the right things right."
> ~ Anonymous

Launching your business plan is clearly the very last and final step of any project and definitely a critical and most visible step as far as success of that initiative is concerned. But that does not undermine the importance of all the other stages in the life of an initiative, i.e. idea conceptualization, planning, designing, forecasting as well as logistical planning. Driving a culture of executional excellence at every stage is clearly what drives your company's competitive advantage and your ability to succeed in today's competitive marketplace. Execution is what turns normal operational plans into lethal campaigns. Lack of executional excellence is one of the key reasons why many powerful and apparently insightful strategies fail.

One needs to take execution extremely seriously at every stage and be personally involved and in-touch with two things, namely what's happening: a) in the company and b) in the marketplace. The first can be done via weekly Monday morning reviews, monthly one-to-one meetings with team leaders and being overtly available to your teams and employees. For the second one, you need to make sure you have constant and timely market research data available to you and your teams, carry out frequent store-checks in all cities and distribution channels, and meet up one-to-one with your distributors, sales teams, customers and consumers.

In Gillette, my team made more market visits then is the norm in the industry. I have personally made road trips once and sometimes twice a year across the country to see first-hand the ground reality in different towns and meeting and spending time with the distributor sales force employees. If you do all this, only then will you truly be in-touch with reality and deliver executional excellence in your company's plans.

Today the business environment is tougher than ever, the financial market is extremely volatile, margin for winning is razor thin, competition is ferocious and only those companies will survive who have built executional excellence into the gene pool of its employees. Others will not be able to cope up with these constant external challenges and will eventually fail vis-à-vis those companies that display executional excellence in everything they do. Why do you think companies like Apple, Coke, Wal-Mart and Southwest Airlines continue to outperform other companies in their sectors year after year, it is because they display executional excellence in everything they do, it is built into their culture and is constantly role modeled by their management team.

One must realize that competing firms also have very smart and talented CEOs who have in many cases been brought onboard due to their exceptional track record. So it is important to remain vigilant and on your toes, but in case any of the CEO's were **not** able to deliver on their vision and promises, they will be booted out without a second thought; in majority of the cases the reason would be that they were unable to indoctrinate quality execution within their management teams as well as among the company's employees in general.

Ram Charan and Larry Bossidy give a classic example of what a difference executional excellence can make in their book *Execution-The Discipline of Getting Things Done*. They share an excellent example, which relates to how Dell consistently outdid its competitors in everything they did due to their hawk like focus on executional excellence. The PC market during the last two decades had gone through immense changes and Michael Dell understood the kind of executional excellence that would help him win vis-à-vis other equally formidable competition like Compaq and IBM.

As the authors state "Execution is the reason Dell passed Compaq in market value years ago, despite Compaq's vastly greater size and scope, and it's the reason Dell passed Compaq in 2001 as the world's biggest maker of PC's. As of November 2001, Dell was shooting to double its market share, from approximately 20% to 40%." Dell beat their competition due to their executional excellence, in-depth knowledge of the computer industry and their ability to remain in-touch as well as their knack to forecast consumer preferences accurately.

One key management strategy that handed Dell the competitive advantage was their selection of the right production model. In the computer industry there are basically two production models in practice today, i.e. Batch Production Model and Built to Order Production Model.

1. *Batch production model* is based on forecasting demand over the next few months. Sales teams make their forecast and pass it to their production teams. They in turn negotiate pricing on the volume required and place orders with component suppliers to deliver to the warehouse. If actual sales fall short of the forecast, then the company gets stuck with high inventory and if sales exceed demand then everyone, including the component supplier, is working overtime and scrambling to meet demand on a very short notice.

2. *Built to order model* works on ordering components only when confirmed orders are placed with the company. This situation requires very close coordination and a strong relationship with your suppliers and a perfectly streamlined system of communication between all parties for it to be effective. Managing customer expectations from order to delivery time is very challenging.

Compaq worked on the 'batch production model' and Dell on the 'built to order model'. The issue that turned the tables on Compaq was the increasingly volatile period faced by the PC market in the mid 1990's. Technology changed very fast, new and faster processors were being introduced, memory prices were plummeting, disk drive capacities were ballooning, value added options were being introduced such as game ports, speakers, cameras, internet ports, wireless net, etc. and consumer preferences became quite fluid and difficult to forecast by the manufacturers.

Dell took full advantage of their unique production model and effectively utilized their strong insights of the computer industry and consumer preferences to beat competition at their own game. They hammered their competition due to their executional excellence, sharp focus on costs and strong knowledge of the industry. Dell's model had no waste, no inventory tied in working capital and total flexibility in meeting the changing demands of its customers. Dell used the concept of 'just-in-time' inventory successfully and squeezed cash and time out of the entire process from ordering to delivery by never investing in inventory. This allowed it to significantly improve their inventory turnover and there productivity resulted in a much higher cash flow from operations.

The utilization of the just-in-time inventory concept allowed their sales force to be extremely flexible in meeting customer needs and they could offer the latest technology while Compaq sales force was unable to match this flexibility. When the computer demand hit a snag right after 9/11, companies on batch production model such as Compaq were stuck with high-unsold inventories.

Their model was double edged as on one end they faced obsolescence on key electronic components as technology advancement continued to gain pace and on the other hand they could not benefit from the rapidly falling prices of components; true victims of obsolescence! According to the authors of the book *Execution*, Dell turned its inventory an impressive, over eighty times a year, as compared to only ten to twenty for its rival. Dell had a negative working capital and an incredible 355% return on invested capital in fiscal year

2001. This provided Dell with immense reservoirs of cash to invest in further research, improving their systems and processes as well as in gaining an upper hand on marketing campaigns, it made them the largest makers and supplier of PC's in the world in the 90's.

What is clear from this example is that executional excellence is extremely important at every stage of a product launch, at every level of management and in every execution of every system and process. The employees at Dell were executing every action with excellence and took extra pains in making sure no stone was left unturned which would help give Dell extra cash flow benefit, time to market advantage or an edge to custom design solutions to meet the ever increasing and changing needs of their customers. To me their ability to remain in-touch with the industry, with technology advancement, and with customers preferences coupled with executional excellence at every stage is what made Dell so successful.

It is pertinent to note that the selection of a production model may vary from industry to industry depending upon their maturity, technology advancement, quality and proximity to their supplier base. The batch production model was ideal when Apple launched its computer in mid 1980's and did very well. The real difference is in how in-touch you are; Dell read the situation spot on and won big. Using common sense and business acumen and driving executional excellence into a company's gene pool, can allow any company to gain a much-needed competitive edge.

9 B. Acid Test of Executional Excellence

The true acid test of executional excellence is when the idea or the initiative is finally launched and seen by the outside world or by the end consumers, or as we sometimes call it *when the rubber meets the road.* This is what some people consider to be the true test of executional excellence. All the steps leading to this one have to be done with excellence in order to have any chance of realizing top quality results in the in-market execution, i.e. brainstorming to meet a challenge, selecting an idea, building a plan, allocating resources, preparing execution materials, purchasing and informing sales force of launch details. Notice that all these steps do not touch the external world or the end consumers (only exception being if any test market survey was carried out to assess the viability of the idea) hence on these stages executional excellence is very much an internal benchmark, which is not seen by other companies.

Once all these stages have been delivered then is the time for the execution stage or the going live stage. The result of the in-market execution confirms whether executional excellence has been displayed and followed throughout the life of the project. One simple way to measure it is to see if all the next steps agreed on have been delivered as planned. If executional excellence is not in a company's culture and is not applied during the various stages of an initiative, then you may work 24/7 but the final execution in the market will never be of top quality. When we are impressed by the launch of a competitor's product or service we rarely realize that it is a result of their superior internal processes, superior team collaboration and superior delivery of executional excellence at every stage.

Do realize that executional excellence is not only required in the final five yards of a hundred yards race but during the entire hundred yards; if this fact is internalized that indeed is a breakthrough insight. Excellence should be applied at each and every yard of the race and that is when you will be able to win and beat competition on a sustainable basis.

"Every job is a self-portrait of the person who did it.
Autograph your work with Excellence."
~ Ted Key (1912–2008),
American Cartoonist, Writer

9 C. Ability to Execute with Excellence

For any vision to be delivered or for any strategy to be executed, if the management does not take into account the organizational ability to execute, having a vision or strategy has no value. From my years of experience and watching teams that have shown the ability to deliver unbelievable stretch goals with excellence and who continue to deliver executional excellence time and time again, I observed that they all have the following four basic characteristics;

a) High level of talent and skills.
b) The right people in the right seats on the bus.
c) Disciplined to do the right things.
d) Visible leadership at every level.

a. High Level of Talent and Skills:
Like they say *a chain is as strong as its weakest link*, the same is true for any organization; a team will be as strong as its weakest member. Hence it is extremely important to hire the right talent, groom and train them properly, make sure they are assigned to the right jobs and given full opportunity to utilize their strengths in their jobs. Companies, which survive the true test of time and prosper for decades if not centuries, are those who display strong internal values in their recruiting and promotion tradition. They are the ones who over time recruit great people who share their values and ethics; this allows values to permeate the organization's culture and impact overall performance positively.

Similarly if you want to have a company populated by talented and skillful employees, you will have to have a robust hiring process, clear job descriptions, a vigorous training program, a learning environment and merit-based career planning and succession program. Consistently driving this philosophy year on year will result in an impressive and formidable organization, which can deter any challenge and fight off any competitive maneuvers.

Another relevant perspective comes from General Colin Powell who states in the *Leadership Primer* his rules for picking people: "Look for intelligence and judgment, and most critically, a capacity to anticipate, to see around corners. Also look for loyalty, integrity, a high energy drive, a balanced ego, and the drive to get things done." Here he mentions characteristics, which go far beyond just intelligence, knowledge and capability building; he talks about gut feelings, intuition, ability to make sound judgments and presence of core values. The former have a lot to do with qualification, level of education and general knowledge but the later, i.e. "to get things done" is most critical on how a person entwines their experiences with their acquired knowledge and that is what makes that person a true talent.

b. Have the Right People in the Right Seats on your Bus:

Jim Collins states in his book *Good to Great* that the right sequence for the leader is "First Who ... Then What." Before we can think of 'what', we must first decide on the 'who', that is, who will do it? Usually what happens in most cases is that we first decide what to do, *before* we make a decision on who will do it. Here two mistakes have been made namely:

a. We have not yet defined the teams and individual roles, i.e. don't yet have the right people on-board and,
b. We are already suggesting where we want to go.

If the team has made the decision on which way to move rather than the leader, it would have driven deeper passion and commitment from the team. Hence, the very *first* thing to do is to get the right people on-board and the wrong people off (if there are any low performers or non-committed people that are present). So it is important to highlight the subtle difference in the old adage "People are your most important asset," people are not your most important asset, the <u>right</u> people are.

Once you have the right people in the right positions, the next step will be to figure out which direction you now need to drive the business.

Jim Collins has used the example of the bus for the **bus**iness, driver of the bus for the leader and passengers of the bus as member of the teams. What Collins states is to assume your bus (your business) is at a standstill and your job as the bus driver (i.e. the leader) is to move the bus in the right direction. Before you even decide which direction to drive the bus, you must first on-board passengers (your team); it's no fun driving around in an empty bus. The leader must make sure that they have the right passengers on the bus and the wrong people off the bus plus have the right passengers in the right seats (their core competencies must match the discipline or function they are assigned to).

This concept emphasizes the strong focus that must be placed on selection of leaders as well as their teams. Once the leader has put together a capable, committed and morally upright team then it is the right time to answer the '*What*' question. What should the company's vision be and what strategies should be pursued in order to deliver this vision?

One of the key advantages of starting with the 'who' rather than the 'what' is that if the bus faces any challenges (i.e. fast changing world) they can easily adapt to the challenges as all the team members were involved in deciding the direction the bus is moving towards. If you move the bus and decide the direction without selecting the 'who' you will inevitably have issues adapting to any changes as the passengers (team) are not aligned and not part of the original decision. Deciding the 'who' before the 'what' will make your reaction much faster and much more adaptive to handle changing conditions.

Also as Collins says, if you have the right people on the bus, you don't need to worry about motivating them. The right people are self-motivating, nothing beats being part of a team that is expected to produce great results. Always remember that a great vision with mediocre people will produces mediocre results, but a qualified and competent team delivers great results. Right people in the right seats are the key for the success of any leader; success breeds success.

c. Disciplined to do the Right Things: Managing Meetings and Emails

I have been part of many meetings where a great idea is born, immense commitment is shown and a lot of excitement is displayed, but all to end up in naught! Execution is lacking in follow-ups, in taking it to the next stage and finally with new and different priorities taking over the participants work life. Companies waste a huge amount of management time and effort on projects that never take off. I am sure we all know of managers who talk a lot in meetings, adding some nuance to every topic but none of the ideas reach the light of day. Such managers need to be discouraged, counseled and groomed as such actions are not only detrimental to their own career but that of their teams as well.

Company's who execute with excellence are those where time and effort is measured, meetings are timely, with a clear agenda and finite duration, frivolous behavior is not tolerated and inept display of ideas or mental games just to impress others is discouraged. Do note that we are not talking about deterring creativity, I am a strong supporter of new ideas, but power games or behaviors that display personal win/lose in meetings should be curtailed. What is critical and much needed is a personal conviction to single-handedly bring ideas to life and make formal closure to pending issues on a timely basis.

One of my previous bosses Vice President/General Manger Philippe Bovay was a master of effective communication and management. One golden tip that I loved and followed was related to managing incoming email, which was: Manage your email inbox as you would a paper inbox. Handle each email once and action it!

According to his laid down principles, when you get a new email you should read it only once and once read you must take one of the following actions:

a. Reply if a reply is asked for, ideally with a decision or with specific requests for more information to allow you to arrive at a decision. This is because taking a decision is the most important thing to do to avoid inaction and procrastination.
b. Forward to others for important information sharing.
c. File crucial correspondence in a mailbox folder for future reference.
d. Delete after reading it if it is just for info. Avoid printing as much as possible as it is a huge waste of resources and has no place in today's world.
e. If the email requires you to put significant time on it in order to progress it, put it into your electronic calendar and set up a specific time and date that you will tackle it on. In other words you are booking an appointment with yourself in your calendar, with the number of hours you plan to spend on it. Just as you would put a meeting date into your calendar.

Always pursue a goal that the inbox should be empty except for new emails.

Vital Tip 24: Never read your email and take no action as then you will come back later and will find it again in your inbox and inevitably waste more time rereading it and end up with new and old emails all piled up together.

The same logic can be applied to meetings and making interactions effective and productive. If an idea is generated or an action is suggested, it should be acted upon and must not lie dormant to be narrated in another meeting as a potentially great business building idea. It should be dealt with right there and then and not postponed or parked to be discussed later.

There are many examples of people procrastinating on potentially explosive ideas, only to find that they lost a critical first mover advantage to a competitor. Focusing and fixing meeting management principles and interaction at this basic level is what drives true productivity and organizational excellence in organizations.

Vital Tip 25: Always make sure that you do not leave a meeting or discussion without assigning someone the responsibility to write its minutes and assigning proper tasks and deadlines for each next step that is aligned in the meeting. There is nothing worse than attending a meeting where a great discussion and a good decision had taken place but only to be forgotten due to lack of follow-up or due to lack of ownership. Even writing minutes does not deliver closure, managers have to take personal responsibilities and ownership for the work identified and deliver it with quality and in time. In every subsequent meeting on the same project, it is paramount that they should always start with the reading of minutes so that there is continuity and we do not ignore the key next steps and issues raised earlier.

Great leaders have an innate ability to make sure that projects remain on track, they make sure they are part of every critical follow-up meeting, they inspire by helping break down barriers, and their personal charisma and commitment is contagious. General Colin Powell has very aptly stated that "Great leaders are almost always great simplifiers, who can cut through argument, debate and doubt, to offer a solution everybody can understand." Such leaders breed cultures where blame games and internal agenda are never played upon, where *the moose is always placed on the table* voluntarily and where people are willing to raise red flags when ever and where ever they may find them. Only in such an environment can executional excellence is bred, merit encouraged and employees strive to do the right thing every time.

d. Visible Leadership at Every Level:
Role modeling is one of the most powerful tools in inspiring your people, setting gold standards of performance as well as to help groom and train young managers on what true leadership is all about. Reason I have used the word 'visible' is to highlight the kind of leadership that is displayed while operating amidst your troops and not by sitting back in your glass towers and mahogany offices and shooting off emails and verbal phone orders. Like they say the best generals are those who lead from the front, in the business world that would be called *management by walking around*. There is nothing more motivational then seeing and watching your team leader or CEO right next to you in time of need. Visible leaders never allow things to fall through the cracks.

Visible leadership is clearly not an easy virtue to have; it requires strong moral fiber and a lot of guts. If you are not the master of your business and do not have all-round capabilities then showing visible leadership is prone to major risks; many such managers are fearful of exposing themselves. It is easy to guide and steer from the comfort of your office, but in team meetings you have no second chances but have to shoot from the hip, make quick decisions and need to evaluate the situation at the toss of a coin. Any reluctance in quick decision making, showing confusion or inability to make tough calls can easily expose chinks in your leadership persona. Only leaders of high moral character, strong confidence in their abilities and having extensive hands-on experience can survive the true test of visible leadership.

Visible leadership is not just about making good decisions and breaking down barriers, you also have to take responsibility for the welfare of your managers, be equitable in your actions and always have the courage to call an ace an ace. Like General Colin Powell who interestingly in his very first lesson states: "Being responsible sometimes means pissing people off." He raises a very important point that you cannot keep everyone happy all the time, you will have to make tough decisions and break serious status quos, which may be derailing your projects. This means that some people will get angry at your actions and decisions. It is just not possible or feasible to keep everyone happy.

Trying to get everyone to like you is a sign of mediocrity and by doing so you will inevitably avoid the tough decisions. If need be, you must confront managers who need to be confronted, else you will end up innately giving recognition to mediocre performers. This will result in demotivating the most committed and productive members of the team and eventually lead to mediocre business results. Remember that everyone's performance and contribution is not equal and they need to be treated as such. Never procrastinate in making tough calls and don't be worried if you hassle or shake up a few people, remember the rework avoided in the future will be ample compensation. Mr. Nice Guy has no place in the corporate world.

An organization with a true visible leader at its helm will have everyone focused towards delivering the company's vision, all employees will value time as well as each other's opinions, team collaboration will be abundant and leadership behavior will be displayed at every level of the organization. Visible leaders are those who are intimately involved with their organizations and their businesses and they energize and inspire their people by the examples they set. Visible leaders don't just preside over but lead the organization. Visible leaders don't just delegate and walk away, they are close by to handle and advise on critical issues.

9 D. Motivation Drives Executional Excellence

There are many reasons why companies are unable to drive executional excellence within their organizations but one common denominator is lack of motivation. For anything to be delivered with excellence there are two type of motivation, which must be present in a company's culture:

a) Deep inner personal satisfactions in what employees are doing. This happens when the company's mission matches with an employee's personal mission in life, employees feel immense personal pride in completing their projects as it brings them closer to their own personal mission.

b) Encouragement or motivation driven by clear reward or recognition if the project is delivered with excellence. This is mostly performance based.

While running your business it is critical that you make sure that both types of motivation are present in all your initiatives or projects. Offering motivation as mentioned in point 'a' above is a much more difficult task as it has to do with the inherent culture prevailing in the company. Studies have shown that linking the benefit of a project to the company's mission or its purpose has a significant impact on the passion of its employees. The level of motivation is directly linked to how closely the company's mission matches employees' personal desires and goals.

On the other hand structuring a reward system which encourages employees who live and display the mission in everything they do plays a critical role in driving appropriate behavior. For proper reward and recognition it is important that in all corporate performance evaluation processes as well as in all internal communication it is clearly highlighted as to who is truly responsible for the various stages of the project. Make sure recognition is merit based and is shared broadly so that everyone is aware of who is a being recognized and why.

If both of the above mentioned motivational energies are present in an organization then the company has a clear path to success and without much cajoling employees will drive executional excellence in everything they do. If neither of them are present then the project will be completed just because it was required by management and will not have the much required 'excellence' written all over it.

<blockquote>
"Excellence is not an act but a habit.
The things you do the most are the things you will do the best."
~ Marva Collins (b. 1936),
Educationist
</blockquote>

Let me take each of the two motivations and expand them for further clarity:

a. **Purpose Driven Corporate Projects:** As mentioned in Chapter 2, the presence of a mission statement helps to guide the organization on why this company is in existence and to make sure that all work plans, its systems and processes are totally in-sync. The mission statement influences and impacts all decision making and projects across different management levels. For example in P&G the mission or as they call it 'Their Purpose' is to 'Improve the lives of the world's consumers'; any P&G project that has a direct link to improving people lives will invariably get top performances as the objective of the project will go far beyond personal motivation, it will touch the employees chords at a much deeper emotional level.

That is one of the reasons that the first major initiative taken by Bob McDonald at taking over as the new CEO of P&G in 2009, was to promote what he calls P&G's "purpose-inspired growth" strategy of "touching and improving more consumers lives in more parts of the world ... more completely."[46] It is extremely important to recognize that the kind of performance a person can deliver if they believe in a cause, is radically different from the performance that person will deliver if a job is assigned to them without them buying or believing into its rational or its benefit.

b. **Reward and Recognition in Corporate Projects:** Here there are two issues to wrestle with, namely:

    a.   What is in it for them, the employees? i.e. reward, and
    b.   Who gets the credit for the project? i.e. recognition.

One common symptom for not having executional excellence is the lack of clarity on who finally gets the credit for that project or initiative.

There are several reasons for this: a) In many cases the true recognition is given to those who came up with the idea and not to those who implement the idea, b) the period between conceptualization of the project and the time when the final in-market results are available to herald success in most cases takes months, if not years and most managers would have moved on by then to new assignments, hence accountability gets a lot fuzzy. It is thus important that unless active effort and focus is placed on giving due credit for executional excellence at every stage of the project, the required behavior will be absent.

Humans are creatures where the right behavior is clearly stimulated via timely incentives and rewards. The company systems and processes need to be designed in such a way so as to cope with this characteristic head-on, human resources must make sure that the performance evaluation process is tightly linked with true accountability. As reward and recognition is in your hands and is something you can impact today, you must act on it right now with complete transparency and clarity.

Let me further elucidate the above mentioned pitfalls so we can get a good grip on how we can truly bring reward and recognition in sync with executional excellence namely:

- ✓ Loopholes when Assigning Credit
- ✓ Giving Credit too Early

✓ **Loopholes when Assigning Credit:** As everyone wants a feather in their cap, hence everyone loves to be the one to be given credit for an idea that they had envisioned, suggested or worked upon to bring it to life. The entire team from the person who is leading the project to the one who does the most routine work should all be equally committed and concerned if the project is to succeed. Unfortunately due to misguided credit where a team effort is ignored and a single individual is given all the credit, results in major de-motivation in future team projects by all those ignored.

The flip side is also important where if an initiative fails than no one person should be made the scapegoat but the entire team be made responsible. Like they say, once you are in it, you are in it for the long haul; the concept of 'all for one and one for all' applies fittingly. The real challenge for top management is to make sure that each and everyone who actually helped make the project a success is rewarded and a note placed in his or her personnel file specifically highlighting his or her contribution.

Casual focus on recognition leads to behavior that does not encourage executional excellence. Hence initiative success rate should be made an integral part of all managers' performance criteria and specially should be on the CEO's scorecard, as only then the proper culture will evolve from top to the bottom.

✓ **Giving Credit too Early:** Another catch that I have observed is where credit for an idea is given to the person or persons who envisioned and worked on the project even before the true results of its success have been properly determined. The actual in-market results can take quite a long time to be collected and tabulated (it may take from six months to a year for properly analyzing market research data), and that's why giving proper credit sometimes gets muddled because of this long duration. This results in improper credit being given, as in a twelve-month period, people may change assignments and some new faces may have taken over during the execution stage. Therefore, it is imperative that proper tracking be put in place for all three stages, i.e. Idea Generation, Planning and Execution.

In my three decades of working in P&G and Gillette, I have seen many instances where a manager was rewarded for a great project, which from the initial results looked impressive, but when the final data was tabulated it got labeled a failure. So clear effort should be placed in determining who gets the credit and credit should only be given when proper results are available and broadly known.

In Summary:

When we talk about what kind of motivation is needed to drive executional excellence in an organization, the first motivation, of having purpose-driven projects, can only be delivered by the top management and their ability to formulate and deploy a truly inspiring mission statement. This mission should be kept alive at all times, in company meetings, and in rewards for those who live the mission to the letter.

This is a long process and it may take years or decades to get it ingrained into the DNA of every employees as well as anyone who joins the company. The other motivation mentioned in this section, i.e. pure reward and recognition, is much simpler and can be implemented in no time. It only needs a strong focus from management, strong collaboration with line management and total transparency in implementing it.

To me execution is in every stage of the race; from the starter's gun to until you break the end ribbon. You have to run the entire race by dotting all the i's and crossing all the t's, immaculate planning, exquisite execution: only then will you deliver executional excellence in everything you do. The final ten yards are extremely important too, as all your good work could be lost if in the final in-market execution stage you go lax or lose focus.

You may have started the race off the blocks very well, taken the lead in the first ninety yards, but if you do not continue to maintain the momentum and execute the final ten yards with excellence, the entire race is lost. That is why executional excellence is the key for any strategy.

"Excellence can be attained if you care
more than others think is wise,
risk more than others think is safe,
dream more than others think is practical,
expect more than others think is possible."
~ Anonymous

Chapter 10 – Rewarding and Celebrating Success

10 A. Celebrating Success

Nothing is more motivating than being given credit for your hard work. Humans have an in-built euphoric spirit, which takes flight when given praise and recognition for a challenging task successfully accomplished. This desire to be praised starts from our childhood, when we do all sorts of antics in order to gain attention and with any luck get praise from our parents.

If you ever try to research corporate icons or meet managers who are known for their success, you will inevitably see that they have a strong desire and a passion to share organizational as well as individual success, across the board. Unfortunately this powerful tool of rewarding success is not effectively used by many corporate leaders and is one of the reasons for attrition as well as for mediocre performance in such companies.

To properly use this effective tool for motivation I have a few effective tips:

a) Reward and recognize all sorts of achievements, big or small. Reward could be as small as a pat on the back or as big as giving out company stock options.

b) Reward and recognition of achievements should be given on a timely basis, ideally right there when the right behavior is displayed or success confirmed.

c) Reward and recognition should be spread to all levels of the organization.

d) Reward and recognition should always be linked to the overall vision of the company.

e) Reward and recognition should be ingrained into the culture of the company.

f) Reward and recognition should be posted on company notice boards, shared in company meetings and included in newsletters.

g) Reward and recognition should be shared with top management when they visit your company and plants.

h) On every special occasion, such as an official lunch or dinner with visiting senior managers, reward these select individuals by placing them at the head-table. Treat them as special as they are special and deserve this recognition and appreciation.

Remember, praise does not cost anything but it goes a long way in motivating and refueling an employee for further success. For this very reason I created the Mission Dugna Tigna Award to reward good work and linked it directly to the vision of Gillette Pakistan. In addition to this yearly award, we also had other rewards such as quarterly silver, gold and platinum awards, annual stock option awards, etc., each linked to a certain period and performance.

"The more you praise and celebrate your life,
the more there is in life to celebrate."
~ Oprah Winfrey (b. 1954),
American TV Personality, Actress and Producer

10 B. Rewarding Good Performance

Whenever employees are surveyed on what they want most out of a job, getting recognition for their quality efforts ranks high among their responses. Employees who get timely recognition show stronger self-confidence, have a much higher level of self-esteem and are more eager to take on bigger and more challenging roles. Experienced managers recognize such people who deliver consistently and who work passionately to deliver their work plans, as their own success as leaders depends on these employees' contribution and commitment.

Rewarding and celebrating performance and employee success in delivering their work plans must take into account the following four factors, namely:

A. Compensation for a Fair Days Work
B. Performance Based Rewards
C. Special Performance Based Rewards
D. Employees Who live the Company Values and Mission

A. Compensation for a Fair Days Work

It is important that we create an equitable balance between the company and its employees. As they say it's a two-way street, i.e. the organization must compensate employees for working hard and delivering on the objectives set by management, and in return the employees must spend their time focused on delivering company objectives and in helping the company move towards its vision. To deliver *Fair Pay* means we pay based on a benchmark job survey vis-à-vis others similar jobs in competitive companies.

The key is not to match job titles but to match job descriptions. The work and effort put in by a brand manager in your firm may not always match the work and effort of another brand manager of a competing firm. The key is to write a detailed job description of each job and when trying to benchmark them, match job description to job description. Your brand manager's work may match the job description of a marketing director in another firm. If this type of matching is not done for compensation, then you will err in not offering proper compensation, which may lead to de-motivation, lack of focus and finally attrition.

It is extremely important that each company carries out a fair and in depth study of their compensation and benefits and offers a compensation package that is competitive. By offering competitive packages your employees will stay focused on work, goals and delivering your dream and not be distracted on whether they are being treated fairly.

B. **Performance Driven Rewards**

People deliver different levels of performance, commitment and ownership while delivering company assigned work. It is critical that management differentiates compensation based on performance otherwise there will be no incentive to work hard, to show ownership behavior or to deliver performance beyond standard company expectations.

To achieve this, in most companies there are performance salary bands and higher the performance, higher is the performance salary band under which that employee is compensated. This allows management to properly reward employees who display higher levels of performance vis-à-vis other employees through their compensation and benefits program. It is de-motivating for high potential candidates who are showing higher levels of commitment and performance to be receiving the same pay scale versus someone who is not that committed and showing lower level of performance. This allows the retention of high performers and encourages them to work even harder and continue to deliver high levels of performance.

Promotion must be directly linked to the level of performance, so people in the higher performance bands get promoted faster than those in the lower bands and therefore take on bigger and more challenging roles.

C. **Special Performance Based Rewards**

For employees who show a marked higher level of performance and if the performance is consistent and sustained over a long period of time they need to be and must be specially recognized and rewarded. Some companies incorporate bonus systems, some have stock ownership plans and while others may have special cash awards to serve this objective. All of these awards are given for showing disproportional level of commitment and performance.

Timing can vary from giving it once a year to offering it on a quarterly basis depending upon the amount or the type of rewards. Bonuses and stock options are usually given once a year, which makes them highly attractive to the employees. Stock options specially, are perceived as having a very high value and act as an effective retention tool for many companies. These options can be exercised over a fixed period of time (ranging from five, ten or fifteen years) and most people tend to hold on to them as their value increases over time (if the stock keeps on appreciating).

D. **For Employees Who live the Company Values and Mission**

In order to keep the company's mission alive and for encouraging employees to display and live within the agreed core values, some companies introduce a special reward. This is given only to those select few employees who display and keep the company's mission and vision alive. These employees act as role models and it is extremely important that they are recognized and that all other employees are kept aware of the company's mission and its core values which must be followed at all times and without exception. Rewarding such behavior is one of the most effective ways of making the organization breath and live within company value's and mission in everything they do or plan.

"Celebrate what you want to see more of."
~ Thomas J. Peters (b. 1942),
American Author and Consultant

..........━━ ━━━━━━......

Chapter 11 – Road Map to Help Deliver your Mission

Strategy is the plan of action to deliver your vision and to accomplish the mission that your organization has signed in to deliver. Each has its own place in the hierarchy of choices. First you have to define the mission,

which literally is the reason for their very existence, meaning what purpose this company has been created to deliver. Once the mission is deployed, next step is to define your vision, where you want your company to be in five or ten years. The vision has to be totally in sync with the mission.

Once the vision is agreed and aligned then the tough job starts of identifying a few critical strategies that will help you deliver your vision. Setting strategies is a two way process and you have to address the following:

a. <u>Where do we want to play?</u> In simple words where do you want your company to operate in order to deliver the vision, which product categories, which geographies, which trade channels, which socio-economic class, etc.?

b. <u>How do you plan to win?</u> This requires you to carry out a reality check to find out if you are building on your core competences, do you have the resources, the financing, and the capability to win in the areas you have identified to operate?

If both these steps check out, you are ready to list down and share broadly the selected strategies that you have identified in your organization.

Once *strategies* have been agreed upon, the next step is to identify a set of *tactics* or action steps that need to be carried out in order to deliver these strategies. To make sure tactics are delivered, as that is the acid test of success,  *measures* and targets are agreed on for each of the tactics. The key is to make sure all your tactics are delivered with *excellence* and that can only be achieved if its planning and its execution are impeccable and of top quality; what we in business lingo call *executional excellence*.

Rest of the game from here on should be focused on keeping the vision alive, following its progress by closely *tracking* its goals and measures, celebrating success whenever a milestone is delivered and having proper checks and balances to make sure we do not deviate from this path. Appius Claudius ('the blind'; 340–273 BC) a Roman politician, who later became a dictator, encapsulated this process very well when he said *"quisque faber suae fortunae* (Latin)" which means, "Every man is the architect of his own fortune."

Remember the Steps to Success

- ✓ Identify a mission that is close to your heart as well as your purpose for existing.
- ✓ Write a clear and all-inclusive mission statement or statement of purpose.
- ✓ Use mission as a foundation for creating a vision for your company.
- ✓ Enroll the target audience into your vision and roll it out to all.
- ✓ Set goals as milestones for your vision.
- ✓ For inspiration define a few BHAG goals.
- ✓ Identify a set of strategies to deliver your vision.
- ✓ Agree on 'where do we play?'
    - Be choiceful; define a set of tactics for each of the strategies.
- ✓ Check on 'how do we win?'
    - Make sure strategies are sustainable and focused on your company's core competencies.
- ✓ Be a strategist and a tactician. Maintain the right balance.
- ✓ Roll out a set of measures for each strategy.
- ✓ Follow the SMART principles in setting your goals and measures.
- ✓ Design a complete balanced scorecard to track progress.
- ✓ Execute strategies with excellence.
- ✓ Never lose faith in your strategies, if they are not delivering, find out why and fix the issue.
- ✓ For proper prioritization of each strategy define its sources of growth.
- ✓ Do quarterly checks of goals and measures in an open and candid manner.
- ✓ Create virtuous cycles and further fuel them for peak results.
- ✓ Embrace change as and when it happens.
- ✓ Never ever lose confidence or stray from your vision despite obstacles.

✓ Confront the brutal facts while keeping unwavering faith in your end results.
✓ Act as an inspirational leader and help in breaking down barriers.
✓ Always keep hope alive as that is the fuel for delivering your vision.
✓ At all time treat people as they are your most important assets.
✓ Reward people on a timely basis for displaying behavior in line with company's values and mission.
✓ And celebrate big as well as small victories.

"Vision is perhaps our greatest strength ...
it has kept us alive to the power
and continuity of thought through the centuries,
it makes us peer into the future and
lends shape to the unknown."
~ Sir Ka Shing-Li (b. 1928),
Wealthy businessman from Hong Kong, who is the
richest person of East Asian descent in the world, and
the sixteenth richest man in the world in 2009.

••••■■■■■■■■ ■■■■■■■■■■••••

PART II

DRIVING ORGANIZATIONAL EXCELLENCE IN YOUR BUSINESSES

Introduction: Part II

Driving Organizational Excellence

In continuation to the Part I of this book, this section is written to act as a catalyst or spark in bringing your vision and strategies to life. To grow a plant you need air, sunlight and fertile ground, similarly for an organization to realize its vision you need a culture where passion for winning, positive thinking, embracing change, leadership behaviour and striving for excellence is a way of life.

An ideal culture is where trust is in abundance at every level of the organization and every employee's DNA is programmed to deliver excellence and peak performance in whatever they attempt to do. This kind of culture cannot be created overnight and has to be nurtured, protected and developed over years. You need to be consistent and disciplined in your approach so that over time you can drive this into the character and DNA of each and every employee. And once that has been achieved, then the sky is the limit as no person or competition can stand in the way of such a highly committed, and charged organization.

In this part of the book, I have captured many of the softer topics of 'organizational excellence' which lie on the periphery but are critical for the success of the entire vision and goal setting process.

What many people miss out on is that delivering a vision is not just about envisioning and selecting strategies and tactics. Factors such as human interaction, tone at the top, inherent culture, value systems and other organizational aspects are equally important in delivering the vision. A vision in isolation has no value and no likelihood of turning into reality if not supported by a strong conducive culture nurtured by committed and dedicated leaders. I have realized that in the majority of cases where leaders have failed to step-change the business, the reasons had more to do with ignoring the smell of the place rather than lack of robust strategies and plans.

A senior manager once came up to me after my presentation on the 'Power of Vision and Strategies' at the Marketing Association of Pakistan (MAP) seminar in Lahore and asked me, "I have set a daunting vision and targets, but no one is excited and committed in delivering it, what should I do?" Unfortunately, strategies can be identified, aligned with proper access to market research and demographic data plus a creative mind, but changing the hearts and minds of the employees who can deliver extraordinary results can take a long time and can be a very exasperating experience.

So my best wishes to you and God speed in your efforts to paint in some much needed color into your 'direction setting' efforts.

Saad Amanullah Khan
August 10th, 2013

Chapter 12 – Organizational Culture

Organizational culture is a set of operating principles or rules under which the organization operates and which collectively help define how people behave within a certain company. Culture as you will agree is not something one can touch or feel; it is invisible but has a profound impact on how decisions are made, how people are motivated, respected and retained. In any company the employees driven by the culture, over time, develop specific ways of interacting and communicating with their peers, bosses, subordinates and external partners.

Underlying all this interaction, communication and observable behaviors is a set of values and beliefs, which drives overall performance. These values and beliefs need to be properly selected, nurtured and developed within the organization. The culture of the company is the outward demonstration of the values that exist in the organization. In larger more established organizations the mission statement and values hold together a company's organizational culture.

A key to the success of any company is the degree to which an organization's values match the values of individuals who work in that company; if it is a good match then chances are that these individual will be able to function at peak performance and remain loyal to the company's mission and values. It is essential that proper focus be placed on building a *Winning Culture*, which starts right from the hiring process. While hiring one must evaluate whether the candidates are a right 'cultural fit' for the company, do they display strong work ethics in their past actions, for this reason explore their previous achievements, find out what challenges they had to overcome as well as any ethical dilemmas they may have faced and how they resolved them.

To me past behavior is a perfect reflection of future behavior. So do remember that the only way a winning culture will permeate the daily operations of a company is on the strength of focus that management places on how employees are motivated and rewarded for their efforts.

First thing you must do is to take a look at the culture that exists in your organization today. Your assessment of the culture may make you happy or sad, depending upon what you find. Do not under any circumstances delay this assessment if you have never formally done it before. The age-old idiom of ignorance is bliss does not stand true in this case. You need to be ready and convinced on fixing this very important aspect of business success. Whatever the assessment reveals, that is your organizational culture; the key now is to focus on fixing it. There are many aspects to an organizational culture about which I will talk later in this chapter, but there are three key aspects which I would like to highlight as being the foundation of any culture.

a) **Trust**: In a company where trust is present, everything else becomes easy. Trust forms the foundation for effective communication, employee retention as well as a source of motivation for employees to function at their peak performance.

b) **Values**: All companies' need a set of values, which create the basis for all interaction and decision-making, they are the starting point for every action taken by employees and dominate and guide the overall culture of the company. In short values act like the soul of the company.

c) **Respect and Dignity**: These are the two basic needs of any human being. They are driven by trust and values, but the reason to especially emphasize these two is to highlight their importance to any organization or society. Focus on respecting people and treating them with dignity, henceforth they will work for you for a very long time and they would voluntarily do things, which may even be outside their scope, and do so happily and with full commitment and determination.

> "Treat others with dignity and make sure
> your behaviors are respectful,
> it will make you a person of quality."
> ~ Anonymous

At the end it is important to note that top management plays a critical role in defining the organizational culture by their actions and leadership, however one must remember that holistically it is the entire employee population, which contributes and brings this culture to life.

12 A. People are the Real Assets

One thing that I have learned by working in multinationals is that people are the real assets of any company and should be treated as such. What amazes me is that many companies or corporate leaders in many developing countries including Pakistan do not follow this simple but very important concept. Developed countries on the other hand have learned the hard way that without quality people, you can never win on a sustainable basis. All successful companies treasure and invest in their people; this ensures their long-term success.

That is why even today you will find companies that are centuries old and doing extremely well (e.g. P&G +178 years, Merck +348 years). When competition is brutal, margins of error are small, and street fighting for every percentage point of market share is fierce, the employees, their capabilities, their commitment, their passion and their inherent desire to win at all cost makes all the difference.

> "No organization can do better than the people it has."
> ~ Peter F. Drucker (1909–2005),
> Writer and Management Consultant

General Colin Powell in one of his many insightful lessons hits at the heart of an interesting fact that, it is not the strategies or the theories that finally makes the difference between success or failure of any project or assignment but the people you hire, groom and retain. He states: "Organization doesn't really accomplish anything. Plans don't accomplish anything, either. Theories of management don't much matter. Endeavors succeed or fail because of the people involved. Only by attracting the best people will you accomplish great deeds."

Vital Tip 26: Finding quality people and training them is merely 50% of the work, retaining them and keeping them inspired and motivated is the balance 50%.To achieve this goal, you must identify people who share your values and passion, place them in the right jobs, compensate them competitively and work towards creating a culture which inspires them to deliver their very best every hour and every minute of the day.

Do remember that quality people do not come cheap and should never be taken for granted; they have to be paid competitively and in line with the best company practices in your country and region. To me employee compensation has always been part of a two-way street, you pay them well and in return they will help make the company successful. One of the best and most effective ways of building quality incentive is to add stock ownership as an integral part of every employee's compensation program, which makes each employee an owner in the company.

The stock ownership can be implemented in any type of company, big or small, public or private, corporation or proprietorship. This way the employee's interests and the company's interests will always remain in harmony. The better the company performs, the better will be its value or stock price and more lucrative will be their ownership of shares in the company. For example William Cooper Procter who was the grandson of William Procter, one of the two men who founded The Procter and Gamble Company, established a profit-sharing program for the company's workforce as far back as 1887.[47] He hoped that by giving the workers a stake in the company, they would be less inclined to go on strike and would show more ownership behavior as they would now be part owners in the company, in its operation as well as its profits. This is one of the reasons that P&G today is 178 years old and continues to do very well.

Competitive and superior compensation is just one aspect of the endeavor by companies to retain quality people. Other aspects, which in some cases are even more important than compensation, are the presence of a value-based culture, mutual respect across all levels, constant capability building philosophy, merit based promotions and a healthy competitive internal environment. These characteristics of a culture are not easy to create, maintain and sustain.

It takes years of nurturing values, fostering a culture of innovation, cultivating a spirit of competition, constant thirst for innovation and a passion for winning against all odds. So my suggestion is that if you are truly passionate about winning in the long-term, then learn from these centuries old companies like P&G

and Merck and implement policies and benefits that truly respect individuals and their contribution to a company's success.

> "I am convinced that nothing we do is
> more important than hiring and developing people.
> At the end of the day you bet on people, not on strategies."
> ~ Lawrence A. ('Larry') Bossidy (b. 1935),
> Businessman and Author

Vital Tip 27: We may call 'our people' our most important assets but interestingly they don't show up in one of the most important accounting records, i.e. the company balance sheet. They in fact show up as expenses in the Income Statement. Assets are defined as items that have some economic value for the company and can be converted to cash. Example includes such items as inventory, machinery, building, etc. Even intangible assets are present, such as trademarks, patents, goodwill, etc.

Regrettably, employees are viewed as expenses in true accounting terms and not assets. As all key management strategies and action takes into account the status of its balance sheet, it overlooks this extremely important asset. If we could somehow treat these alternate yet progressive assets in economic terms and not expenses, all the company's commercial apprehensions will be a thing of the past.

On the other hand if you do not treat people as assets, then you may win in the short-term due to some unique market niche or some other temporary competitive advantage, but it would not be sustainable. As a consequence your employees will not show high level of commitment for the company, and you can be sure that you will lose that advantage as the business world is dynamic and competition will learn of your advantage and counter it quickly. Competition will immediately analyze the situation, read the market trends and take away your advantage or leadership.

Always remember that the company that values people the most will eventually win the game, as it will be its people who will help in winning by analyzing the situation, finding competitors weaknesses and reacting with ferocious speed. Therefore to strengthen your company, you must inculcate a culture of ownership behavior and passion for winning in all your employees.

> "Tough times don't last. Tough people do."
> ~ Robert Schuller (1926–2015),
> American Televangelist, Pastor, and Writer

12 B. Smell of the Place

Professor Sumantra Ghoshal was a teacher, author and a management guru. His ground breaking work on setting the tone by the top management for improving the 'smell' of the workplace to dramatically change people's performance is a very popular concept and is practiced in many companies even today. Crux of his research states that you cannot change an organization without revitalizing its people.

According to him revitalizing people is an attitudinal change. For productivity improvement, attitudes as well as the mindsets of the employees has to change. The challenge is that amongst adults, due to their maturity and past experiences, it is very difficult to change their mindsets.

> "I really believe, revitalizing manufacturing,
> revitalizing a business, revitalizing a company,
> takes, among other things, the revitalization of people."
> ~ Sumantra Ghoshal (1948–2004),
> Indian Organizational Theorist and Academician
> in the field of Management

Knowing that you cannot teach old dog new tricks, how do you expect to change people's mindsets? Ghoshal's theory to revitalize people is grounded in the ability to change the context that management is created around people and for that he uses a great example from his personal life.

The smell of the place: Ghoshal was a native of Kolkata settled in UK. Each year he and his family would visit Kolkata to spend time with his parents and extended family. Before moving to London where he lived until his death, he had taught at INSEAD for nine years and lived in Fontainebleau, France.

As he recounted, while living in France, every year in July he and his family used to visit Kolkata for almost a month as that is when his kids had their long summer break. What does downtown Kolkata look like in summer? In July downtown Kolkata looks awful, the temperature roamed around 100°F with humidity at 98%. Due to the awful weather he would end up spending most of his vacation indoors as he was too exhausted and tired to do anything else.

On the other hand while at INSEAD he lived in Fontainebleau, which was a pretty little town, forty miles south of Paris, and had the most amazing scenery, weather, and environment. Fontainebleau was surrounded by one of the prettiest forests in all of Europe. According to him whenever he would visit the forest in the spring he would go with a firm desire to have a leisurely walk but ended up doing something totally different. That was because the smell of the air, the trees and the general ambiance made him want to run, jog, jump up and catch a branch, throw a stone, or just do something; to him the fact that you entered the forest to have a leisurely walk but end up doing something totally different was the essence behind the issue of revitalizing people.

If you enter any factory or a head office, you can grasp in just the first fifteen twenty minutes the 'smell of the place', from the quality of the hum, in the eyes of its employees and workers, and in how they talk and interact with each other. Most large companies in India and abroad unfortunately end up creating downtown Kolkata, in summer, in their organizations.

He goes on to explain that in most large organizations people work long hard hours but in an environment of constraint. What is the 'smell of the place' when a worker is a part of such a large organization? The person on the factory floor looks up at his boss, top managements and all the systems they have created, i.e. human resource systems, manufacturing systems, planning systems, budgeting systems – each by itself is totally justified, but has been created to control him. He has to comply at all times and this burden hangs on him like the Sword of Damocles.

Within the worker's circle of influence he cannot see the justification of the sixteen levels of management other than to control him and to make sure he does not do anything wrong. The job becomes a contract and his environment is full of constraint, compliance and control - that is the 'smell of the place'.

However, if you talked to the top management in that organization you will be surprised to see that they want a different behavior from him. They want him to take initiative, to cooperate, to volunteer, to learn, to continuously improve things in his domain and to make the company succeed in its objectives. How does one create the right 'smell of the place' to get these behaviors out of the worker?

Organizational Renewal: This is the heart of his research. He talks about a pervasive disease, which he calls 'satisfactory underperformance'. Let me explain, after a crisis hits a company, the problem is easily identifiable and addressable, but long before the real problem pops up, the company is usually coasting along in a mode of satisfactory underperformance. In most cases the organization is aware that given the resources, brands, technology and equipment the company could be doing much better. But instead of confronting reality, top management rationalizes and brings down the level of aspirations to that of satisfactory underperformance. What needs to be done is to create a mentality of stretch, discipline, commitment, constructive confrontation and collaboration.

He goes on to explain this concept through an analogy of 'yin yang'. Yin and yang is a concept taken from Chinese philosophy, which literally means shadow and light, or a way to describe how seemingly opposite or contrary forces are interconnected and interdependent in  the natural world. Mr. Ghoshal uses the concept to describe the forces between stretch and discipline, i.e. the combination and the tension between the two. With stretch but without discipline, you just float up and lose touch with reality. Without stretch, and only discipline, you become corrosive over time and too rigid in your approach. But combine those two and the mutual tension between them leads to the magic of individual initiative and the spirit of entrepreneurship, which goes right through the organization.

His assertion is that ordinary people can deliver extraordinary results if and only if the top management can create that smell and by doing so they protect a unique culture, as well as allow employees to deliver peak performance over a long period of time. For a management team that inherits "downtown Kolkata in the summer," it is possible to create a "Fontainebleau forest in the spring?" In fact based on many case studies it has been proven, that changing the 'smell of the place' is possible in a reasonably short period of time. The key is to focus and consistently apply principles and values to create the right culture.

Remember that companies cannot win merely on the strength of their brand, service, size, patents or technology. These are important factors but sustainably winning will only be possible if the organization has the knack to enhance the individual's motivation, capacity and ability to take initiative. Ghoshal's contention is that in the majority of organizations employees are asked to use 5% to 10% of their capacities at work. Hence it is not a matter of hours or effort, but how does the management get more out of the missing 95% human capabilities? This in fact is what allows top management to get ordinary people to deliver extraordinary results.

The 100 Minute Culture Test

Time and again when I hear of a company whose performance has dropped or is facing problems, it is invariably due to organizational or people related issues rather than having a weak strategy or a poor game plan. I would challenge you that 'you' can forecast whether a company will deliver strong results or not, just by doing the 100 Minute Culture Test.

The only prerequisite for this test is that you need to get official approval from that company's management to visit their premises and to walk around, meet managers and see and observe their employees in various situations. For your own company you can carry out this test today. What you need is checklists where you mark each item on a scale of 1 to 10 where 10 is the maximum score and 1 the lowest. You can make your own list, but do include such items as:

a) Do people look confident (you can see it in their eyes and their demeanor).
b) Sound of the place (is it positively noisy).
c) Watch interaction between bosses and subordinates as well as between peers to observe the presence of trust in the culture.
d) Find out if they celebrate success and if so, how.

e) Discover how the employee's work-life balance is and whether the management really cares.
f) Layout of the office: does it have open offices, lounging and reading areas.
g) Is top management easily accessible, and are there any visible differences for hierarchy.
h) Find management emphasis on training.
i) Is driving simplification a way of life in the company.
j) How empowered does each employee feel in taking decisions.
k) Check notice boards: does what is displayed reflect a positive and healthy culture.
l) What is the level of caring and team spirit within the company?
m) What role does HR play and are they are in touch with their employees as well as the external world?
n) Watch role modeling by senior managers.

I think you have got the idea of what I mean by the 'smell of the place', it alone drives motivation, commitment, empowerment and consequently breakthrough results and peak performance from the organization. If you carry out a 'smell of the place' survey based on the above-mentioned list of fourteen items, resulting ratings would show,

✓ If your score is above 85% i.e. 119 points, you have an organization with a *Great* smell of the place.
✓ If the score is between 85% and 65%, i.e. between 119 and 91 points, the organization has a *Good* smell of the place.
✓ If the score is between 65% and 50%, i.e. between 91 and 70 points, the organization has a *Fair* smell of the place and needs to be looked into and fixed.
✓ If the score is below 50% or below 70 points, then the organization has *Poor* smell of the place or smells like 'downtown Kolkata in the summer,' i.e. the organization

is not effective at all. A clear plan needs to be put in place by Human Resource and top management to address the issues and improve the score.

To do a quick personal check on the 'Smell of the Place' in P&G and Gillette, I always tell my people "the day you get up in the morning and you do not feel like going to the office, come straight to me, as something is clearly wrong." I want my people to feel excited and motivated everyday in the morning when they came to office. I want their minds to be focused, racing with ideas, with next steps, what they need to achieve today even before they leave their home. Only then, in my mind, I have the winning team spirit, which is capable of delivering larger than life breakthrough results and enabling it to function at peak level.

To me a de-motivated or confused employee is a sure sign that something is wrong and in most cases it points towards a serious issue which would clearly create hurdles in the company's path to success. Whenever I delved deeper into the issue of why someone was not excited about coming to work, I found, in most cases, was that it had to do with the wrong 'smell of the place'. And every time this happened, I found some rare insight, which helped me make the working environment more conducive and receptive for outstanding performance.

To me, you as the leader of an organization own the 'smell of the place'. The higher you are in the organization, the more essential it is to make sure you do not delink yourself from the workforce and always remain in-touch with their feelings and motivations otherwise by the time you hear of a problem, it would probably be too late and a lot of damage would have already been done.

An ideal time to link into your organization informally is during lunch (if you have a common eating area), try to sit on different tables each time, vary between senior and junior managers and people from different departments. Remember the only way you and your leadership team will have a finger on the pulse of the organization, is by making yourselves more approachable and accessible to the organization.

Not just HR but you and your management team should jointly own the 'smell of the place'. A permanent feature of all formal leadership team meeting's agenda should have active discussion on the prevalent culture in the workplace. In P&G and Gillette, whenever our regional Vice President would visit Karachi, he always sets up separate meetings with the CEO and the HR manager to review the status of the company's 'smell of the place'.

The key is for you and your management teams to always remain in-touch with your people, have an open door policy, are easily accessible and constantly strive to create an environment in the company that breed's team spirit and where each and every employee feels proud of being part of the company. Below are a few points that will help in improving the 'smell of the place'. They are:

A) Make Winning Contagious.
B) Can Do Attitude.
C) Positive Thinking.
D) Be Approachable.

A) Make Winning Contagious

There is nothing more potent than an organization programmed to win. If any organization can get to the level where winning becomes contagious, there is nothing stopping it from succeeding. The day you realize that the absence of a winning culture can stop you dead in your tracks and its presence can take you to great heights in your efforts to deliver your vision, then to me, 'that' is when you have found the true insight into business success. To get this insane passion for winning into the organization's DNA, a lot of long term and sustained effort has to be put into place.

"Good leaders guide the willing and persuade the stubborn."
~ Anonymous

How do you program a passion for winning into your employee gene pool?

Here are a few guidelines and ideas:

1. Have a purpose, which is close to the heart and minds of your employees. Everything the company does or executes should always be in line with this purpose.
2. Make sure that the vision and goals are deployed and owned by everyone. That each and every employee's work-plan has a direct link to these vision and goals.
3. Create a culture of transparency in performance, equal treatment for all levels (if management travels business class then everyone must do the same, only have one cafeteria for all employees, parking access based on time in company and not seniority, etc.).
4. Celebrate success and build reward and recognition systems that go all the way down to the junior most employees. Celebrate their hard work, determination and passion for winning; only then will it be replicated again and again.

Using these four ideas as guiding principles is the best way of motivating your employees and encouraging a winning culture.

In addition, as they say, practice makes perfect; carry out internal competitions to nurture this winning spirit. You can start by doing activities such as:

1. To me sport is a great approach in driving winning spirits as well as in improving the energy levels of the organization. Ideas include:
   a. Carry out an Olympic style sports championship once a year. Take a day off, book a stadium and gym, and divide up the organization into teams taking care of diversity (gender, department, age, etc.). Give awards to all the winners and celebrate with a grand party at night.
   b. Take up the most popular team sport in your country such as soccer, cricket, hockey, etc. and have quarterly championships between departments or between the plant and general office. In Pakistan we use cricket as everyone plays and enjoys it.

"Those who truly have the spirit of champions are
never wholly happy with an easy win.
Half the satisfaction stems from knowing that it
was the time and the effort you invested
that led to your high achievement."
~ Nicole Haislett (b. 1972),
American Freestyle Swimmer and Winner of
three Olympics Gold medals in 1992

2. Clearly highlight who is the best in the company in different fields, both in sports and in company processes.
   a. Sports: Identify who is the fastest person on ground and in water, who can jump the highest or the longest, who can run a marathon, etc. Encourage employees to challenge each other and take the ultimate title. Display their names prominently in a prominent public area.

b. <u>Business</u>: Identify who is the best recruiter? (highest success rate of interviews vs. offers made), who is the best trainer? (highest scores in post training surveys), and so forth. In P&G we have a special award, which we call the Excellence Award, which was given to only one individual who has delivered the best all round results and displayed outstanding leadership skills in doing that.

c. <u>Diversity</u>: Respect diversity and work towards creating an inclusive culture. Highlight talents other then sports and business. Showcase musical geniuses, eloquent writers, natural painters, talented dancers and anyone with a unique and interesting skill.

Driving winning behavior in various ways will help drive the winning spirit deep into the organization and eventually show up in business results and in your battle to win in the market place.

"Few men during their lifetime come anywhere
near exhausting the resources dwelling within them.
There are deep wells of strength that are never used."
~ Rear Admiral Richard E. Byrd (1888–1957),
American Polar Explorer and Aviator

Vital Tip 28: You must understand the difference between being competitive and having 'an insane' desire to win. Many people confuse the two. The true way to win is to achieve victory while operating <u>within</u> the rules of engagements and while <u>keeping</u> the value system intact. Those people who start looking at everything as a game, it may be business, interpersonal relationships or sports and would like to win at any cost, they have an unhealthy competitive spirit, which would undeniably lead to trouble.

B) Can-Do Attitude

If like the frog on the right, each person in an organization is infused with the attitude that anything can be achieved and everyone believes that they can take on any type of challenge, then you as a leader are sitting on an explosive organization. This is what I call having an organization that has a can-do attitude, i.e. having the confidence and the self-belief that I can do anything. This however requires a special type of culture and management style to help breed this attitude in an organization and once it is achieved you have a potent weapon, which will increase the probability of success on various projects.

Never Give up!

"Attitude is a little thing that makes a big difference."
~ Winston Churchill (1874–1965),
British Politician and UK Prime Minister

Here are some ideas on how one can drive a can-do attitude in your organization:

1. Management Style: Control versus Coach.
2. Question Why Not?
3. Find Out What You Cannot-Do.
4. Identify and Expand your Circle-of-Influence.

1. **Management Style Control versus Coach:**
   Having an organization with an abundance of can-do attitude comes out of your management style; control versus coach. In a corporate environment where bosses are control freaks, there is lack of delegation and empowerment and the decision making remains at the top. In such circumstances a can-do attitude cannot exist. By coaching, you empower your teams and give them an opportunity to deliver and prove their competence.

   An excellent example that comes to mind is of a situation where a business team comes to you with a serious issue. You have two options, you can either give them possible solutions or you can request them to come up with a few potential ideas by themselves. Instead of providing answers, it would be a better idea to help guide and carry out a brainstorming session and help them identify possible solutions.

   Coach them on how to look for solutions rather than give it to them on a silver platter. Just like a famous Chinese Proverb says "Give a man a fish and you feed him for a day. Teach a man to fish and you feed him for a lifetime."

   "Champions are not super humans,
   they just fight for one extra second when everyone else quit.
   Sometimes one extra second of effort gives you the success!"
   ~ Anonymous

2. **Question Why Not?**
   A wise man (my father in this case) once told me that the best way to generate a can-do attitude was to ask why not? Question yourself: "What is stopping me from doing this or that?" Once you get this ability into your organization every time they come across a challenge, which seems impossible, they look at it with a different yet positive attitude; the can-do attitude has taken root!

Moving in this direction and nurturing this why-not ability will build confidence in your team to take on bigger and tougher challenges and to bring a step-change in your employee's capability to deliver projects. Your personal confidence in their ability to surmount hurdles is also a key factor and every time you watch them overcome hurdles and challenges, overtly appreciate and highlight the presence of the can-do spirit in the teams.

"If we all did the things we are really capable of doing, we would literally astound ourselves."
~ Thomas Edison (1847–1931),
American Inventor, Scientist and Businessman

3. **Find Out What You Cannot-Do**:
Another way to improve your can-do ability is to make two lists of action items under the title can-do and cannot-do. Then review the cannot-do list and find out why a specific action is present there. Think of how you can move that action to the neighboring column of can-do. In fact, you should find ways of not having anything in the cannot-do column. Of course you will need help, support, capability building and guidance but what you have to believe in is that there is nothing within your circle-of-influence that you cannot do. Some times when we are being proactive and facing frustration, it is extremely important to appreciate if the issue is within your circle of influence, if not then pull back as you have little or no real control over rectifying it.

"The greatest pleasure in life is doing what people say you cannot do."
~ Walter Bagehot (1826–1877),
British Journalist, Businessman and Economist

4. **Identify and expand your Circle-of-Influence**:

To further help you in reducing your cannot-do list, you must understand the concept of the circle-of-influence and the circle-of-concern' (see diagram). All of us have a wide range of concerns in our lives and within this universe of concerns there are certain things that  we can influence; the others remain untouched as we can only stay concerned about them but cannot influence them. For example my circle-of-influence is my family, friends, my social work, my two foundations (on entrepreneurship and innovation) and my two start-up businesses. However, my circle-of-concern is Pakistan politics, US foreign policy, etc., issues on which I can do nothing other than feel frustrated and concerned.

This concept drives its strength from how we choose where we want to focus our attention and energy. Once you determine which things you can take action on, they will make up and help define your circle-of-influence. By focusing our attention and energy on our circle-of-influence we become increasingly proactive and get immense satisfaction in resolving those issues. These two circles also help define what you can-do and what you cannot-do, but the key is to expand your can-do circle or the circle-of-influence and reduce cannot-do or the space in your circle-of-concern.

Once you get to a point where there is nothing falling in the cannot-do column of your list, you have achieved a huge win in your personal and professional life. But this usually happens when one has reached the peak of one's career and has spent the majority of one's life expanding the horizons and getting experience in variety of fields.

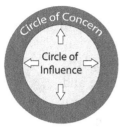 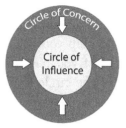

PROACTIVE FOCUS
Positive Energy Enlarges
Circle of Influence

REACTIVE FOCUS
Negative Energy reduces
Circle of influence

Proactive and Reactive Focus: A simple definition is that can-do is a proactive attitude and cannot-do is reflective or a reactive attitude. Reactive attitude results when you don't fix an issue and it rebounds back and hits you and then you have no option but to react and resolve it.

Let me deep dive into each: Proactive is when you are master of your discipline, upbeat, hands on and willing to fix things, you will invariably over time continue to expand your circle-of-influence and take more and more space away from the circle-of-concern – left circle in the diagram. The inverse is also possible where a person is not on top of their discipline; symptoms of problems are not addressed on a timely basis and consequently the circle-of-influence shrinks (see right circle). This is true for a person who is reactive; they handle issues after the fact and after damage has been done!

So if you want be an effective leader, be proactive and increase your circle-of-influence, which in turn will give you larger responsibilities and will invariably result in your moving up the ladder of success at a much faster rate.

"The important thing in life is not victory but combat;
it is not to have vanquished but to have fought well."
~ Pierre de Coubertin (1863–1937),
French Pedagogue, Historian, and considered
the Father of Modern Olympic Games

Vital Tip 29: Let's not take this can-do and cannot-do concept out of context. In everything we do or think, our experience and our level in the hierarchy makes a difference. You cannot on day one of your job decide that a certain strategy on a certain category is not correct. You must understand the difference between your circle-of-influence and circle-of-concern. There may be many things in your circle-of-concern that you may or may not like, but many of them you cannot influence directly. Circle-of-influence is your domain. You have to master organizational norms and the business systems and processes to be able to fix things properly. If you see an issue outside your circle-of-influence you can always inform someone for whom that specific issue is within their circle-of-influence.

Can-Do Advice from an Expert: In an article by Ed Sykes titled "Success Starts with a Can Do Attitude" he gives some very valuable tips on how to build your can-do attitude. Let me for your benefit summarize Sykes three key points:

1. Set Can-Do Goals: Set goals that move you towards successful results. Many people fail because they don't know what they want or what they don't want. Ask anyone, a friend, family member or an associate of what they want in life and you will be surprised how unaware majority of the people are about their goals and wants. Many will pause and say "Ah, never thought of that!"

   However if you ask the opposite "What don't you want in life?" you will get some crisp and clear answers. The reason is that we concentrate on what we don't want to happen instead of what we want to happen. In life, as in sports, we concentrate on *not losing* instead of concentrating on *how to win*.

"The greatest mistake you can make in life is
continually fearing you will make one."
~ Elbert G. Hubbard (1856–1915),
American Writer, Publisher, Artist, and Philosopher

2. <u>Take Care of Your N-E-T-S</u>: Sykes explains that you must network or meet people that will support your can-do attitude. N-E-T-S stands for 'Network with Everyone Today for Success.' These people, while supporting your goals, will also help you pass roadblocks to achieve your goals. You will also make your NETS stronger by supporting their goals to create a mutually supportive situation.

   Sykes goes on further "Clean your NETS of people who have a cannot-do negative attitude, and who don't support your quest to achieve your goals. The more junk (negative people) in your NETS, the less room you have for treasures (positive people). Take a close look at friends, family and co-workers and ask, do they support me and my can-do attitude? If they don't, remove them from your NET. Keep your NET strong with positive people." (I love this concept).

"Keep away from people who try to belittle your ambitions.
Small people always do that,
but the really great make you feel that
you, too, can become great."
~ Mark Twain (1835–1910),
American Author and Humorist

3. <u>Concentrate on the positive</u>: This is the easiest step and is in your total control. In our daily life we are bombarded by too much negative news. Open today's paper and believe me 75% of the news on the front page will be something depressing. You need to make sure this does not get you down. You need to take control of your life and your mind and focus on thinking

positive and be responsible for your own can-do attitude. You can start with the following:

a. Concentrate on self-talk with positive solutions: Start your mornings with meditation. Concentrate on positive thoughts with positive results. Visualize, involving as many senses as possible to intensify the visualization and make it real for you. Ask, "What does my success feel, look, sound, and taste like?" Be aware of negative self-talk, and replace it with positive self-talk.

b. Control the communication: If it is a conversation, reframe the negative conversation into a more positive conversation. If someone is complaining endlessly, say, "Sarah, I hear what you are saying. What solutions do you see to this problem?" If the media is negative, tune it out or turn it off. You can always walk away. You have that right.

c. Walk the talk: Be consistent in your behavior, and act on your can-do attitude.

d. Fake it till you make it: Act like you are already achieving your goals and you will rise to a higher level. Others will also see you as achieving your goals and interact with you accordingly.

C) Positive Thinking

One thing that clearly separates leaders from others is their ability to look at the positive side of a situation even under seriously adverse circumstances. One must remember that in any business or corporation having a positive tone, pace, and confidence while delivering goals, must be omnipresent; the leadership team should drive this. If the employees see their leadership cracking under pressure, from that day onwards the company performance is going to go downhill. The leaders have to be steadfast, confident in their plans as well as their own and their team's capabilities and must live and exude this attitude 24/7.

One of General Colin Powell's key lessons accentuates this view when he states, "Perpetual optimism is a force multiplier." Positive thinking is clearly a hidden weapon for any leader and should be in your grip throughout the workday.

> "The greatest discovery of my generation is that a
> human being can alter his life by altering his attitudes."
> ~ William James (1842–1910),
> Pioneering American Psychologist and Philosopher

An interesting bestseller, *The Secret* written by Rhonda Byrne released in 2006 highlighted this fact in a very mysterious and spiritual manner. The key precept of this book is that an individual's positive thinking can result in life changing results on such things as wealth, health, happiness and more. The book also received a lot of criticism as many claimed that positive thinking alone would not result in improved health, wealth and happiness. Many felt that too much credit is being given to positive thinking.

I personally liked the emphasis the author placed on positive thinking and the role it plays in making things better. Of course positive thinking has to be taken in conjunction with reality, as on several occasions I have personally experienced how merely utilizing positive thinking has averted confrontational situations.

Vital Tip 30: <u>Opportunity in Adversity</u> – The famous quote by Thomas Edison "I have not failed. I have just found 10,000 ways that won't work." clearly underscores an important reality; every event and every action has a positive side, the key is to have the ability to see the positive side, as that is where the true opportunity lies.

"Change your thoughts and you change your world."
~ Norman Vincent Peale (1898–1993),
Protestant Preacher and Author
most notably of *The Power of Positive Thinking*

I do believe that many of today's problem stem from people who have given up hope on the future and it is due to this severe dearth of positive spirits to improve the world around us that we as a civilization are in this current quagmire. A case in point is Pakistan where just a decade ago, majority of the people were very positive about its future prospects, but now are actively thinking about wanting to migrate to a different country due to the unending bad news they hear every day. Unfortunately, this is the type of mind set and thinking which will lead us nowhere.

Same fact is true for companies, the day you give up hope in turning it around or making it profitable, you will eventually drive it into the ground. What these negative thinkers don't realize is that thinking positively will keep the hope alive and taking action to move in the right direction despite obstacles, can and will make a difference.

As I like to say, "The ocean is made up of an immense number of drops all put together one by one." So don't ever think that if a few employees are not positive thinkers it is okay. You are then missing out on an opportunity where the sheer volume of positive thinking people or employees can create a momentum that will turn the tide; each will add up to create a powerful ocean and keep competition at bay.

Personally I had positive thinking wired into my DNA from a very early age, thanks to my father who always made us look at the bright side of things. Anybody who knows me professionally or personally can vouch for this immense amount of positive energy and positive thinking that I exude in everything I do. I can always find a positive side in the most depressing and difficult situations.

I strongly believe in the philosophy that adversity breeds' opportunity and that you can never achieve any advantage by looking at the negative side of an issue. Negative thinking to me is synonymous with termites, leaves behind a weak shell.

"It is amazing what you can accomplish if
you do not care who gets the credit."
~ Harry S. Truman (1884–1972),
33rd U.S. President

Food for Thought:

Positive Intelligence

Shawn Achor coined the word Positive Intelligence in an article in *Harvard Business Review*[48], in which he shares research, which shows that when people work with a positive mind-set, performance on nearly every level, productivity, creativity, and engagement, improves.

Shawn goes on to explain how the impact of happiness on 'human success' is underrated, he says: "Yet happiness is perhaps the most misunderstood driver of performance. For one, most people believe that success precedes happiness. Once I get a promotion, I'll be happy, they think. Or once I hit my sales target, I'll feel great. But because success is a moving target as soon as you hit your target, you raise it again; the happiness that results from success is fleeting." He then goes on to suggest that if we try to do one brief positive exercise every day for a few weeks, one will see that it will transform that person's ability to out-perform and out-think all those who do not indulge in looking or believing in positive thinking.

A historical fact that I once read helps in answering the question of the strong correlation between positive thinking and success, i.e. does the probability of success of your initiative, project, or effort improve significantly with positive thinking? The example is again related to Thomas Edison who among many things is also the inventor of the electric light bulb. While working in his laboratory and testing different metals as filament for the bulb he kept on failing. Despite the failure Edison strongly believed that his theory was correct and that he was on the right track.

Edison's positive thinking kept him on the path of discovery. I don't know how many of you know but he tested over 2,000 different metals, alloys and their combinations before he happened to test Tungsten – which finally worked and he ended up making the world a much brighter place. Now if he had not been a positive thinker and a true believer in his capabilities, his spirit would have given up after 50 tests, or 500 tests, or say even 1,999 tests – the fact that he did not give up is a clear testament of his positive thinking. He had confidence in his theory (plans) and believed in his success (positive thinker). And this attitude resulted in one of the biggest inventions of our time, the light bulb. I hope that from this simple but impactful example, you have been able to appreciate the strong correlation between success and positive thinking.

"Our greatest weakness lies in giving up.
The most certain way to succeed is always
to try just one more time."
~ Thomas A. Edison (1847–1931),
American Inventor, Scientist and Businessman

Let me share another example of a famous person who achieved his goals by the sheer strength of positive thinking and overcame decades of failures and disasters in his life. Imagine a person who lost his job, got defeated in a legislature election then started a business, which also failed. On the personal front, his fiancé died of a fatal disease, later his second son died of tuberculosis at the age of four, his third son also passed away at the early age of eleven and he himself experienced a nervous breakdown.

Subsequently he contested elections for speaker in legislature and lost, he applied for the post of land officer and did not get it, he again contested for senate and lost, then again contested for vice president and faced defeat. Once he again contested for senate and lost but due to his continued determination, two years later in 1860 he got elected as the President of America!

I am talking about no other than Abraham Lincoln. His sheer belief that he had what it takes and never giving up is a true testament of his positive thinking. He went on to become one of the most respected US presidents and is credited with ending slavery in USA.

Vital Tip 31: In an article on *Good Communication that Blocks Learning*[49] the author highlights some key watch-outs on positive thinking, and I quote: a) In the name of positive thinking, managers often censor what they see as a Pandora's box of problems. What we see here is managers using socially "upbeat" behavior to inhibit learning. b) With the emphasis on being positive, they condescendingly assume that employees can only function in a cheerful world, even if the cheer is false. There is nothing wrong with contented people, if contentment is the only goal. My research suggests it is possible to achieve quite respectable productivity with middling commitment and morale.

Be aware of these pitfalls and don't push problems under the carpet but face them head-on. Don't just assume that your organization has a great culture of positive thinking if in fact it does not. Work on creating one.

Giving Up Too Early: I sometime wonder how many inventions got delayed or never materialized, how many initiatives failed because the person or the team pursing it lost their spirit and gave up before giving it enough time; although the idea was correct and they were on the right path. One example that I can share is from P&G and is of Pringles potato crisps (they are not potato chips as some may believe them to be but are potato crisps). Pringles actually came out of our experience in papermaking and market research insights into potato chip eating habits.

Many of you may not know the interesting fact that Pringles in its first decade of launch was a major success as it met the unmet need of potato chips consumers, which were chips being broken, greasy and sometimes stale with air in the bags. However, in late 70's and 80's it gradually lost its charm and was labeled a major failure and was being put on the block to be discontinued. All this changed when a group of P&G'ers who passionately believed in the merit of the Pringles concept continued to push and turn it into one of the biggest global raves of the 90's.

The point I am making is that we in our own daily corporate life will face many failures and challenges. What is critical is not to lose confidence. Of course one must make sure that the assumptions are correct, the data is accurate and that the concept holds water. Take my word for it, keeping a positive attitude will invariably turn the tide towards success, it has been proven multiple of times.

Closely connected to positive thinking are two other concepts, which I would like to share. One is what I call 'Shine or Whine' and the other is known generally as 'Half Full Glass of Water'. Both reflect a different aspect of positive thinking and can make a significant difference if you can appreciate the concepts and internalize them.

i. **Shine or Whine:** Here the basic concept is that the future is defined and shaped by your own actions. Every time we react to an impulse or crisis, we have two ways to respond, a positive way and a negative way; consequences of both are diametrically different. Always remember that you are the custodian of your actions and depending on how you react to a specific situation, you are solely responsible for its consequences. Imagine one of your top rated female managers who is leading an important project comes up to you and gives you some extremely bad news. You have two ways of handling the situation:

→**The whine way:** As you were having a rough day, this news is the last straw. You scream at her, you tell her that she is incompetent and useless. You take out your entire frustration on her even before understanding the reason behind the failure. You cannot believe that such a capable manager has messed up your project!

→**The shine way:** Despite the fact you have had a rough day, you control your frustration on hearing the news and you immediately get up and ask the subordinate to accompany you to a huddle room to have some privacy. You sit down and tell her that you are very disappointed in her but want to know what happened and why the project failed. You listen to her and want to know if you can help and control the damage. Based on the facts of the case you will decide whether to reprimand the manager or not.

Consequences of Both: In the whine scenario your top-performing manager feels humiliated, depressed and shamed. She decides to leave the company, as she will never want to work in a place where she is not respected. She did try her best but things just happened which hurt the project. You lose that manager just a month later. In the shine scenario your top rated manager feels very bad that she let you down but works with you to figure out how best to salvage the situation. The fact that you kept a positive outlook towards the crisis and the fact that you listened to her despite the bad news, she is even more committed to never let such a situation reoccur. She later turns out to further shine and drives the business to new heights.

"The only disability in life is a bad attitude."
~ Scott Hamilton (b. 1958),
American Figure Skater and Olympic Gold Medalist

ii. **Half Full Glass of Water:** There are situations where two people see the same situation in two diametrically opposite ways. Imagine there is a half filled glass on a table, which can be seen either as being half full or as half empty? How can the same fact (i.e. a glass which is half full) look different to two individuals? Reason is if an individual is a pessimist they would view the glass as half empty however another individual who is an optimist will view the glass as being half full. The point is that like the half filled glass, in a business situation, it can also be viewed in a positive as well as a negative manner depending upon if the person is an optimist or a pessimist.

The consequences of how one views an opportunity or a crisis is very different, the positive thinker will turn the situation to their advantage while the negative thinker will feel depressed, dejected and miserable and miss out any opportunity that may have arisen as a consequence of the crisis. In an office environment the outlook of the people who are leading these projects will impact them either positively or negatively. Always look at any situation in a positive light, so that you can see opportunities and solutions rather than barriers and constraints.

"If we think happy thoughts, we will be happy.
If we think miserable thoughts, we will be miserable."
~ Dale Carnegie (1888–1955),
American Writer and Lecturer

Food for Thought:

<u>Optimism in Life</u>

No one's life comes without difficulties. Whether difficulties are few or come in scores, it is about how you deal with it once a situation has arisen. Those who can see an opportunity in a difficulty are true optimists. When you are an optimist, you are actually attracting opportunities. Try to see the silver lining whenever faced by a difficulty. Know that this difficulty is to go. Be optimistic and feel yourself victorious over your troubles. After all, nothing is permanent in the world. So whatever you are going through is not here to stay. It will go. Repeat positive affirmation to yourself so that you can hold firm and stay focused.

Published in Sunday Times of Daily News (Issue 38, dated: 12-19 September, 2009)

D) Be Approachable

To many this may sound as a non-issue, but I strongly believe that any manager who is approachable by his subordinates irrespective of how junior they may be or how important a project they are working on does wonders to the empowerment and confidence of the team. They consider you not just as the leader but also as the most knowledgeable team member. Issues get resolved faster when dealing with managers who are approachable, easy to talk to, friendly and accessible. If a team has to deal with managers who are not easily accessible then an evolving problem, which could be nipped in the bud at an early stage, tends to grow into an even bigger one.

General Colin Powell very eloquently states that "The day soldiers stop bringing you their problems is the day you have stopped leading them. They have either lost confidence that you can help them or concluded that you do not care. Either case is a failure of leadership." That is the downside of not being available to your troops or teams; they lose their confidence in you if you are not there to help them in their time of need. They will also over time stop treating you like a member of their team and in such a situation you have clearly failed as a leader. So be approachable and be overtly known for being right there at the front to help and guide your teams through challenges and in time of trial.

So try to think it through; "Why any leader would not want to be involved especially when his team is facing barriers and issues?" For me the answer to this question has many facets, namely:

a) It could be an ego issue: "Resolving issues is my team's responsibility and below my dignity."

b) Overconfidence in your subordinates to break barriers: "My people are capable and will be able to break all types of barriers, they don't need me."

c) Lack of passion for the company's vision: "One of these days we will deliver our goals, what's the hurry?"

d) Lack of confidence in their own ability to solve problems: "I am lucky to have made it so far, and hope my capability is not put to a test."

e) Simply did not occur to them to get involved: "My team is so capable that I am sure they can handle any crisis situation."

f) I am just too busy to worry about my team's issues: "I am so stuck in much bigger issues and challenges that I don't have time to help my teams."

The answers highlight different perspectives that could confront any leader. To me none of these examples are acceptable except last, in which case the manager should work on improving his priority setting.

> "The world is a great mirror. It reflects back to you what you are.
> If you are loving, if you are friendly, if you are
> helpful, the world will prove loving
> and friendly and helpful to you. The world is what you are."
> ~ Thomas Dreier (1884–1976),
> Author and Inspirational Speaker

Approachability is an attribute, which takes shape by role modeling. You have to, through personal example, make your teams feel comfortable when they come to you for help, show them empathy and understanding. Remember you are the most experienced and capable member of the team and if your expertise and experience is not utilized on a timely basis, then you are letting go of a key competitive advantage. It is like having information available on your fingertips but refusing to use it (how very sad).

People are very perceptive and they can figure out in seconds whether you are only putting on a face that you are okay at being approached or if you are genuinely happy that they have come to you for help; this contradiction can make all the difference whether they will approach you again with a problem or not. So either you like being approached or you don't like it, you need to look at your management style and personal preferences. Whatever the true findings, either way you need to ingrain approachability into your system and believe that it is good for the team and the company and role model that behavior; your team needs you and even more so in crisis situations.

In an interesting article in the *Harvard Business Review* titled *"Why Should Anyone Be Led by You?"*[50], the authors highlight an interesting paradigm that affects us all. He says that if you want to silence a room of executives, try this small trick and ask the following question, "Why would anyone want to work for you?" They say that they have asked this question many times during the ten years they have consulted with companies in US and Europe. Without fail, the response is a sudden, stunned hush. All you can hear are knees knocking! Executives have a good reason to be scared. You can't do anything in business without followers, and followers in these 'empowered' times are hard to find. So executives had better know what it takes to lead effectively—they must find ways to engage people and rouse their commitment to company goals.

So executives need to know what it takes to lead effectively; they must find ways to engage people and rouse their commitment to company goals. The author shares four unexpected qualities of inspirational leaders that they had discovered, namely:

1. They selectively show their weaknesses: By exposing some vulnerability, they reveal their approachability and humanity.
2. They rely heavily on intuition to gauge the appropriate timing and course of their actions: Their ability to collect and interpret soft data helps them know just when and how to act.
3. They manage employees with something we call tough empathy: Inspirational leaders empathize passionately and realistically - with people, and they care intensely about the work the employees do.
4. They reveal their differences: They capitalize on what's unique about them.

To me these qualities highlight some soft qualities, which can make you approachable and likable as a leader such as humility, empathy, and a caring nature. Also they can gain the confidence of their team by exposing their own vulnerability (no one is perfect) such as, a weakness they may have or a unique difference about themselves; this would clearly build trust and help them focus on their strengths to resolve issues and break barriers.

> **Vital Tip 32:** It is pertinent to remember that you won't achieve your leadership aims if you sacrifice yourself by neglecting your personal needs. You have your priorities and no one will do your work. Don't spend all your time fixing other peoples issues. Don't run yourself into the ground; take care of your health, and your ability to think straight.
>
> You must invest in yourself, help create a proper work-life balance, control your diet and work towards honing your physical, emotional and mental energies. You don't just have to manage your time, but also your energy. This investment in yourself will help you to be alert 24/7 and hence be ready to handle any crisis as and when they happen.

12 A. Family Businesses

There is a unique class of businesses that continue to prosper and grow, but the distinctive feature is that they are family-owned. In majority of cases the family is very protective about their company, they are involved in every strategy, they are nose deep in the operations and running of the organization and at the end they also enjoy the fruit of success as the company is wholly owned by the family; there are no external shareholders.

The smell-of-the-place is very critical in such organizations as the alternatives between merit based promotions (motivational) versus family favouritism (demoralizing) can make all the difference between long term success and failure. Organizational cultures in such circumstances take yet another twist, family members have a special place in such companies and the environment is disheartening to majority of the employees as merit takes a backseat to lineage. If the owners of the company are not careful in how they select the leadership team, the long-term survival of such companies can be doubtful.

For long-term sustenance it is critical that merit plays a pivotal role in deciding who leads the company. It takes a lot of guts and courage to hand over your company to a non-family member, it is just like allowing some stranger to come and live in your house.

There are ways of keeping a balance between keeping ownership and still driving selection and promotion on merit. P&G is a classic case which started as a family-owned business by two individuals married to two sisters, William Procter (1801–1884) and James Gamble (1803–1891), way back in 1837. Initially the baton of leadership continued to be passed from father to son, until William's grandson William Cooper Procter (1862–1934) who led the company from 1907 to 1930, handed over the reins of P&G to Richard Dupree who became its first non-family CEO.

To me a lot of credit for P&G success today has to do with William Procter's vision and personal humility. William Cooper Procter, despite his higher education, started his tenure in P&G as a production labourer and worked his way up through the ranks to become the CEO in 1907. William is remembered for his radical and unconventional labour practices such as creating a profit sharing trust, introducing a dividend day, and moving to a five-day workweek. In 1890 when William saw a dire need of cash to fund new equipment, capital expenditures and development of new products, which was beyond company's resources, he suggested the company become a corporation and issued stock valued at $4.5 million in an effort to raise capital. By 1889, he headed the entire Ivorydale factory in Cincinnati, Ohio and prudently used the funds for additional plants, new equipment, and the development of new products.[51]

This was a turning point in P&G's history, as P&G ownership was offered beyond the family members and employees of the company, directly to the public. Finally on his retirement, when William could not see a capable member of the family to lead the company, he went and gave the helm to a non-family member, Richard Dupree and thus laid the foundation of a great company that is older than many countries in the world today (including Denmark, Australia, Pakistan, etc.) and continues to do well. William's legacy of introducing humane business practices and his unrelenting focus on devising systems that would reward employees for their loyalty as well as efficiency, are present even today in every subsidiary where P&G operates.

Today P&G is over 178 years old, no original family member is part of the management team and its presence is clearly a result of the legacy and principles left behind by the founding fathers and their children. But even today, the principles and values infused by the owners are still alive and impact every decision and every initiative. If William Cooper Procter had not handed it over to a non-family member, P&G would most certainly be led by a non-performer and may not have existed today.

To me this is a great example to all family business owners; it is very prudent and smart to let the business be led by a non-family member rather than to hand it over to an incompetent family member.

> **Vital Tip 33:** For any company to be successful and be sustainable in the long term, it is extremely important that appointments and promotions of all employees be based on merit. In family business there is an inherent bias towards fitting family members as managers and executives irrespective if they are capable or not. The downside of this practice is that good talent, when they realize they will be superseded by the company's family members, leave to find opportunities elsewhere.

One structure, which has been used very successfully to protect family interests as well as retain quality and capable human resources, is the inclusion of an Executive Board on top of the official Board of Directors. The company is run totally independently from any influence from the family, quality people are hired on merit, which may include family members if they meet the minimum requirement of education and experience. Like any other corporate, BOD sets the company's direction, keeps an eye on business progress, sets controls and check and balances, reviews compensation, etc.

The role of the executive board is to set the overall vision and approve investment plans over and above a certain value. Any major acquisition or diversification of business, or expansion plans have to be pre-approved by the executive board, but it has no direct interference into the daily business activities or the hiring and firing of executive and employees.

"It is worthwhile for anyone to have behind him a few generations of honest, hard-working ancestry."
~ John Phillips Marquand (1893–1960),
Pulitzer Prize winning American Novelist

Unfortunately family-owned businesses are the most non-culture friendly especially in developing countries like Pakistan and the Middle East. "Seth" culture (Seth actually means the owner of a business in Urdu language and Seth culture means where every action is dependent on the owners whims and fancies) sadly goes totally against the spirit of empowerment and rewarding good behavior and is very predominant in developing countries where the wealth lies in the hand of the few. The family members in such countries use company cash and assets as their birthright. The 'smell of the place' reeks of nepotism and family biases.

With the younger generation getting educated and their subsequent exposure to successful global business models, many family-owned businesses have started to re-think and are moving away from traditional Seth cultural norms; such as accepting that the leadership will not remain forever within the family due to incapable heirs. This is the biggest 'Aha!' and a recipe for success.

In most cases these companies have qualified and capable managers present in the company but they are never given the top slot due to which they invariably leave and the company is left without experience or leaders. So my hats off to those family-business owners who consider people as their key assets and make promotions only on merit.

"Between plans and reality lie years of habits,
customs, unwritten ground rules,
parochialism, and vested interests: the corporate culture."
~ Larry E. Senn and John R. Childress, in their book
"The Secret of a Winning Culture: Building
High-Performance Teams"

·········· ·········

Chapter 13 – Values

13 A. Why Values are Vital?

The most critical and yet the most overlooked aspect of organizational and corporate effectiveness is the role values play in any culture. To me values are like the soul of a company, something which cannot be seen or touched, but which is ever present in every strategic decision, in every action of the employees and which dominates and guides the overall culture of the company. No words, no actions and no management assurances will have as much of an impact on a company's success as a simple set of values deeply ingrained into the company's culture.

One of the most oft spoken words by management are "people are our most important assets." Most companies will say this to attract new talent as well as to retain their existing employees. Their employee's experiences, decisions, judgments and capabilities will eventually make the difference between success and failure. But can you honestly say how many of these companies actually believe and act in the true spirit of these words? Very few indeed!

These words are a clear expression of the values of the company, and these values are visible via the action of the management and not just by spoken words. Do they respect diversity, do  they focus on work-life-balance, do they have a transparent performance evaluation process, and are their salary and benefits competitive – this kind of action and focus makes the real difference. To me values are like an *anvil*, solid, firm, reliable, heavy, and permanent; something that will always remain – and will never ever change.

> "Values are not just words, values are what we live by.
> They're about the causes that we champion
> and the people we fight for."
> ~ Senator John Kerry (b. 1943),
> US Presidential candidate for the Democratic Party in 2004

Let me ask you a question: Does the company you work for have well defined values? If your answer is no, then your organization is missing a critical characteristic of organizational effectiveness and your company's long-term sustainability is questionable.

When you look at companies like P&G, Merck and Walt Disney who have been very successful for over a century, the key reason for the strong consistent performance is the presence of values in their culture. Values are like an umbrella under which the employee's function, where the umbrella protects the employee's from having to indulge in corruption or unethical practices to further business interests, to do things against their personal beliefs, or making decision under pressure, which they may regret later.

> "Being truthful when you know it will cost
> you is the true test of honesty."
> ~ Air Commodore (R) M. Amanullah Khan (1931–2003),
> Air Force Fighter Pilot, my father and my role model

13 B. What are Values?

What are values and how do they impact a company's success and sustainability? Let me start by giving you a few examples:

Procter & Gamble[52] is a multinational consumer goods manufacturing and distribution company. Its product range includes personal care, household cleaning, laundry detergents, prescription drugs and disposable nappies. In 2015 P&G completed 178 years in existence and touched $83 billion in total global revenues including having twenty-three billion dollar brands and another 14 with sales between $500 million to $1 billion, many of those with billion-dollar potential. P&G community consists of over 138,000 employees working in over eighty countries worldwide. Its values drive and fuel its purpose and today it is the custodian of hundreds of products, which clearly help, improve the lives of its consumers all over the world. Its values, which are publicly shared and have been intact for over a century, are:

- ✓ Leadership
- ✓ Ownership
- ✓ Integrity
- ✓ Passion for Winning
- ✓ Trust

Each of these values stands on its own merit and for each P&G employee it is mandatory to appreciate, own, display, live and practice each one of these values at work. Tolerance of not following these values is literally zero and any exception is taken extremely seriously. In my nearly three decades of experience in P&G and Gillette, I have no doubt in my mind that our nearly two centuries of successful functioning is clearly credited to the presence of these values in the company's culture. Let's visit each one of them to get a feel of how they impact the daily functioning of the company and its employees:

Integrity:

- ✓ We always try to do the right thing.
- ✓ We are honest and straightforward with each other.
- ✓ We operate within the letter and spirit of the law.
- ✓ We uphold the values and principles of P&G in every action and decision.
- ✓ We are databased and intellectually honest in advocating proposals, including recognizing risks.

Leadership:

- ✓ We are all leaders in our area of responsibility, with a deep commitment to delivering leadership results.
- ✓ We have a clear vision of where we are going.
- ✓ We focus our resources to achieve leadership objectives and strategies.
- ✓ We develop the capability to deliver our strategies and eliminate organizational barriers.

Ownership:

- ✓ We accept personal accountability to meet our business needs, improve our systems and help others improve their effectiveness.
- ✓ We all act like owners, treating the Company's assets as our own and behaving with the Company's long-term success in mind.

Passion for Winning:

- ✓ We are determined to be the best at doing what matters most.
- ✓ We have a healthy dissatisfaction with the status quo.
- ✓ We have a compelling desire to improve and to win in the marketplace.

Trust:
- ✓ We respect our P&G colleagues, customers and consumers, and treat them, as we want to be treated.
- ✓ We have confidence in each other's capabilities and intentions.
- ✓ We believe that people work best when there is a foundation of trust.

Merck[53] is a very old company made from the merger of Merck and Schering-Plough in 2009 and today is the second largest pharmaceutical company in the world by market share. Merck dates back to 1668 when E. Merck in Darmstadt, Germany created it. Schering on the other hand was founded by Dr. Ernest Schering in 1851 and started operation by developing pharmaceuticals based in Berlin, Germany. Merck was the first company to create the measles and mumps vaccine back in 1963. Today the merged company produces pharmaceutical products and provides insurance for pharmacy benefits.

This company has stood the test of time due to its strong values, which are publicly shared, and they are:

Our core values are driven by a:

- ✓ Desire to improve life,
- ✓ Achieve scientific excellence,
- ✓ Operate with the highest standards of integrity,
- ✓ Expand access to our products and
- ✓ Employ a diverse workforce that values collaboration.

"Do not separate personal values of what is right and wrong from the values you put into practice at work."
~ Peter F. Drucker (1909–2005),
Writer and Management Consultant

Values are the basic set of beliefs under which all employees are required to function. Values form the foundation for everything that happens in the workplace, from strategic decisions to simple tasks such as ordering stationary for office use. Values permeate from top down. If you are the founder or the CEO of a company and you are very ethical and show high level of integrity in your dealings with everyone, the same values will be imparted into everyone that works for you as well as in every business decision. Living these values will allow them to permeate the workplace culture and the company will over time naturally hire people who will share the values–just like what Darwin meant when he coined the concept of *natural selection*.[54]

Consistently hiring such people over decades will create an inherent culture which will be principled, ethical and honest and in line with your values. Consistency and zero tolerance are the two most critical aspects, which will bring these values to life and sustain them for a very long time. The key is to 'walk the talk' and 'practice what you preach'; role modeling is the right way to implement values just like they say, "actions speak louder than words."

> "One of the greatest challenges of businesses today
> is creating a culture that is both values-
> centered and performance-driven.
> Many business executives believe they must make
> trade-offs between the two. I don't buy it."
> ~ Bill George (b. 1942),
> Retired Medtronic CEO and Academic

Employees must be able to see that no one is above the corporate value system; everyone from the CEO to the tea boy is expected to live by these values. Only then, over time, these values will become part of the culture. Merely saying that these are our values, publishing them and implementing them selectively will never be effective. In P&G my personal experience is that values are kept in very high regard, are applied equally across all levels and functions and are the very reason P&G has been successfully operating since 1837. Albert Einstein stressed this very well when he stated: "Try not to become a man of success, but rather try to become a man of value."

One of our ex-CEOs John Smale who was instrumental in taking P&G from $11.4 billion to $24.0 billion in top-line growth during his nine years tenure as CEO stated the following about the character of P&G and the strength it gave the company to succeed by pursuing an ethical existence.

> "The company has always seemed real to me - almost like a living thing. Certainly, it has character - a meaning - and somehow, although the essence of what the company is - its personality and character - are the sum parts of the people who have been a part of it; it has always seemed better than us. We have faults - we make mistakes. But, the company doesn't. Its principles reflect the best of us as individuals - without the faults."
>
> John Smale, 1995

"Sometimes the poorest man leaves his
children the richest inheritance."
~ Ruth E. Renkel (b. 1955),
Author

Food for Thought:

<u>Value Self-Test (VST)</u>

If you look at the culture of the company in which you are currently working and if you are generally happy and at peace within, then you have clearly selected an organization whose values are congruent with yours. If you are not happy and feel troubled at the workplace, then there is clearly some disconnect existing between your values and those of the people running the company. In such cases it is always better to change jobs and find a company that respects your values; otherwise every time you are required to go against your personal value system, you will feel unhappy and depressed.

Always look for a company whose values are in-sync with yours. Only in that situation will your heart and mind function at full throttle and you will succeed in your career and your life.

13 C. Values in Action!

Let me substantiate the impact of values through some personal examples:

<u>Making employee life worry free</u>: I had left Pakistan in 1978 for higher studies. After earning two engineering degrees I worked for two years in Saudi Arabia, and then left for the US to complete my MBA from the University of Michigan, Ann Arbor. In 1987 I joined P&G in Switzerland and subsequently was moved to the P&G operations in the Arabian Peninsula based in Jeddah. In 1994 I was offered a move back to Pakistan as the Finance Manager of P&G Pakistan.

Everybody I met was surprised and would say "Saad you have been abroad for sixteen years and have never worked in Pakistan, you have no idea how difficult and corrupt the business environment is over there – how will you survive?" My answer was simple, "I have nothing to worry about as I am sure P&G will never expect or want me to compromise my values." I was able to say that with full confidence, as I knew the five core values of P&G included integrity and trust, were very close and congruent with my personal values.

In my tenure as Finance Manager P&G, than as Deputy General Manager P&G and later as CEO of Gillette, I had many interactions with government and public officials and I would go to these meeting knowing very well that I will never have to compromise my values. This naturally made my life worry free, helped me make the right business decisions and allowed me to continue functioning effectively and most importantly operate within my own personal value system.

"It is not who is right, but what is right, that is of importance."
~ Thomas H. Huxley (1825–1895),
English Biologist

Below is an example, which will help make my point clear:

➢ When I joined P&G Pakistan as Finance Manager, I informed our clearing agent that under no circumstances was he to grease the palm of any customs official or the port authorities to expedite the clearance of P&G shipments. The clearing agent informed me formally that in that case he would not be able to guarantee how long it would take to clear the imported containers. I told him that was fine as long as we knew that he was trying his best and working within the P&G value system.

We faced many issues during the first few years during clearance but later something my clearing agent mentioned was like music to my ears. He said "Now all P&G shipments are cleared very fast as all officials know that there is no chance they will make any money by creating hurdles as P&G never gives in." To me this is an excellent example where our values have helped our business processes become more efficient and also in making life for our employees as well as our suppliers easier and worry free. I sometimes wonder that if all companies followed this route we could eradicate corruption from its very roots.

"Be always sure you are right - then go ahead."
~ Davy Crockett (1786–1836),
American Folk Hero, Frontiersman, Soldier and Politician

There is a very real aspect of a company that follows and implements a strong value culture, which I want to share with you. In such cases you end up working and interacting with colleagues, suppliers, contractors, etc. who share your values and interestingly these values do not just permeate into your professional life but they also permeate into your personal life. You cannot be Dr. Jekyll and Mr. Hyde, i.e. be good and ethical in your professional life and corrupt and unethical in your personal life – it just does not work that way!

Let me share a personal example of when I was returning from Cincinnati, USA after attending P&G year-end meetings and as an avid aero modeling enthusiast I had ordered and was bringing back three large boxes of aero-models to build and fly in Pakistan. At Karachi airport I came across a custom official who desperately wanted to make some easy money from me by saying "Aero model kits are banned in Pakistan as they can be used for surveillance and other such suspicious activities." I knew this was hogwash and tried to argue that these are just toys and nothing more. I knew he wanted a few hundred or a thousand rupee bribe and then he would let me go. I also knew that if I left my stuff at the airport, it would be an administrative nightmare, as I will have to visit custom counter at Karachi airport a few times for hearings and other formalities. But my personal value system locked in and I refused, as I knew that I was not doing anything wrong for which I should be afraid of or which should compel me to do something unethical.

On my return to office the next day, I asked to see our clearing agent who said "Sir why go through such a huge hassle, you only had to pay a few hundred as that is all he wanted. Now we will have to drive to the airport and back a few times for hearings and to get the items released." I said that if he had asked me to pay government levies or custom duty, I had no issue, but I was just not interested to discuss the options to what he was suggesting, This news very soon permeated the office as employees recognized that their CFO did not just preach and role model ethical behavior in the office but he also did so in his personal life. To me it was natural and totally in line with my character and value system; I had not done anything special or unusual.

Remember that your reputation as a leader, who holds himself to high standards and constantly sets examples for others to role model, will do more to drive proper ethical behavior in and out of office than anything else you can do. Always fight the temptation to compromise on your values and beliefs, as it will help make your life easier and hassle free in the long run. Always follow your conscience instead of 'following the crowd' as that will always be the right thing to do. The up side of such behavior is that it makes you stronger and helps build a strong character for others to emulate and respect.

> "Choose rightness over ease and convenience
> – It will give you pride ... and peace."
> ~ Anonymous

13 D.   How do I implement Values?

If after reading about the benefits of a value based culture, you are interested in implementing values in your company then you have clearly stumbled upon a game changing idea! These values have to be well thought out and closer to your heart then anything you will ever decide to implement in your company. You must believe in these values wholeheartedly and role model them in your daily life.

I will give you a list of values as examples that you can use as a starting point in case you want to start a discussion within your organization. Some typical values that you can use include: Integrity, respect, courage, quality, discipline, loyalty, equality, competency, diversity, challenge, compassion, dedication, efficiency, passion for winning, stewardship, collaboration, trust, flexibility, ownership, excellence, responsibility, trustworthiness, innovation, honesty, accountability, credibility, empathy, dependability, commitment, teamwork, wisdom, fun, coaching, leading, risk taking, inspiring, in-touch, and optimism.

Select a maximum of five or less values, which are relevant to your business case as well close to your own value system. Selecting any more than five will make it difficult to rollout and keep them alive within the entire workforce. Once values have been rolled out, first you must make sure that each and every employee properly understand each one of them. Secondly, you must work towards nurturing and rewarding those employees who share and display these values in their daily work; will send the right message across the organization.

"Open your arms to change, but don't let go of your values."
~ Dalai Lama XIV (b. 1935),
Religious Leader of Tibetan Buddhism

Identifying relevant values is just 10% of the job; implementing them and bringing them to life is the real challenge. For the second part you need people who live, practice and believe in the values. To make the values impactful the following must happen in the company's culture:

- ✓ The leadership team must role model these values at work, in decision-making and in inter-personal behaviors.
- ✓ Everyone must use them to guide all decisions made in the organization.
- ✓ Employees who exemplify value-based behaviors are singled out and rewarded.
- ✓ Make sure all new hires as well as existing employee's behavior is congruent with the company's values.
- ✓ Zero tolerance for any behavior that is not in line with agreed values.

"To outperform you must out-behave,
and by out-behaving you achieve not just performance,
but principled performance, something at the
center of any truly sustainable business."
~ Dov Seidman (b. 1962),
CEO LRN Corporation, helps businesses
develop ethical corporate cultures
and inspire principled performance

I came across a very impactful story narrated by Norman Ralph Augustine (b. 1935), which he calls the Boa Principle on the criticality of zero tolerance when it comes to ethical behavior and company values. Augustine is a US aerospace businessman and has served as Under Secretary of the Army from 1975-77. He once also served as a member of the P&G Board and as Chairman and CEO of Lockheed Martin, a well-known aerospace firm.

Augustine once believed that a boa constrictor makes its kill by quickly crushing its victim in the powerful folds of its body. However, his quick look in the encyclopedia instead revealed the following: "The snake places two or three coils of its body around the chest of its prey. Then each time the victim exhales its breath, the boa simply takes up the slack. After three or four breaths, there is no more slack. The prey suffocates and is then swallowed by the boa."

Augustine went on to note that this deadly phenomenon, of the victim becoming the unwitting accomplice of its own destruction, is not just confined to world of reptiles. The *boa* we have to face, and sometimes fail to fight, is this whole concept around "following our ethical values." Each lapse or abuse of our accepted ethical or moral values is very similar to the tightening of the coils by the boa. Every time we tolerate anyone breaking a single value, however junior or senior he or she may be, it sends a wrong message across the length and breadth of the organization inferring that values are not considered to be sacred and revered by everyone. If we continue to show tolerance and let people exploit and not follow the values actively, it would be just like the boa victim, our business would eventually suffer and die.

The very concept of using values as an effective and potent tool to drive the culture is short-circuited! Values once shared and agreed within an organization must be kept sacrosanct and must be treated as untouchable and followed by the CEO to the peon without exception. Otherwise like the boa, it will slowly destroy your culture of values with every violation that you tolerate.

> "All that is necessary for the triumph of
> evil is that good men do nothing."
> ~ Edmund Burke (1729–1797),
> Irish Orator, Philosopher, and Politician

In summary, values are a core concept to drive proper ethical behavior across thousands of your employees. Values act like a safety net over which the organization functions, they work as a guidebook to handle ethical conflicts, they influence how we handle business decision-making, they help build trust inside and outside the organization and with continual focus and use, they create a culture that permeates our everyday life and makes the employee's life focused and worry free.

You have a choice to make today, you can start by making a commitment to yourself that you will always do the right thing; that you will uphold the values that are dear to you and in doing so you will leave behind a legacy which will live long after you are gone.

"Culture makes all men gentle."
~ Menander (342 BC–292 BC),
Greek Dramatist

•••••▬▬▬▬ ▬▬▬▬▬•••••

Chapter 14 – Leadership Topics

Leadership is a subject very close to my heart as I have been a Lead Trainer of the Leadership Training Module in P&G for decades. Leadership is a very wide topic, but I have kept the dicussion in this handbook focused only on how it impacts the process of vision setting and its eventual delivery.

14 A.   Leader vs. an Ordinary Person

While working as Plant Accounting Manager at the P&G Diaper Plant in Jeddah, Saudi Arabia in 1988 I attended a course on leadership. The trainer shared a very impactful yet simple example on how leaders differ from ordinary people, which has stuck to my mind, and I share it broadly every time I get the opportunity. I always get oohs and ahhs on the crispness of the metaphor and its application to real life. Let me share this insightful example:

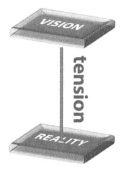

If you imagine that there are two planes, one at the bottom which we shall call **Reality,** i.e. the current state of affairs, and another higher plane above it which we shall call **Vision,** or where you want to see reality in say five or ten years. Now imagine there is elastic tied to the two planes. The distance between the two planes defines the tension in the elastic. If you want to make your vision more challenging, you move the upper plane higher, which in turn will increase the tension in the elastic.

Consequently, if you want to lower your vision, by lowering the upper plane, you will automatically reduce the tension in the elastic. Now imagine if the tension in the elastic is synonymous with stress in a person's mind, the higher the tension, the higher will be the stress in the leader's mind. This links very well with vision setting and its associated stress. The higher and more challenging the vision, higher is the stress in the minds of its leaders. Similarly the lower the vision, which means it's much closer to reality; the lower is the stress in the minds of its leaders.

Now imagine you have set a vision of becoming a billionaire by 2010 and today is year 2000 and your net wealth is $100 million. This is a very aggressive and challenging vision for any person and the stress in that person's mind (or the tension in the elastic) will be immense; you have to increase your wealth ten times in ten years. Just by lowering your vision from a billion dollars to say $500 million, you will reduce the tension significantly.

Now let's assume you start with a billionaire vision and as we know from experience, money makes money, so the hardest part will be to make your first $500 million dollars. For simplicity sake let's assume that you grow year to year at a constant rate; this means that you need to increase your wealth at a constant annual growth of 26% per year for ten years to become a billionaire (this is also called CAGR or Cumulative Annual Growth Rate). Based on this trend, mid-way in 2005, you should be having a wealth of approximately $316 million. Let's assume it is 2005 and that you were able to accumulate a wealth of only $250 million, i.e. you grew at a CAGR of only 20% over the five years and hence fell short by $66 million versus your vision's 2005 milestone. If from here you plan to continue growing at the original planned CAGR of 26% then you will only reach $790 million by 2010 and will not realize your vision of being a billionaire in ten years.

However, if you do not want to compromise your vision, you will have to now increase your growth rate in the future to a CAGR of 32%, which will in turn significantly increase the tension in your mind even further.

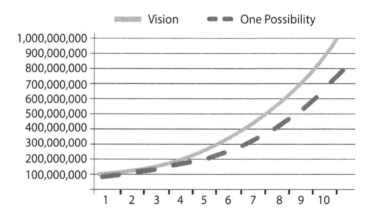

If you are an ordinary person, you will not be able to live with this high level of tension and will start thinking of compromising your vision. You know that from 2000 to 2005 you have grown your wealth only 2.5 times or a CAGR of only 20%. Looking at ground reality, you are convinced that growing 32% is insane, and a more realistic and achievable goal will be to grow at a still aggressive 26% per annum or doubling wealth every three year. However, this will drastically alter your vision and instead of being a billionaire by 2010, you will only achieve three fourth of the Goal, i.e. $790 million (lower line in the graph).

Nonetheless by lowering your vision you have significantly reduced the tension in the elastic between reality and vision, and as a result reduced the stress in your mind. This is a classic example of an ordinary person.

Every human's natural instinct is to reduce the tension in one's life. No one enjoys tension of any kind. Now in our model there are two ways to reduce this tension, namely a) lowering the vision (as the case above) or b) raising reality to get closer to the vision. If you are a true leader, you would not compromise the vision you have created under any circumstances.

In the current situation, as a leader you will rise to the challenge and try to grow your wealth at an even faster pace to overcome the shortfall in the first five years. You will need to raise it to 32% CAGR, which clearly is an extremely aggressive and risky proposition but will get you to your billionaire vision. For this you need to go back to your drawing board, brainstorm ideas, learn from your past mistakes, review current strategies and portfolio investments and come up with a new strategic plan. If you have true leadership qualities you will never compromise on your vision. You will want to reduce the stress in your mind, by raising reality to meet your vision rather than lowering your vision to get closer to reality. This is the genuine mark of a true leader.

"Leaders aren't born they are made.
And they are made just like anything else, through hard work.
And that's the price we'll have to pay to
achieve that goal, or any goal."
~ Vince Lombardi (1913–1970),
Legendary American Football Coach

An ordinary person reduces tension by lowering their vision and a true leader reduces tension by raising reality to meet their vision. Martin Luther King, Quaid-e-Azam Mohammad Ali Jinnah and Nelson Mandela are all examples of true inspirational leaders – they had great dreams and visions, the tension and the stress in their minds must have been intense. The challenge and the opposition to their vision was real, daunting, organized and calculated and in most ordinary people's viewpoint the probability of their vision coming to a successful ending was extremely low.

However these people strived, continued to slowly and surely raise reality until the reality rose and hit their vision, taking stress levels and tension to zero. But never in their struggle did they compromise their vision for a single day. Mandela took thirty-one years to realize his vision, twenty-seven of which were spent locked up in jail. But Mandela never compromised his vision to reduce tension in his life despite all the hardship, challenges and difficulties.[55]

The aim of this example is to explain in layman's terms the difference between a true leader and others. Leaders set visions, visions that significantly change and enhance reality. They constantly strive and struggle to deliver this vision. They cherish challenges and live with the tension that the vision has created in their mind. Due to the toughness of their character they never compromise the vision to reduce the tension until they have changed reality to match their vision even if it takes their entire life and even beyond.

This belief and confidence in the vision is what makes them unique. Their faith in the vision is so overpowering, their commitment so high, that they never waiver from their resolve to deliver the vision or to compromise the vision to reduce the vision-to-reality tension. They rest only once the vision has been delivered. A wise man once said "The idea is not impossible for the people who believe in it."

"Don't be afraid of the space between your dreams and reality.
If you can dream, you can make it so."
~ Belva Davis (b. 1932),
Newscaster and Journalist

14 B. The 5-E Leadership Model

Many of us have grown up believing that you are born as a leader and leadership is not a skill that can be learned or coached. In P&G, this myth was quashed when I found out that through years of research and testing they had created a Leadership Model which goes by the name of 5-E Model; using this model P&G is able to teach their employees the fundamentals of leadership and to fine tune and polish their leadership skills. Recall that in P&G one of the five core values is leadership. As it is a core value in P&G, therefore it is critical that each and every employee must display this value, use it in his daily work and utilize it to help deliver company goals and strategies.

> "The most dangerous leadership myth is that
> leaders are born – that there is a genetic factor to leadership.
> This myth asserts that people simply either
> have certain charismatic qualities or not.
> That's nonsense; in fact, the opposite is true.
> Leaders are made rather than born."
> ~ Warren G. Bennis (1925–2014),
> American Scholar, Organizational Consultant and Author

In June 2009, in an exclusive interview with Xinhua, Robert McDonald, chief operating officer of the Procter & Gamble Company (P&G), talked on many topics including leadership. He talked about the challenges companies are facing due to the rapidly changing environment and crises, such as the global volatility and change, which saw consumer spending down, and costs up. "What is critical is leadership," he said. "What makes good companies is leadership."

He further went on to explain the concept of leadership in P&G by stating[56], "At Procter & Gamble, the leadership and its behaviors are watched, and they will become models, the models we call five E's," he said, referring to Envision, Engage, Energize, Enable and Execute." He was referring to the Leadership Program in P&G, which teaches leadership skills to all employees and later by using advanced leadership courses they further fine tune and sharpen their individual leadership skills.

Let me give you the concept behind what Bob was explaining, i.e. the 5-E Model. P&G has through research and experience split leadership roles into five distinct and separate behaviors and teaches each of them in separate modules.

1. **Envision**: To Create a Future. Ability to envision the future is a key characteristic of any leader. To be able to see the possibilities, to be able to stretch ones imagination and see the future. To be able to create a mental image of the vision, so that it is clear, crisp and distinct.

2. **Engage**: To build relationships and collaboration. To be able to involve or on-board other people onto your dream or vision. The leaders cannot deliver a corporate vision by themselves; you need to convince and get other people to join you on the journey to deliver your vision.

3. **Energize**: To inspire others. Once you have engaged your organization, next you need to energize and excite them about the vision. Having a sapped or de-motivated team does not help. In order to energize the team you will have to create a meticulous image of the vision as well as its benefits so that everyone can picture the vision clearly, get inspired and get excited and get energized to deliver it.

"There is little success where there is little laughter."
~ Andrew Carnegie (1835–1919),
Industrialist, Businessman, and Entrepreneur

4. **Enable**: To build capability. Once you start on a journey to realize your vision, you must make sure that the team has the right capabilities, skills and knowledge to achieve the vision. In addition, to enabling your team to deliver the vision, you as a leader must breakdown any barriers, which may exist and are beyond the scope and ability of your teams.

5. **Execute**: To deliver outstanding results. This is one of the most critical roles of a leader, you can plan all you want but until you execute the plan nothing will be realized. Execution has to be done with quality and excellence; else all the good work will go to waste. You must have bias to action in your DNA to be an effective leader.

Using various techniques and surveys, the model identifies which of the 5 E's are the strengths and which are the opportunity areas for each individual in the company. This involves two sets of data, 1) what your perception is of how you rate your 5 E's, 2) feedback from your peers, subordinates and bosses (control group) based on their experiences of working with you and how they rate you on the 5 E's. Based on these two sets of data, a report is generated and the following facts are highlighted:

a) Whether your perception of your leadership 5 E's is in-sync what others think that you display in real-life? The higher your perception versus the control group, the bigger is the opportunity that exists for you to improve yourself, i.e. you think of yourself on certain E's to be far better then what others felt. It is important to have a reality check and sometimes it can be a rude awakening when you realize that your personal perception of your leadership skills are far from ground reality. Remember what is important and what ultimately matters is what others think about your leadership skills and not what you think they are.

b) <u>Where do you stand on each of the five leadership E's?</u> A report is generated which highlights in which E you are weak, in which you are ok and in which you are strong. To improve your leadership qualities you need to continue doing what you are doing on the E's you are rated strong on. On the other E's you will have to work on them and you may need to attend training programs, get coaching or read relevant literature on how to improve these leadership behaviors. Having all 5 E's as strong is a sure sign of a person who has strong and well-rounded leadership skills; that is where you ultimately want to be.

> "Management is doing things right;
> leadership is doing the right things."
> ~ Peter F. Drucker (1909–2005),
> Writer and Management Consultant

14 C. The Most Important Job – People Focus

One of the most critical jobs for a leader is to own and supervise the hiring of the right people and placing them in the right jobs. Without a proper, qualified and experienced organization no company can deliver any vision, any strategy or any tactic. This fact was most boldly displayed by an earlier CEO of one of the oldest and most successful consumer goods company in the world, Procter & Gamble. Mr. Richard Dupree while discussing in 1947 P&G's belief about the role employees played in the success of the company had stated: "If you leave us our money, our buildings and our brands, but take away our people, the Company will fail. But if you take away our money, our buildings and our brands, but leave us our people, we can rebuild the whole thing in a decade."[57]

This quote clearly highlights that the key assets of P&G are not its famous trademark brands such as Pampers, Tide, Head & Shoulders etc., the technological advancement or the cutting edge manufacturing processes. The key assets are its people who developed these as they can still develop new and more innovative products, processes and inventions if given the challenge. I feel that this quote is as true today as it was six decades ago; P&G's continued success is built on the foundation of its real assets, its people.

As a corporate leader what is the one thing that you have under your control at all times? You cannot predict where the exchange rates will be a year from now, you cannot forecast global economic growth, oil prices evolution, interest rates trends or even competitors reaction, but what you can control is the quality of people you will have a year from now or even a decade from now. Recruiting, training and grooming is in your hands and to me that is the most reliable barometer of a company's success. Your employees experience, judgment, knowledge and skills will help define your company's future.

Those leaders, who delegate this critical responsibility or just rubber stamp anything their human resources department does, are short selling the company's future cheaply. To me leaders have three core responsibilities that cannot be delegated,

a. Setting the vision and its associated strategies
b. Selecting and developing future leaders
c. Driving executional excellence.

In the book *Execution - The Discipline of Getting Things Done* Ram Charan and Larry Bossidy touch this very important topic in a chapter titled *"The Job No Leader Should Delegate - Having the Right People in the Right Place."* It is a must read. They go to the very core of why in many companies the 'right people are not in the right jobs'. Reasons include situations where leaders pick people who they are more comfortable with or where leaders do not have the courage to discriminate between strong and weak performers.

This happens mostly where the leaders are not deeply engaged in managing the people development process; you have to personally remain involved, committed and supervise the process.

The authors of *Execution* list down four reasons in which they summarize the key symptoms why leaders fail to deal with this very important philosophy that the people are the most important assets. The symptoms include:

1. **Lack of Knowledge**: Where leaders make assignment or promotion decisions based on superficial facts. The authors use an example where a leader takes a '*fuzzy and meaningless*' recommendation from a person's boss to decide his or her future. Just because someone's boss states that Ameen is right for the job as he is "a great leader" or " a great motivator and very smart" is not enough. These are very superficial attributes and not supported by facts. The boss without getting into deeper attributes and real life examples can end up making a wrong decision on people assignments. The boss needs to describe Ameen in terms of three or four important criteria – things that the person must be able to do in order to succeed in a new position in the company or for a promotion.

2. **Lack of Courage**: This is the case where despite management knowledge that someone is not performing, the person continues to keep his or her job year after year. The usual reason according to the authors is that the person's superiors do not have the emotional fortitude to confront them and take the correct decision or action. Such failures can results in considerable damage to the motivation of the organization in general as well as damage to the business. If such a mediocre performing person is in a high-level leadership position, they can end up destroying the business in the long run.

3. **The Psychological Comfort Factor:** Here the issue is where leaders assign the wrong people to a job just because they feel comfortable with them. It is natural for many leaders to get comfortable and develop loyalty with managers who they have worked with for extended periods of time. This association can sometime overshadow a leaders' judgment as they fail to be objective as performance varies year to year. Many leaders over time start to give preference to certain subordinates who do not challenge their decisions or have developed skills to insulate their bosses from conflicts. This is a very serious and damaging leadership weakness, which if left unchecked by senior management can seriously damage an organization.

4. **Lack of Personal Commitment:** Failure to put the right people on the right jobs is not difficult to identify for any smart leader. However, we see that alarmingly many leaders do not do anything about it. The only way to fix this problem is for the leaders to get personally involved and committed to the peoples' process. According to the authors, leaders need to commit as much as 40% of their time and emotional energy in selecting, appraising and developing people. The benefit on such investment is not seen overnight but is clearly the key success factor to long-term success and sustenance of a company.

P&G Focus on Leadership Development

P&G is a company very close to my heart where I have spent majority of my adult life and where I have seen with my own eyes the focus management places on leadership development and in treating people as their most important assets. To help identify their future leaders P&G has a unique and rare philosophy that has being followed for decades across the world, i.e. promotion from within. Recruiting is carried out only at entry level (exception being where educational qualification and experience is mandatory for the job like in certain research and product development, external relations or for some specialized engineering jobs). All other job openings in middle and higher management are filled through promotions and not hiring.

The key advantage is that by barring lateral hiring at middle and higher management they enhance motivation at every level of the organization as everyone knows that any upper level position will always be filled by them or their peers and not by an outsider who will jump in from another company and become their boss. P&G through their grueling recruiting processes makes sure they hire only those who share their values and mission, thus preserving the company's strong ethical and moral character in the long term.

An unwritten benefit that I realized overtime of the promotion from within philosophy is the immense network that a person creates through various assignments, cross collaborations, regional meetings and by being part of the same company from day one. After working in P&G for nearly three decades, plus having met hundreds of managers who like me have grown from entry level, today I practically know someone in every country and in every function across the world.

In situations where I needed any urgent business info, I did not need to search the company database and write to people I had never met, all I had to do was just pick-up the phone and get the information within seconds from my huge network. If I heard of a great business idea in another low-income market, I could call the CEO or CFO of that country and get that information within minutes, as we had known each other for decades. Imagine the immense saving in time (time is money), quality of collaboration (networking) and free flowing knowledge (data is power) that this philosophy brings to the table and gives an important competitive advantage to P&G.

If P&G hired laterally, this would not be true. All of the P&G CEO's have been hired from entry level and internally groomed and in entire history it has had only twelve chief executives, all insiders, and among them only two family members (the very first two). Just a few companies can boast of having the ability to groom top talent which clearly gives them a solid competitive advantage vis-à-vis others as they understand the business better, know their people, and have lived through success and failures in that industry.

It is noteworthy to note that the very first thing that is shared with any new recruit globally and consistently in P&G is the company's purpose, values and principles document or as we call it the PVP's in our local lingo. Here I want to shed light on P&G values, which start with a stark and single-minded focus on people being their real assets. The values section of this documents starts by stating:

> P&G is its people and the values by which we live. We attract and recruit the finest people in the world. We build our organization from within, promoting and rewarding people without regard to any difference unrelated to performance. We act on the conviction that the men and women of Procter & Gamble will always be our most important assets.[58]

Later the document goes on to state the five core values which all have to do with human virtues, i.e. Leadership, ownership, integrity, passion for winning and trust.

Promotion from within has its pros and cons; for the companies that follow and implement this concept, the benefits outweigh the pitfalls. Paul Spiegelman in his article titled "Should You Always Promote From Within Your Company?" sheds light on this other viewpoint, he states,[59] "For most companies, the best solution is to strike a balance between internal promotions and strategic outside hires. While fresh hires may require some time to adjust to your company's unique culture, these hires have several advantages. Bringing people in from outside the company ensures you're hiring someone with the right skill set for the position. These hires can offer a fresh perspective, mentor existing employees and help your team develop crucial skills. Hiring externally can also motivate top performers to work harder because it sends the message that there are no guarantees for promotion." In such cases, special emphasis has to be taken to preserve the company's culture, values and leadership norms for people who did not grow within that company.

In addition, for leadership development, 'succession planning' is an extremely important exercise. Succession planning is taken extremely seriously across P&G with strong programs in place to identify replacements of every key position especially those in the leadership positions of its many global operations. Also, for every employee there is a plan to identify what his or her next potential assignment will be.

For the very top tier, the company maintains what they call a Talent Portfolio, which contains names of P&G's up-and-coming leaders, who have been compared against one another over the past six years in financial performance and the ability to lead and help others. There are lists of who is ready to be promoted next, who will be ready after the current assignment, or who will need more time. There are at least three possible candidates for each major job. In addition, every February one entire board meeting is devoted to reviewing the high-level executives, with the goal of coming up with at least three potential candidates for each of the top thirty five to forty jobs. This is the kind of focus a company like P&G places on leadership development and in truly treating people as their most important assets.[60]

Food for Thought:

<u>P&G rated No. 1 in the World for Leadership</u>

In the eighth annual Top 20 Best Companies for Leadership survey announced on Sep 19th, 2013 by the global management-consulting firm Hay Group, Procter & Gamble Co. had surpassed General Electric as the number one company in the world for leadership. "Passionate people are central to Procter & Gamble" the Hay Group said. The rankings were based on a survey of more than 18,000 employees of 2,200 organizations spanning 125 countries.

Key considerations in the survey were on how companies foster innovation and nurture talent. "People development is a strategic choice for P&G," the Hay Group said. "Integrated into the way it manages the business, developing career paths for employees is both intentional and flexible." P&G was ranked number two in six out of the last seven years. GE (General Electric) held the top spot for seven years. In 2013 GE dropped to number three, behind P&G and Microsoft.

A few other facts that clearly highlight the importance P&G gives to the function of human resources and people management are:

a. The office of P&G's global human resources officer is next to that of the CEO.
b. Every employee goes through a 360-degree performance evaluation every year; senior managers have an option to do it once every two years. 360° means to get performance feedback from bosses, peers and subordinates.
c. Based on performance of the respective managers each is rated on a scale of 1 to 3 with 1 being (excellent), 2 (good) or 3 (poor). Their respective ratings drive everything from salary management, assignment planning, all the way to career progression.

d. A Work and Development Plan (W&DP) is reviewed every year for everyone. This includes deciding on a detailed work plan which contains a list of projects expected to be delivered in the upcoming twelve months, i.e. each employee knows clearly what they need to work on and the various milestones they will be evaluated in a year from now.

e. In addition, as part of the W&DP, a development plan is agreed and initiated. Based on the past twelve months performance each manager is informed about his or her opportunity areas; this development plan is put into place in order to make them even stronger performers.

f. All managers who make it to general manager level are evaluated every six months with what is called a GM Performance Scorecard, which not only reviews the financial performance measure but also assesses their leadership and team building abilities.

g. Their bosses' carryout career planning of every employee yearly as part the W&DP process in which their preferences as well as their interests are recorded. This helps in providing a reality check on whether these career expectations are possible considering their current skills and experiences.

h. A robust in-house training program on every aspect of the business as well as other softer skills like presentation skills, memo writing, managing subordinates, work life balance, etc. are taught to make them well rounded and effective managers.

These are just a few of the many efforts that are put in place to hone the P&G employees skills which eventually helps the company face on-going challenges and win in the market place.

14 D. Tone at the Top: Role Modeling

True leaders are role models for their organization. They act as examples for their employees to follow. They are fair, consistent, passionate and empathetic managers. For them caring for their people is as important as the struggle for driving disproportional growth for the company.

The leadership team must walk-the-talk. Once a vision has been established and shared with the organization, it is then up to the leaders of the company to live up to the vision. It is their 'tone at the top' that will drive proper behavior within the company; it will be the leader's passion that will drive their team's performances; it will be the leader's commitment to the vision, which will keep the organization united and confident under difficult circumstances and not compromise the vision under any condition. This kind of role modeling to me is a true testament of strong inspirational leadership.

> "You have to set the tone and the pace,
> define objectives and strategies,
> demonstrate through personal example
> what you expect from others."
> ~ Stanley C. Gault (b. 1926),
> Chairman of the Board and CEO of Rubbermaid

Every company has certain values and principles that are converted into a Good Practice Manual, which drives the company's code of conduct. Every employee of the company irrespective of their hierarchy follows this code. It is imperative that the entire management overtly follows these principles and policies, demonstrate them in their daily dealings and adheres to them without exception. Without the top management buy-in to company polices other employees will not take them seriously and will not comply with them consistently.

Remember in today's world you cannot have one rule for senior management and another for all other employees. Also if the employees do not see the leadership team follow rules and regulations, it becomes increasingly difficult to impose the same rules on the rest of the organization. Role modeling is a lethal and effective tool if used properly.

In the book *Good to Great* by Jim Collins there is a very fitting example of the tone at the top. Collins calls it "Level 5 Leadership" which he defines as: "Builds enduring greatness through a unique blend of personal humility and professional will." He continues to further explain this unique Level 5 Leadership behavior by giving four examples, using situations as they relate to the leader's will and to a leader's humility.

Professional Will	Professional Humility
Creates superb results, a clear catalyst in the transition from good to great	Demonstrates a compelling modesty, shunning public adulation, never boastfull
Demonstrates an unwavering resolve to do whatever must be done to produce the best long term results, no matter how difficult	Acts with quite, calm determination, relies principally on inspired standards, not inspiring charisma, to motivate
Sets the standard of building an enduring great company, will settle for nothing less	Channels ambition into the company, not themself, sets up successors for even greater success in the next generation
Look in the mirror, not out the window, to apportion responsibility for poor results, never blaming other people, external factors, or bad luck	Looks out the window, not the mirrior, to apportion credit for the success of the company - to other people, external factors, an good luck

I cannot think of a better example of tone at the top other then as Collins says in the last example that when something good happens, the leaders look out of the window, i.e. at team members to give them credit, and when things go wrong, a level 5 leader looks at the mirror, i.e. assigns blame to no one but himself.

"Leadership is the art of getting someone else to do something you want done because he wants to do it."
~ Dwight "Ike" Eisenhower (1890–1969),
34th US President and five-star General

To set the tone at the top, the leader must make his expectations, principles and beliefs known. People must know what he stands for and what is closest to his heart as far as professional and ethical priorities are concerned. On July 1, 2009 P&G CEO A. G. Lafley retired and the company got a new leader Bob MacDonald. One of the first things Bob did was to share with the organization what he calls "What I Believe In".[61] He states: "Throughout my education, military, and business careers; there are a few principles in which I believe deeply that drive my behavior everyday"

1. Living a life driven by purpose is more meaningful and rewarding than meandering through life without direction.
2. Companies must do well to do good and must do good to do well.
3. Everyone wants to succeed, and success is contagious.
4. Putting people in the right jobs is one of the most important jobs of the leader.
5. Character is the most important trait of a leader.
6. Diverse groups of people are more innovative than homogenous groups.
7. Ineffective systems and cultures are bigger barriers to achievement than the talents of people.
8. There will be some people in the organization who will not make it on the journey.
9. Organizations must renew themselves.
10. The true test of the leader is the performance of the organization when they are absent or after they depart.

It is interesting to note the importance that experienced leaders place on people. Notice that nine of the ten beliefs are people or leadership related in one way or another, i.e. how to make your people succeed, putting people in the right job, how to create a culture where you can obtain the best out of your people, etc. To me this is clearly a confirmation of the fact that 'people are the real assets' is alive and practiced by top management in P&G. No doubt this company continues to do well and is being rated amongst the list of great companies in Collins book *Good to Great.*

We must always remember that business success is directly correlated to recruiting the right people, having the right people in the right jobs, empowering the people to make the right (even tough) decisions and building a culture that drives all of these. Successful companies believe in this and implement it with urgency and discipline.

> "First test of a leader is that he leaves behind in other men the conviction and the will to carry on."
> ~ Walter Lippmann (1889–1974),
> American Writer, Reporter and Political Commentator

14 E. Lonely at the Top

A unique aspect of being a leader is that you are all alone at the top, the pyramid gets smaller the higher you go. At the very top there is no one to share responsibilities, no one to lend a hand or share the burden. There are no back-ups and no second chances. As they say 'You the Man'. You are solely responsible for the performance of the company, for every initiative that is rolled out and for maintaining the motivation and enthusiasm of the organization that keeps them moving towards the company goals. In fact the 'buck' stops with you, literally!

Top management or the board of the company will question you and only you if the goals or financial targets are not met. The burden of setting the vision, deploying it and finally delivering the associated strategies with executional excellence, all lies on the leader's shoulder alone. Yes, the team is accountable and should feel responsible for the goals and business results. But for the outside world, you are the one who will be questioned and whose credibility as a leader will be at risk if the company fails to deliver.

"I studied the lives of great men and famous women;
and I found that the men and women who got to the top
were those who did the jobs they had in hand,
with everything they had of energy,
enthusiasm, and hard work."
~ Harry S. Truman (1884–1972),
33rd President of the United States

Being a leader has its pro's and con's. Biggest pro is the euphoria you get on seeing the expected business results roll-in and seeing your company succeed under your leadership and direction. The biggest con is if things don't go as planned and if you fail to drive a culture that accepts challenges and strives with full commitment in delivering them. The impact of all decisions made across your company, is at the end, your responsibility. To succeed, it is your responsibility to create a culture, which inspires fast and proper decision-making, trust, ownership behavior and passion for winning.

To me personally, watching my team function effectively, feeling empowered, displaying can-do attitude and exuding positive mindset in difficult times was a true pleasure. Impact of true leadership is displayed when the boss is not present. Without the presence of such a culture, no leader can imagine delivering their vision and feeling confident about the organizational capability in overcoming challenges. This is what I call the 'smell of the place' phenomenon. The presence of a true inspirational leader can be felt and seen by any external visitor merely by visiting their organization and by spending a day or two with the different teams and departments of the company.

14 F.   Discover the 90/10 Principle

Stephen Covey is the owner of many personal development and organizational excellence concepts such as the 7 Habits of Highly Effective People, Emotional Bank Account, First Things First, Principle Centered Leadership, etc. His conceptualization of the '90/10 Principle' is probably the simplest and most powerful; it impacts your daily life more then you can imagine. For a leader, knowing and internalizing the '90/10 Principle' is essential and will help him to be more effective. What is this '90/10 Principle'? According to Covey, 10% of your life is made up of what happens to you and 90% is decided by how you react to a stimulus.

What does this mean? What it means is that we really do not have any control over 10% of what happens to us. We cannot stop the car from breaking down or the plane from arriving later or for the rain to spoil your party. Basically we have no control over this 10% of our lives and for the remaining 90% you are the one who determines what we do or how we react to a situation.

How do we do that? By our reaction to whatever has happened! You cannot control a driver from cutting you off in traffic but what you can control is your reaction to that situation. Don't let people fool you; YOU can control how you react.

Covey gives an excellent real-life example to exemplify the '90/10 Principle', and I quote,[62]

> "You are eating breakfast with your family. Your daughter knocks over a cup of coffee onto your business shirt. You have no control over what just happened. What happens next will be determined by how you react. You curse. You harshly scold your daughter for knocking the cup over. She breaks down in tears. After scolding her, you turn to your wife and criticize her for placing

the cup too close to the edge of the table. A short verbal battle follows. You storm upstairs and change your shirt. Back downstairs, you find your daughter has been too busy crying to finish breakfast and get ready for school. She misses the bus. Your spouse must leave immediately for work. You rush to the car and drive your daughter to school. Because you are late, you drive 40 miles an hour in a 30 mph speed limit.

After a 15-minute delay and throwing $60 (traffic fine) away, you arrive at school. Your daughter runs into the building without saying goodbye. After arriving at the office 20 minutes late, you find you forgot your briefcase. Your day has started terrible. As it continues, it seems to get worse and worse.

"A quick temper will make a fool of you soon enough."
~ Bruce Lee (1940–1973),
Actor, Martial Expert, Philosopher, Film Director and Producer

You look forward to coming home. When you arrive home, you find a small wedge in your relationship with your spouse and daughter. Why? Because of how you reacted in the morning! Why did you have a bad day?

A) Did the coffee cause it?
B) Did your daughter cause it?
C) Did the policeman cause it?
D) Did you cause it?

The answer is "D". You had no control over what happened with the coffee. How you reacted in those five seconds is what caused your bad day.

Here is what could have and should have happened. Coffee splashes over you. Your daughter is about to cry. You gently say, *"It is ok honey, you just need to be more careful next time"*. Grabbing a towel you rush upstairs. After grabbing a new shirt and your briefcase, you come back down in time to look through the window and see your child getting on the bus. She turns and waves. You arrive five minutes early and cheerfully greet the staff and have a nice normal day.

Notice the difference? Two different scenarios: Both started the same but both ended different. Why? Because of how you **reacted**! You really do not have any control over 10% of what happens. The other 90% was determined by your reaction."

"Anger is short-lived madness."
~ Quintus Horatius Flaccus (65–8 BC),
Roman Lyric Poet

Excellent example and it clearly highlights how much of what happens to us is really how we react to a stimulus. Hence we and no one else is responsible for what happens next. Like the famous saying goes "You get what you give," so you must always remember that you make your own destiny and you cannot blame others for what you have or for what you have become.

How does one go about applying these wonderful '90/10 Principles'? Here are a few suggestions:

- If someone says something bad or negative about you, you don't have to react and don't have to act like a sponge. Remember you are in control of your actions, so don't react to any such comment especially if it upsets you or makes you angry.

"Silence is a source of great strength."
~ Lao Tzu (571 BC–531BC),
Philosopher of Ancient China and a Central Figure in Taoism

- If you have to react in case the circumstances requires you to do so, then take a minute of silence and give your brain's neurons time to slow down. These seconds of silence will have two impacts, a) the other person will realize something they said or did has really hurt you; b) they will help you react in a proper way. Remember a proper reaction will not ruin your day, but a wrong reaction can result in you losing a friend or getting fired from your job. Not to mention the associated stress and hardship that will follows.

"An inability to stay quiet is one of the most conspicuous failings of mankind."
~ Walter Bagehot (1826–1877),
British Businessman, Essayist and Journalist

- Silence is a powerful tool which is free and I feel is quite neglected; people don't use it that often. Silence has no major downside, in fact if used in an argument, it usually helps to resolve the issue, lower the temper and it helps in finding a win-win solution. Unfortunately when faced with confrontation, we forget that we have it in our system. So remember silence is available at all times and you should use it to your advantage.

- An unplanned comment or something said in anger can have much longer lasting impact. It is said that "the tongue is sharper then the sword," Why? Because spoken words and broken commitments have done more to damage this world than swords. Always remember that the tongue being one of the smallest members of our anatomy, but it boasts great power. It can hurt others more than any other organ in our body. In the Bible it is said in Psalm 64.3 and I quote "Who have sharpened their tongue like a sword. They aimed bitter speech as their arrow." If you can remember that the tongue is to be feared more than the sword, it will help you use your words more effectively.

Let me ask you a question, how would you or how should you react if someone cuts you off in traffic? People who know me call me an aggressive driver; I had the habit of quickly losing my temper while driving and would love to show the other driver exactly how he had made me feel! With experience and age I have changed and realized it was sheer immaturity and this adverse reaction of mine did me no good. Getting upset only hurts you, your blood pressure goes up, you mentally cannot focus, etc. The key objective of driving is to get to your destination, so what is the big deal if you get late by five minutes! Why do you let driving ruin your day? Remember the '90/10 Principle', and be conscious of how you react at all times.

Food for Thought:

Tale of the Two Wolves

One day an old Cherokee (a Native American Indian) was talking to his grandson about the battle that happens inside all of us. He said: "Son, there is a battle happening between two wolves inside all of us. One wolf is evil – it is beset with anger, envy, selfishness, failure, jealousy, greed, lies, sorrow, regret, arrogance, self-pity, guilt, resentment, inferiority, false pride, superiority, and ego. The other wolf is good – It is awash with faith, joy, peace, love, hope, happiness, prosperity, success, serenity, humility, kindness, benevolence, empathy, generosity, truth, and compassion." The grandson listened to his grandfather and after thinking for a minute asked: "Which wolf wins?" The old Cherokee replied simply, "The one you feed the most." We all in our daily lives must always be aware and conscious of which wolf we are feeding and giving energy too.

As a leader I would strongly urge you to use this '90/10 Principle' in all your interactions with your teams and I promise you that you will be amazed with the results. The first negative outburst you experience in the office next time, think of this principle and believe me you will have a better day. One bad comment or an unwarranted remark to your subordinates, colleagues or even your boss in the morning and you would have spoilt theirs as well as your own day.

Remember you will lose nothing if you try it. The problem is that very few are even aware of this principle and hence are suffering due to undeserved stress, useless heartache and a never-ending list of problems. Believe me when I say that this '90/10 Principle' will change your life. It is simple and incredibly impactful. Covey very aptly calls it "Changing your life made simple."

Chapter 15 –
Individual Performance Insights

"Hire the best, retain the top."
~ My Philosophy

Here is a tip that I have shared with all the employees that have worked with me at P&G or Gillette. Recall that both companies have a very grueling recruiting process, a very competitive internal culture and end up hiring simply the best of the best. Interestingly in these two companies they follow a philosophy of 'Promotion from Within', which means that they hire only at entry level and all future leaders of the companies come out of these batches.

A few characteristics that accurately describe the attributes of graduates hired include ambitious, hard working, competitive, committed, innovative, risk takers, collaborative, and having strong leadership traits. Once in the company they all have to fight the proverbial battle of 'Performance Rating' in order to get promoted and climb the ladder of success. A key question many of these new hires asked was "What can I do to succeed in this highly competitive and volatile environment?"

My response to their concern was:

"When I look at all of you from my vantage point,
I see a crowd of people, all well qualified, all

working their hearts out but the only way for you to catch my eye is for you to stick your head out from the crowd and get noticed. The key question here is how does one get noticed? The best way to get noticed by your supervisors is to consistently deliver your projects on four non-negotiable factors, namely:

A. Beyond the Scope.
B. Ahead of Deadline.
C. Impeccable Quality.
D. Minimal Supervision.

A basic expectation from all new hires as well as existing employees is that they will deliver their agreed work plan as it relates to timing, scope and quality. Let me now explain what each of the abovementioned factors means and entails:

15 A. Beyond the Scope

To me a top rated employee is the one who does not get bogged down by the scope (meaning project boundaries or the range of key issues that need to be addressed) given in the project guidelines and has the ability to change and find creative ways on how a good and impactful a business solution can be found. They have the ability to take calculated risks rather than playing it safe and operating within pre-defined boundaries. While analyzing the project if he/she feels that the final results will be compromised if the scope is not expanded to include some new factors that they have come across in their research, then these factors must be included. They must have the ability of looking at the problem or challenge from a totally new perspective. Don't just blindly go and deliver the scope because that is what your supervisor has asked you to do.

Always remember that the true intent of the project is to deliver the objective and not the scope. Scope is given to get you started, to let you know what factors and what variables one needs to focus on so that you don't end up going all over the place trying to collect the initial data and research information. However, if your research highlights new factors that need to be included to deliver the objective, then include those factors and expand the scope. If you end up treating scope as a limiting factor then you are not doing justice to your project and the quality of your results or findings will be compromised.

This behavior of expanding your scope or looking at totally new opportunities that have never been tested will clearly show the top management your ability to think out-of-the-box, take calculated risks as well as your commitment for getting quality results and a strong command over the subject matter. Remember the potential return rises with an increase in risk; high risk should be calculated but not reckless. To your managers this aspect will become visible over time as their basic expectation would be that you will deliver the project based on the initial scope; but they will notice it at the final stage that if you had not voluntarily expanded the scope, the company would have missed out on an opportunity and that will put a much needed feather in your cap and get you noticed.

By constricting yourself to the initial scope, thus missing out on key opportunities that may lie just beyond it, you will hurt the projects effectiveness and in turn it will show poorly on your ability as a professional. So question, learn and ask as many questions as possible at the design phase in order to avoid falling into this trap. By doing this consistently you will have a great chance to get top ratings and start moving towards being not just a good but a great manager.

"Choose a job you love and you will never
have to work a day in your life."
~ Confucius (551–479 BC),
Chinese Teacher, Editor, Politician and Philosopher

Vital Tip 34: Scope vs. Objective: While expanding the scope of the project do not lose sight of the objective of the project. Don't convert the project into your own personal pet project where the original objective is lost. Always keep the objective in mind and use the scope only for the initial fact finding mission and then go wherever you need to go to deliver the objective.

On the other hand don't expand the project's scope just to impress your management. There must be some tangible benefits or clear advantages for making the project bigger than its initial scope. Frivolous and non-value additions will do nothing but add complexity, delay the project, compromise your credibility and will eventually impact the quality of your results.

---

15 B. Ahead of Deadline

Everyone over their lifetime develops a personal style or a habit in meeting deadlines. Timely completion and the quality of the project depends upon how you plan out the project from the time it is assigned to you to the time when you finally submit it. For example there are three ways on how project planning can span out and I call them the 3 P's of Project Delivery: The Planner, The Procrastinator and The Permanently Late.

"You can't overestimate the need to plan and
prepare. In most of the mistakes I've made,
there has been this common theme of
inadequate planning beforehand.
You really can't over-prepare in business!"
~ Chris Corrigan (b. 1946),
Australian Businessman

1) <u>The Planner</u>: They are the ones who start working on their project the day it is assigned to them, plan everything way ahead of time and complete it with time to spare so that they can review and polish it even further.

"You can't build a reputation on what you're going to do."
~ Henry Ford (1863–1947),
Founder of Ford Motor Company

2) <u>The Procrastinator</u>: As apparent from its name, they are the people who drag their feet and postpone working on the project. They put off things, defer and start late but do ultimately complete the project with barely any time to spare. Compared to the planner they start working on the project very late and are left with no time for last minute reviews. Remember, the quality of your assignment can clearly be compromised due to procrastination.

"Procrastination is the art of keeping up with yesterday."
~ Don Marquis (1878–1937),
American Humorist, Journalist and Author

3) <u>The Permanently Late</u>: These types wait until the very last moment and cram the entire work into a few days and nights. They spend long sleepless nights at the tail end of the delivery date and due to the shortness of time end up compromising its quality and submit poor conclusions. In majority of the cases there is lack of analysis, deficiency of authentic data and the final report is clearly not of the best quality.

"Everybody in the real world will agree - the
moment a project is behind deadline,
quality assurance tends to go out the window."
~ Alan Cox (b. 1968),
British Computer Programmer (Linux kernal Designer)

In top multinationals, due to the high level of focus and pressure on business results, there is no margin for error and in fact tolerance for error is zero. A botched project can easily result in a loss of thousands if not millions of dollars and such a blunder could easily leave your career in virtual doldrums. Here I would strongly recommend to get started on your project the day the project is assigned to you; be a planner. In majority of the projects you have to collaborate and collect data from a variety of sources and locations (having sourcing plants and centers of expertise spread all over the world). Procrastination will not get you anywhere.

Remember people in today's global business environment travel for business meetings, go off on training to different locations or simply could be on vacations; hence if you wait too long and cannot locate the right person in time to obtain relevant data, you will be in a tight spot and the quality of your analysis will clearly be compromised. Permanently late will barely survive a couple of months or even a year in a professional company, as mediocre or under-par work will be noticed early on. In fact in most cases your supervisor will be coaching and guiding you and if he/she feels you are not on top of your discipline, you will be warned and if this is not rectified, sidelined and eventually booted out. Excuses at this level are non-existent as the expectation from you is that you will get the job done despite all obstacles. It is a very competitive world out there, so be at your best and come prepared.

15 C. Impeccable Quality

Poor quality and sub-standard work will not get you anywhere in any company! I have found out that quality is a virtue, which gets built into a person's character overtime. It starts taking shape right from your childhood and gets more entrenched during your education and in your interaction with others. You can always work on building this virtue into your character if you are conscious of your shortcoming and work diligently towards improving them. Nothing is more embarrassing as an error that changes the entire outcome of a project.

We are not perfect and we all make mistakes but the key is not to repeat them. For people who learn from their mistakes and single-mindedly focus on delivering quality, then the probability is high that this habit will become part of their character and DNA.

> **Vital Tip 35:** Sit back and look at your conclusion. If the conclusion looks too good to be true with immediate payout or looks simply awful, has no respectable IRR, especially when the data is relatively stable then you must question the conclusion.
>
> Do not submit until you are comfortable with the final recommendation and can support it fully. Always review before submitting, do a deep dive, recheck all your assumptions, relook at your analysis and worksheets with a fine-tooth comb, and crosscheck the information provided by other departments. It should all make sense and only then should you go ahead and submit your project report. Sometimes our gut feelings can save our career, don't ignore them. It saved mine a few times ☺
>
> Let me share a classic example where my gut feelings saved the day. In 1992 when I was the Manager Financial Analysis of Health and Beauty Care and Paper Products categories in Jeddah, one of my freshly hired financial analyst shared with me a cash flow analysis which he had just completed on an investment in the Beauty Care category and was about to email it to his brand manager. As I reviewed his analysis on the printout he was carrying, I saw that the incremental volumes were healthy, good gross margin, and a favorable payout of 2.5 years but a very poor IRR (Internal Rate of Return), much below P&G official benchmark; hence a recommendation of 'no go'.

> My gut feelings told me that something was wrong with this analysis and that the IRR should have been healthier. I asked my analyst to bring his laptop as the numbers were not making any sense. I saw no issue even after reviewing the spreadsheet but my gut would not agree with the recommendation. By further troubleshooting I realized that the analyst had hidden some columns for proper formatting and these columns were empty. As the IRR formula is based on a range of cells and the empty hidden columns act as 'zeros', hence the cash flow gave an IRR that was significantly depressed. My rookie analyst learned a serious lesson that day on going in deep and to look at numbers and not accepting results blindly.

Even today I can count on my fingers the names of the employees who never compromised on the quality of any project assigned to them. I knew that as far as quality and integrity of data is concerned, these employees will never compromise even if the project is delayed. Incidentally these were the same employees who eventually got the best and most challenging projects and moved up the corporate ladder. Three of them, who I had personally hired and groomed, ended up becoming Chief Financial Officer's of P&G Pakistan.

Here are some tips on how to ingrain quality into your corporate life and have a good shot at getting top rated:

1. Be a planner. Plan out your work in detail and leave enough time to check for mistakes and to cross check the data and your findings with appropriate people and experts.
2. Never hand in your project report or an important memo without proof reading it and checking all facts and figures meticulously. In fact I would suggest that once you have completed a project (and if you are a planner you will have the time), sleep over it and the next day review it with a

fresh mind. You will invariably be able to see things better with a clear and rested mind.

3. Ask for help when needed. If you feel that something is not correct, then don't just submit the report assuming that asking would make you look less qualified, in fact mistakes tend to overshadow people's career more than asking for help.

4. Check your assumptions and data integrity multiple times and as they say, dot all the i's and cross all the t's.

5. Sit back and look at your conclusion. If the data is relatively stable, but the conclusions are too good to be true or simply awful, question it. Do a deep dive into your assumptions, analysis, worksheets, inputs, etc. Only when it all makes intuitive sense should you go ahead and present your conclusions. Always remember that your gut feelings can save you from embarrassment, so don't ignore them.

"A man should never be ashamed to own
he has been in the wrong,
which is but saying, in other words, that he is
wiser today than he was yesterday."
~ Alexander Pope (1688–1744),
English Poet

15 D. Minimal Supervision

This is something only you and your manager will see and notice. And as your career progresses your rating will get impacted by what your manager perceives as your performance, hence working independently and with self-confidence is an essential trait. This does not mean that you do not ask your boss for clarification, data and information. But if you expect your manager to repeat the clarification or correct your mistakes and review conclusions at every stage of the project, you will not succeed in a highly competitive company where individual performance is the true barometer of success.

As I mentioned earlier, making mistakes or asking for clarification once is human, but doing it repeatedly shows lack of capability and lack of internal passion to be the best. Focus on building your competence and skill base right from the first day on the job, as a strong early start is a sure fire way of avoiding disappointment later.

> **Vital Tip 36:** Do not take the concept of minimal supervision as something where you do not ask for help or clarification. Nothing is worse than delivering a project that is not in line with your manager's outline and expectations. When you start a project, hound your manager so that you thoroughly understand the scope, challenges, expectations, etc. of the project, but later do it mostly by yourself.
>
> Remember asking questions early on in the project is expected, but raising basic queries at a later stage shows lack of professionalism on your part. Only exception being when you need your manager's help to break down barriers due to the non-collaborative behavior of other departments, lack of resources or funds to complete your project.

In Summary: At the end let me paint a picture of a top-rated manager. He/she is a person who consistently delivers their project beyond the defined scope, with top quality analysis and data, with no or minimal supervision and invariably ahead of time, they are the planner's. Instead of just growing the business, they change the way the game is played. They blindside the competition and create real sustainable value from within the existing paradigm. They are game-changers rather than those who remain within the boundaries of how business is being done. They are focused, they leave a legacy behind when they leave their jobs, and they take calculated risks and do not like to play it safe. Such kind of performance, time after time, will make your boss realize who in their team delivers the best quality results and does it consistently.

Consistently does not mean that you deliver this high quality performance only on projects assigned to you over the next two to four months, but you do it on the majority of projects over a span of year or years. Slowly all important and urgent projects will start flowing to the few who outshine all others on these four dimensions.

Coincidently, these will be the few who will also start to climb the ladder of success at a much faster rate versus the rest of the crowd.

"Success comes from good judgment.
Good judgment comes from experience.
Experience comes from bad judgment."
~ Arthur Jones (1926–2007),
Founder and Inventor of the Nautilus Exercise Machines

••••••-----   ----------••••

Chapter 16 – Insights from Good to Great by Jim Collins

As a result of extensive research carried out by Jim Collins in analyzing the companies he categorized as having achieved *greatness*, he gained a wealth of knowledge into their management styles and the unique strategies that allowed them to gain competitive advantage, and the financial challenges they faced as they grew disproportionally. While dong his research he noticed something incredible, an insight that on face value is incredibly simple yet extremely powerful.

This insight has intrigued me from the first day I read about it in Collins book "Good to Great". The insight was simple yet profound, i.e. "Good is the enemy of Great." The reason that many companies although doing quite good will never get into the category of greatness is because "they are doing so well." Complacency digs in! Due to their current healthy status there is no dissatisfaction with the status quo within the ranks of the company's leadership team; they all feel quite happy delivering good results and never feel the urge or the drive to move the performance needle to greatness. Being good is one of the key reasons why they are not great.

The same concept applies perfectly to individuals as it does to companies. Many employees never take their careers to new heights as they are already good and that makes them complacent, a clear barrier in developing into great managers. Becoming great is not easy; it requires disproportional focus and an unrelenting internal drive to excel, without which people or companies cannot step-change their performance. The key insight here is that if you are good in your work and doing well in your career, without a healthy dissatisfaction with the status quo there is no effort and consequently no chance that you will endeavor to further your career or raise the bar of your performance. Don't get me wrong; being good is not bad.

My personal experience is that nearly 80% of employees in any organization are in fact good. Majority of the employees do their work very well, they meet the needs of their job, they help the company deliver its goals, but that is the minimum performance expected from all employees in any case. What would make them great is if they strive to deliver way above their job expectations, if they bring a paradigm shift in the quality of results or if they bring in disproportional but sustained growth or profit improvement. To achieve the greatness status requires a mindset change, a never-ending desire to continuously improve performance, a total discontent with the current status quo, only then will you or anyone else can and will move, from *good to great*.

"Heart is what separates the good from the great."
~ Michael Jordan (b. 1963),
Former Pro Basketball Player and Businessman

Inspired by this "Good to Great" book and its unique insight, I took the concept one step further and designed a course by the name of "How to get from being a Good

How to get from being a Good manager to being a Great one!

Manager to being a Great one?" and offered it to a cross-section of young managers at P&G and Gillette. The course was very well received and even after many months and years, I kept getting

positive feedback on how it had helped some of my managers to realize their true potential, drove them to change their behavior and to help bring a step-change in their performance. Let me take you through the concept and the flow of the course and how I approached its designing.

"Outstanding leaders go out of the way to boost
the self-esteem of their personnel.
If people believe in themselves, it's amazing
what they can accomplish."
~ Sam Walton (1918–1992),
American Businessman and Entrepreneur, founder of Walmart

16 A. Prelude: Good to Great Managers

Have you ever thought of why there are so few *great* people, great institutions, great companies or great schools? The reason is because we have so many *good* schools, good governments, and good people; it's just that simple. It is easy to settle for a good life. Majority of companies never become great, precisely because they become quite good. Same principle can also be applied to managers; the majority of employees never become *great* managers, precisely because they are quite good; that is the central theme here.

16 B. Who are Good Managers?

By good managers I mean the people who deliver on expectations, help drive business growth, help train people, work hard, are committed, live up to the purpose and the value system of the company, and love their people and their work. This is an impressive list of attributes and many of us may be struggling to figure out what more can one do, to move to a great status.

What are we missing here? What more can we add to the profile of the good manager that will help them move to the greatness status?

From my personal experiences the reasons why so many managers are only good is because:

- ✓ They probably work nine to nine and do not have a good work-life balance. ☹
- ✓ Once they move from their assignment, people quickly forget them.
- ✓ They are more focused on their own success rather than of their subordinates.
- ✓ The hand-over to a new person is invariably a painful and complex process.
- ✓ They are not the masters of their job; key facts are not always on their fingertips.
- ✓ Have never been able to change the name of the game, they just inherited the business and drove it well.

Everyone at the back of their mind would love to be classified as a great manager but most of them never really strive to get there. Nothing in this world comes for free; everything has a certain price tag associated with it. The next question that invariably comes is: "How does one move from good to great?" Before I share my insights, let me share what some of the good managers I surveyed thought was needed to achieve greatness. The questions I asked was:

Q: What are some characteristics, which will move you from being good to great?

Insights shared were:

- ✓ To be top-rated !
- ✓ To work hard 24/7 !
- ✓ To sell yourself to your seniors !
- ✓ To be cutthroat in everything you do !
- ✓ To have a strong career sponsor in high places !

✓ To be extremely ambitious about ones career progression !
✓ To deliver outstanding results without worrying about the consequences !

"But the real great man is the man who
makes every man feel great."
~ G. K. Chesterton (1874–1936),
English Writer, Poet and Philosopher

16 C. How to get from being 'Good' to being 'Great'?

You will be pleasantly surprised to know that the right answer to the above question is "None of the above." To me the core issue is much deeper than what meets the eye. To me great managers are those who truly ...

✓ Deliver 100% expectations by only working nine to five.
✓ Leave behind a legacy in their previous jobs.
✓ Have an inherent dissatisfaction with the status quo.
✓ Are compassionate and empathetic to their people and teams.
✓ Have an exceptionally balanced work and personal life.
✓ Have teams and organization that deliver sustained top results.
✓ Constantly striving to 'Raise the Bar' to new heights.
✓ Leverage diversity to optimize business results.
✓ Former direct reports continue to aspire to work for them.
✓ Can manage both their time and energy efficiently.
✓ Make sure they groom successors before moving to their next role.

From my experience in grooming managers and driving businesses in top multi-nationals, I have six tips, which if you master, will eventually move you to the greatness category. The six tips are:

a) Make current job Best-in-Class (BIC).
b) Become a great People's Champion.
c) Focus on Succession Planning.
d) Display exceptional Leadership Skills.
e) Efficient manager of Time and Energy.
f) Display passionate Ownership Behavior.

"Leaders don't create followers, they create more leaders."
~ Tom Peters (b. 1942),
Management Expert and Writer

a) Make Current Job Best-in-Class (BIC)

The first and foremost virtue you have to master is to fully champion your current role. People will listen to you and follow you anywhere if you can help them succeed in their jobs, if you can help solve their problems, break down their barriers and help them to be successful. If they feel that they know more about your job then you do, there is a risk that they will not respect your decisions and that faith, which is required to drive peak performance from your teams, will be missing.

In addition, you must approach each activity with a high level of inquisitiveness and with the mindset of fixing or improving every process and system in your department. You must also be a good listener; you must be willing to appreciate diverse points of view and then using your experience come up with the best game plan. Ability to see through things and to identify and fix opportunity areas will be the key for you to get full support from your team and organization.

As I mentioned in Chapter 6 which is on 'Setting Measures and Tracking Them', I strongly recommend using scorecards to track your organization's performance. Only continuous focus, unrelenting support and celebrating success via proper tracking techniques, will help deliver best-in-class results. Don't just focus on growing the business you inherited, but look for ideas to step change the game dynamics and grow disproportionally. In parallel you have to make sure that there is accountability at every level, including your own. If you took it upon yourself to do some part of a project, then you must track it and if not delivered on time then highlight it as such.

Be consistent in your handling of all your team members. Use the same performance yardstick and make no exceptions or have favorites. Being one team one voice will be the only way you will step-change the quality of results and make your job best in class. Delivering above and beyond the call of duty is what will help you classify among the best managers of the company.

> **Leave a legacy, which lasts long after you have left the position**

"Excellence is the gradual result of always striving to do better."
~ Pat Riley (b. 1945),
NBA Player, Coach, President of 'Miami Heat' Basketball Team

b) Become a Great People's Manager

Greatness only comes to those who are more concerned about the success of their subordinates, other people and teams rather than being focused on their own success. This is not easy; our personal ego coupled with cultural and peer pressure's makes us focus on our success and our own career growth. What people fail to remember is that you are as successful as the people that work for you! You will deliver nothing impressive if you do not have talented and qualified people working under you.

Invariably great leaders are those who attract skillful and capable people around them. You need to invest and become a great trainer and a champion of people and their issues. You will notice there is always someone in your office that everyone looks up to, who people go to for help and advice; they may not be the top managers or members of the leadership team, but they invariably are the people's person.

It is heartening to see that the kind of commitment and work that these managers can obtain from their teams can only be imagined! Connecting such people's passion with a potent ability to set visions and identifying and implementing strategies is a sure fire formula for a true leader. Motivation to go the extra mile by any team is more driven by their respect for an individual, appreciation for his character and capability and a deep desire to give back to that person from their emotional bank account.

Vital Tip 37: The following example exemplifies the importance of knowing your team at a much higher plane. In a Human Resources MBA course exam there was a question: What is the name of the janitor who cleans the hall every day? One student asked the professor whether this was a joke. The professor answered that it carried ten marks and highlighted the importance of knowing every member of your team and that is when you become a true people's manager.

To be a champion of people, you as an individual will have to reach a maturity level, which many psychologists call 'Self-Actualization'. A person has achieved self-actualization when they embrace reality and facts instead of denying the truth. They are spontaneous, they have a bias towards action, can see the big picture, are natural people motivators, are interested in solving problems and are accepting of themselves and others and lack a prejudicial attitude. Try to be such a people's manager.

> **To be remembered as an ideal mentor and the person they most want to work for**

'A big man is one who makes us feel
bigger when we are with him.'
~ John C. Maxwell (b. 1947),
Evangelical Christian Pastor, Author and Speaker

c) Succession Planning

An essential action that any manager must deliver in order to
graduate to the greatness status is the ability to plan out his
or her own succession. It takes a great person with a lot of self-
confidence and maturity to develop a successor for them self.
Many people are afraid to teach their subordinates or peers all
the tricks of the trade, knowledge and insights of the business, as
they feel threatened. Only a genuine leader and a self-confident
person will do such an act.

Planning out your succession is a complex project and as a start
requires for you to identify the right person or persons to groom.
You must make sure that they all have well defined workloads
and comprehensive work-plans, which test them in a spectrum
of leadership roles. The manager's who are being groomed must
always know what is expected of them and should get performance
feedback on a frequent basis.

You must also start to delegate important and critical work to the
potential successor's in order to test them out and to develop their
mental and cognitive abilities. While delegating work one should
always keep in mind not to hand over work, which is beyond
the influence of your subordinates; don't set them up for failure.
Close supervision, active grooming, providing timely training and
advice should be carried out on a daily and weekly basis.

Delegation is an excellent way to train, groom and empower your
organization but has to be properly managed; delegation should be
conferred in a planned manner over time. I remember when I took
over Gillette Pakistan in March 2007 the organization was very

young and inexperienced. For the first year or so I did everything and involved myself in every decision and meeting. I had my hand in every project, was reviewing every CPS (critical path schedule), preparing and making every presentation and monthly letters to top management, and leading rollouts of all initiatives. But once I felt that my team was up and running, I pulled back as I knew that if I did not, I would be hindering their growth.

After July 2008 I consciously started to delegate my work and I did it in a well thought-out, planned manner without anyone actually realizing that more responsibilities were being placed on their shoulders. My concurrent focus on multiple fronts, such as encouraging ownership behavior, striving to be their best and building inherent desire to win, clearly made a stark difference in them maturing in their roles and made this transition successful. I am proud to say that the majority of managers who worked under me, were groomed and coached effectively and today are handling such senior positions as finance managers and general managers of various P&G subsidiaries. In fact, since I took early retirement from P&G Pakistan to take over as CEO of Gillette Pakistan in 2007, the three Chief Financial Officers' that have now followed me, were all hired, groomed and trained by me.

It is also important to note some pitfalls of doing everything yourself and not delegating, a) People don't get empowered. b) There is lack of ownership as you make all the decisions. c) No one is getting groomed as a successor. d) There is no proper accountability as the buck always stops with you. In order to empower your people you have to focus, on both a) delegating key projects/responsibilities in a planned manner and b) on increasing their capability level to handle complexity as well as dynamic business decision-making. To further this effort I strongly urge you to get personally involved in training and development, not only in areas of your business expertise but in areas of personal development.

To succeed they have to develop all sorts of skills needed to be a leader and know how to break down barriers. For this they must be exposed to business challenges as well as leadership soft skills. An ideal way is to get involved in training personally, you may not realize it but you already have well-rounded knowledge and experience. I was the master trainer in courses as diverse as the Leadership Module, Corporate Athlete, Interviewing Skills, People Supporting People, Developing Subordinates, etc. Majority of these are non-core or non-business courses but are key for developing healthy, capable and collaborative human beings. Personally I am very proud of being rated amongst the top trainers in P&G Pakistan for nearly a decade and being nominated as the top trainer on a few occasions.

> **Succession planning is twofold. One is an emotional one – the desire to leave a legacy – and one is a financial one – Carl Alongi**

"A little spark kindles a great fire."
~ Spanish Proverb

d) Display Exceptional Leadership Skills
Here we are not talking about normal run-of-the-mill leadership qualities but as Jim Collins calls it in his book *Good to Great*, 'Level 5 Leadership'. This level goes far beyond the regular leadership qualities such as being a visionary, exciting and enrolling the team in your vision, inspiring them, helping them overcome challenges, and helping them deliver the vision – the Level 5 Leadership is about being a selfless role model whose ambition is foremost for the company and not for themselves.

Such leaders are rigorous but not ruthless in people decisions. They have an unwavering resolve to do what must be done and nothing comes in their way in delivering their project, their dream. They are those who drive people to deliver their very best

Chapter 16 – Insights from Good to Great by Jim Collins

while being empathetic to their needs. They have the ability to seek peak performances from their teams on a consistent basis. They are sensitive yet tough, emotional and caring on the inside but tough and strong on the outside. In addition to being a well-rounded corporate leader, it is extremely critical that they focus and take on responsibilities on three facets of business excellence, namely:

a) <u>Building the Business:</u> Setting vision and strategies and creating executional excellence standards. Breaking down barriers to help the teams operate freely, as well as monitoring their performance to make sure they remain on track to deliver the vision and strategies.

b) <u>Building Peoples Capabilities</u>: Create a set of values and a culture where people are nurtured and respected. Create a learning atmosphere and robust on-the-job and formal training programs. Be *approachable.* Act as a role model and personally 'walk the talk' by taking the most difficult challenges yourself. Be empathetic and a peoples champion.

c) <u>Building Organizational Capacity</u>: Continued focus on improving systems and processes in the company as well as eliminating non-value work. Have a never-ending desire for innovation and latest management techniques. This will help make, both work and people more efficient and business systems fine-tuned for optimal performance.

Humility + Will = True Leaders – Jim Collins

"Thinking will not overcome fear, but action will."
~ W. Clement Stone (1902–2002),
Businessman, Philanthropist and Author

e) Efficient Managers of Time and Energy

Another aspect that is extremely important to be a great manager is to have proper discipline in everything he or she does. They should value time and utilize it efficiently. Having a mindset that time is limited is critical to make any person effective. The very reason to have clear deadlines and milestones is to create timelines against which people must work, deliver and can be measured. There are various aspects to being an efficient time manager. They are organized, they have extremely efficient filing systems, they plan-out all their activities well in advance, they are the master of their discipline, never allowing anything to fall through the cracks and have an unrelenting desire for executional excellence. In short, they work nine to five but deliver disproportional in terms of both quality and quantity; they are master in managing both, their time and energy.

Managing your Energy: Managing time as well as managing your energy are two distinct but critical concepts. Many of us are quite good in managing our time, but are terrible in managing our energy. A very insightful book *The Power of Full Engagement* written by two psychologists Dr. Jim Loehr and Tony Schwartz gives some very useful tips on how to optimally manage your energy and hence deliver peak performance when most needed.

Dr. Jim Loehr later partnered with Dr. Jack Groppel and founded the Human Performance Institute (HPI) in Florida. HPI pioneered a science-based training solution where they help individuals to increase their performances in high stress arenas and in turn significantly enhance organizational performance. Some notable athletes that they influenced included such famous names as Jim Courier, Arantxa Sanchez-Vicario and Monica Seles in tennis; Mark O'Meara and Michelle Wei in golf; Dan Janson in ice-skating; Ray "Boom Boom" Mancini in boxing, and many more.

Their experience and insights in obtaining peak performances from world class athletes and seeing how they applied these to the corporate world brought them into the world of business; they specifically designed a course which they called Corporate Athlete. They recognized that business leaders and their employees had to learn the same concepts that helped bring peak performances in sports athletes. Many companies impressed with their success in obtaining peak performance from business executives starting sending their employees to HPI for learning energy management techniques, these included such famous Fortune 500 companies such as Procter & Gamble, Citibank, PepsiCo, Dell, etc.

Food for Thought:

Life of Corporate Leader vs. Athletes

Sports heroes who achieve global recognition fascinate us all. In our minds their life appears to be much tougher than of normal business people. They train hard, they exert more and hence they enjoy the fruits of their intense focus and labor. What we fail to realize is that as corporate leaders, our life is much tougher than that of athletes.

Try to compare various aspects and you will be surprised; a) their careers span ten to fifteen years maximum, ours span thirty five to forty years minimum; b) athlete's work six to eight months a year (they have their off seasons), while we work eleven months (and in some cases fail to even take our thirty days vacations); c) everyday an athlete trains for four to six hours max, we in the corporate world work anywhere from eight to twelve hours a day.

So you can now well imagine that corporate life is as tough if not much tougher then the life of any athlete and one must invest and devote quality time to increase ones energy capacity.

The crux of the book is related to 'managing your energy' throughout the entire day more efficiently. They teach you the key principles of managing your energy, help identify what are the energy management barriers and then based on these take you on a journey of change. Let me give you an example, which will help you to understand what I mean when I say managing time versus managing energy.

Imagine that your twenty-fifth wedding anniversary is just round the corner and you have been planning it for months. You have bought a very nice expensive gift, booked yourself for a lavish dinner at a top restaurant, made sure you were not travelling on that day and kept your evening free so that you could spend some quality time with your spouse.

Now imagine a serious business crisis that threatens your company emerges just a day before your anniversary and you and your leadership teams have to work long hours in order to resolve it. Imagine that on the day of your anniversary you started with a six am conference call (due to a four hour time difference with HQ located elsewhere), a daylong meeting with your bankers, you missed your lunch and replenished yourself with just a bag of potato chips and some cookies. Later in the afternoon you go straight into a crisis meeting with your auditors and regulators which took longer than expected and you finally made it home by 8:10 pm. Still not too late as the dinner booking is for nine pm.

However when you come home, you fall into your favorite couch and try to recover your lost energy. Your energy level is incredibly low and soon you start feeling sleepy and your brain suddenly goes into hibernation mode. All you have eaten since morning is some potato chips and cookies; not great energy boosters! Your wife who is looking forward to this day has been impatiently waiting for your return, is all dressed up and looking amazing. She looks at you and out of her love and concern says "Why don't we skip the dinner at the restaurant and let me put something together at home." You want nothing of this sort as you want to celebrate your anniversary in style. So you call the restaurant and tell them that you will be late by thirty minutes, as you want to recover some of your lost energy.

You finally make it to the restaurant by 9:50 pm. You order food and drinks but do not have much energy left to chitchat with your wife or even smile and you sadly turn the evening into a boring chore. You even forget to give her the gift, which you realize is still in your jacket pocket when you get ready to hit the bed at night. You will agree that this is a very sad story but a realistic one.

> "The key is not to prioritize what's on your
> schedule, but to schedule your priorities."
> ~ Stephen Covey (1932–2012),
> Author, Professional Speaker and Management Consultant

Another relevant example, which highlights the difference between managing time versus managing energy, is the case where you have an important early morning presentation in front of the company's Board of Directors. But as there were last minute changes you worked all the way to 2 am the night before and hit bed by 3 am. In the morning you crawled out of bed at 7 am, felt busted but still got ready and sped off to office. Disappointingly you end up making a terrible presentation due to lack of sleep and a fuzzy mind. In addition, due to last minute changes, the presentation also had many typos and all the hard work was wasted and you left behind a bad impression in front of some very important people.

> "Time is the coin of your life.
> It is the only coin you have, and only you
> can determine how it will be spent.
> Be careful, lest you let other people spend it for you."
> ~ Carl Sandburg (1878–1967),
> Writer and Editor

What happened here? You managed your time the best you could within the events of the day, but you definitely ran out of energy and spoiled an important event in your life. If you only had a bigger reservoir of energy that could have lasted you throughout the day! How many times have we heard this statement before that most of us do not have much energy left for our commitments and responsibilities outside the office, after working hours?

In fact most of the time we work so hard that even our business starts to suffer due to our lack of energy. How many of us have messed up a presentation due to lack of sleep, kept postponing a doctor's appointment, going to the gym or meeting friends and relatives. Just like we manage our time, if we also had the ability to manage our energy, then our productively will increase manifolds and will help us meet more of our commitments and even have energy left at the end of the day to handle crisis situations or family commitments.

This book by two eminent psychologists will help you to figure out the best way to create energy reserves, which you can then access at the time when it matters the most (like on the anniversary or the early morning board meeting).

The ability to manage our energy is what separates the *ordinary* from the *extraordinary*. Being present at the anniversary dinner is a matter of time management, but being alert, smiling and relaxed after a long busy day is a totally different matter.

Remember managing time 'gets you there' but managing energy is 'what makes you shine'.

> "Your first and foremost job as a leader is to raise
> your own energy level and Then, to help raise and
> orchestrate the energies of those around you."
> ~ Peter Drucker (1909–2005),
> Writer and Management Consultant

Concept behind Energy Management:

Our life, from our birth to the time we die, has a unique physio-psychological trend. Our energy capacity continues to increase from the day we are born until the age of thirty, and afterwards it starts to decrease until we die (solid line in graph). On the other hand the demand on our body and mind continues to consistently increase from our birth until our death (dotted line in graph).

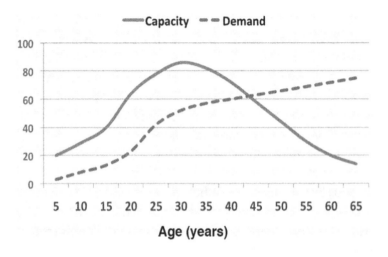

The physical bodies we live in continue to deteriorate and lose capacity, as we get older. Unlike our energy capacity, which starts to deteriorate after thirty, demand on our body and mind continues to constantly increase beyond this point as we take on more business responsibilities, get married, start a family and take over the responsibility as head of the family. It is estimated that these two lines, i.e. demand and capacity of energy, will cross each other around the age of forty or forty-five and that is when true crisis or panic hits our lives; *Demand* increases beyond our *capacity*. Many of us face emotional crisis, nervous breakdowns or stress related ailments.

Now that you are young, invest and grow your energy capacity before it is too late. The key is to move the crossover of the two lines beyond the forty to forty-five years to fifty or even sixty and beyond. The only way to do it is by investing and enhancing your energy reservoir today.

The solution to this problem is not rocket science nor complicated, but to survive post-forty challenges you must work on increasing your energy capacity as early as possible. As per the authors the only way to increase your energy capacity is to improve not only your physical energy capacity but also your spiritual energy, emotional energy as well as your mental energy capacities.

Reason to work on all types of energies is that if you are unfocused (low spiritual energy), or emotionally disturbed or depressed (low emotional energy) or mentally distracted (weak mental energy) then being physically fit does not help much, you need to be at the peak on all the four aforementioned energies; like the famous saying goes "have all your four cylinders firing at the same time to get peak performance." The way to increase capacity is to go into a disciplined and formal training on all four. For each type of the stated energy the training program is quite different:

- ✓ For Physical Capacity: you need to join a gym and start exercising and eat well-balanced and timely meals.
- ✓ For Mental Capacity: you need to start meditation, doing crosswords, quizzes or Sudoku, finding creative ways of challenging your brain.
- ✓ For Emotional Capacity: you need to start handling adversity and take on emotionally challenging projects, such as charity work or helping and caring for older or special people.
- ✓ For Spiritual Capacity: you need to strengthen your faith, live by your values and have specific and clear goals in your life.

Only then will you be able to meet the increasing demands on your body, mind, and emotions and allow yourself to deliver peak performance day after day, month after month and year after year. So I urge you to read this book and get into the habit of investing in your future by increasing the capacity of all four of your energies, i.e. spiritual, emotional, mental and physical.

> "Success is almost totally dependent upon drive and persistence. The extra energy required to make another effort or try another approach is the secret of winning."
> ~ Denis Waitley (b. 1933),
> Motivational Speaker, Consultant, and Author

f) Display Passionate Ownership Behavior

This is the final ingredient in my list on how to make a great manager. You have to have an innate desire to win. In team sports one of the key reasons why certain teams win consistently while others lose, is because each individual member of the winning teams wants to win so fiercely that they will do just about anything to win. They train, they practice, they psyche up each other and they believe in themselves that they will win.

The same is true for us in the business community; if we are going to win the 'Market Leadership Championship' then we have to have a burning desire to win and commit to what it takes. We must be ready to struggle, strive and not give up until we have ensured victory. You will agree that in all of us, deep inside, we have an inborn desire to win but unfortunately many of us lose that desire somewhere along the way. This could be a result of facing failures in the past or because you just don't have it in your anymore, i.e. the desire to be the best in everything you do.

Motivation to win, the desire to win at everything you do must exist within you at all times. Like the famous saying goes that "the chain is as strong as its weakest link," which means that your team is as strong as its weakest member; hence the key is to strengthen each and every link of the chain or each and every member of your team. All have to be running on all four cylinders in synchronicity.

A very inspirational movie showing this passion for winning goes by the name of *Any Given Sunday*, a 1999 drama film directed by Oliver Stone. The movie is about an American football team that has excellent talent and players but is on a losing streak and the team is struggling to make it even to the playoffs of the football conference. Overall the morale of the entire team is extremely low.

However, they have a very inspirational coach (Al Pacino) who gives a very moving speech to motivate and wake up his players during the halftime period. In his speech he talks in a very unique way at how to look at things around you. In American football if you have possession of the ball you have to cover ten yards in four tries in a fixed amount of time, so every inch and every second is extremely important. Let me narrate to you the coach's speech to see his unique approach to winning. The coach says:

> "...The margin for error is so small. I mean one half step too late or too early and you don't quite make it. One half second too slow or too fast and you don't quite catch it. The inches we need are everywhere around us. They are in every break of the game every minute, every second. On this team, we fight for that inch. On this team we tear ourselves and everyone around us to pieces for that inch. We CLAW with our fingernails for that inch. Cause we know that when we add up all those inches that's going to make the difference between WINNING and LOSING between LIVING and DYING ..."[63]

"Inches Make Champions."
~ Vince Lombardi (1913–1970),
Legendary American Football Coach

I would like to apply the same logic to the business environment where we have brand share points, distribution opportunities and consumers all around us. You have to fight for every share point, every new store, every shelf, and every consumer as this will make the difference between winning and losing at the end of the day. You must have a burning desire to win on all fronts, whether it is about growing market share, distribution, improving margin points, or driving executional excellence. After adding up all the new consumers that you wooed to your franchise, every additional distribution point you added and every new store that agreed to carry your product that is what will make the difference between you winning and losing.

Remember that it is the little things we do, day in and day out which will give you the ultimate edge. It is the executional excellence in everything we do, the passion we show to our work and our goals. That is the kind of aggressiveness and deep-rooted focus we need on 'winning' in order to inculcate the winning spirit into the very culture and gene pool of a company.

> **Vital Tip 38:** Here we are talking about winning fairly and within the rules of the game, as only that 'win' is sustainable and true. There is no fun in winning the wrong way. Those people who win using illegal methods end up hurting other people and alienating themselves and in the long run will not even enjoy the trophies of their wins.
>
> So have an unquestionably winning spirit but keep your desires under control and within limits of what is right and what is wrong. We must work towards finding and nurturing this desire to win in our teams and organization, all within the proper rules of engagement.

Purpose-Inspired Growth Strategy:

It is extremely important to realize that the kind of performance a person can deliver if they believe in a cause is radically different than the performance that the person will deliver if a job is assigned without them buying or believing in its purpose. Having a deep-rooted belief in the benefit resulting from your action drives passionate ownership behavior. That is one of the reasons that the first major initiative taken by Bob McDonald on taking over as the new CEO of P&G in 2009, was to promote what he calls P&G's "purpose-inspired growth" strategy of "touching and improving more consumers' lives in more parts of the world ... more completely."[64]

Logic is simple but could be a bit counterintuitive to some, i.e. the way it works is that the company values and sense of purpose, invokes the passion to help and care for the consumers. In the heart of its employees this in turn drives strong ownership behavior, and that results in profitability business growth for the shareholders. This strategy is now growing into 'Purpose-Driven-Colleges', 'Purpose-Inspired Partnerships', etc. all focused on making each and every employee reaffirm their understanding and commitment to the company's values and purpose.

> "Many people have a wrong idea of what
> constitutes true happiness.
> It is not attained through self-gratification but
> through fidelity to a worthy purpose."
> ~ Helen Keller (1880–1968),
> Educator and Writer was both Deaf & Blind

Twist in Ownership Behavior:

As mentioned above and I reaffirm this fact through personal experiences that if a person is just assigned a project versus the person being assigned a project which they believe to be close to their personal values and principles, the individuals performance between the two options will be radically different. The difference in performance emanates from the display of deep-rooted passionate ownership behavior.

Here I would like to share a short example about Mr. Fuad O. Kuraytim who led P&G MEAGE (Middle East Africa and General Exports) as its President during the 80's and 90's (he in fact offered me my P&G job in Geneva back in 1987 and later was my mentor until his retirement). P&G Pakistan started its operations in August 1991 and I arrived in February 1994 as they're second Chief Financial Officer from the company's Saudi operation based in Jeddah. Pakistan was still a relatively small market and had a very young and inexperienced organization. I give Fuad full credit for building the foundation on which P&G Pakistan's operation is built upon. Fuad was instrumental in driving the early exponential business growth as well as in driving strategies to stop its initial bleeding.

What I want to share is the strategy that Fuad always used to follow in his management reviews and which I call "Twist in Ownership Behavior." The young managers would patiently wait for his arrival and passionately present to him their ideas on market exploitation, promotion and media plans and other thoughts on how to disproportionally grow the Pakistan business.

Fuad's style was very motivational; when he did not like a certain idea or he felt strongly that the plan being presented will not work, he would never say "that is such a silly idea" or "that would never work," instead he would applaud the innovativeness of the idea and would build upon it by suggesting alterations or modifications and then would listen for reactions. By the end of the meeting the young managers would walk away very happy and excited about 'their' plans.

What these young managers would fail to realize was that during the back and forth discussions and concept sharing, Fuad had very nicely and sublimely booted out the bad ideas based on his deep experience and planted some of his own ideas into the plans in such an ingenious way that the young managers felt it was still their own idea. Fuad always believed that in order to succeed and to obtain peak performance from his very young teams in Pakistan, he had to make sure they believed in and owned the concepts. So he used to 'twist back' the ownership of the idea back to them by building on their concepts and implanting his views and inputs along the way, an ingenious yet effective management style for motivating a very young and inexperienced organization.

> "Coaches who can outline plays on a
> black board are a dime a dozen.
> The ones who win, get inside their player and motivate."
> ~ Vince Lombardi (1913–1970),
> Legendary American Football Coach

Chapter 17 – TRUST

During my roughly three decades with P&G and Gillette one thing that has stood the test of time and has never wavered, is the presence of 'TRUST' in both the companies. Trust is the foundation of everything we do and stands heads and shoulders above everything else; either it is the trust that consumers bestow on us or the trust we have built with our customers and suppliers over time or the trust within the company between employees or bosses and subordinates. From the day I joined P&G in 1987 I have never ever had a single day where anyone has ever questioned my trust in the company or in what I was doing.

However, the flip side is equally important that I have also never given my company any opportunity to question my trust. Remember, the day you breach the company's trust there are no second chances. Trust is kept in the highest regard and I believe is one of the key reasons that P&G as a company has survived for over 177 years and is still as strong as it was a century ago.

> "Our distrust is very expensive."
> ~ Ralph Waldo Emerson (1803–1882),
> American Essayist, Philosopher and Poet

A. G. Lafley (P&G CEO 2000–2009) in his recent book *The Game-Changer* states: "Trust is critical in a company that must have world-class innovations and world-class execution to grow sustainably. Innovation and execution are team sports. They demand high levels of collaboration. Collaboration requires trust – trust in management, trust in one another, and trust that what is at the core of P&G's business model and company culture will remain unchanged."

So if you have a business or a company, spend some time thinking, "What is the level of trust in my company between the various stakeholders?" Trust between co-workers, between you and your customers and between management and the employees. Think of ways on how you can increase the level of trust, as the success of your business is directly proportional to the level of trust present between different players of your business. You may have a great strategy and an excellent ability to execute it, but lack of trust in the organization can torpedo the results and a high level of trust in the organization can multiply the probability of success.

Trust is a very valuable commodity and does not come cheap. The downside of trust can be very expensive. However, the sky is the upper limit of trust, so you decide. Trust also plays a critical role in your personal life. Marriages and relationships only survive if there is an immense amount of trust. I would not refrain from saying that trust is what keeps the world going round and life, as we know it, to survive and prosper.

What can we do in order to build trust? For me it is a four way process:

1. Define Trust.
2. Find Your Blind Spots.
3. Make a Commitment.
4. Create a Win/Win Attitude.

1. **Define Trust:** One must understand what trust means, what it entails and what it can deliver. Some of the key ingredients

of trust include lack of suspicions or doubts, having a strong faith and belief, maintaining a positive attitude and having high levels of confidence amongst the participants. Many people when evaluating whether they should trust someone always look at their track record and past experiences, which is a good method as the past behavior is a fair reflection of future behavior. The problem arises when we are unforgiving or inflexible, we can make the life of a person in repentance very difficult. Remember nobody is perfect. It is healthy to understand ones intentions, correct mistakes and above all to communicate.

Once you trust someone, you must trust them fully; there are no grey areas in trust. Putting faith in someone you have forgiven after proper probing will go a long way. One must approach trusting someone with true purpose and a clear mind for achieving success.

"A man without trust is a man without faith.
And a man who does not fulfill his
promises is a man without faith."
~ Hadith of Ahmed Ibn Hanbal (164–241 AH)
on the authority of Anas Ibn Malik
Muslim Scholar and Theologian

2. **Find Your Blind Spots:** We live with biases and melancholic life experiences and based on them create opinions and beliefs. If we ever get cheated or betrayed, our trust is shaken and we invariably don't recover from such incidents and keep it in our subconscious for a very long time.

    If the experience involves a subordinate, we stereotype and stop trusting other subordinates. I personally know many people whose trust was betrayed and today they are afraid to trust anyone. Such experiences create subliminal perceptions, which subconsciously persuade us to act in a certain way and create an artificial barrier to trust. As a result one ends up being suspicious and inflexible which leads to confusion in decision-making and reduced productivity.

In such a situation one needs to put on the 'Trust Glasses' to help alter the thought process and to start trusting. This will only happen if one makes a genuine personal commitment, to have faith and to communicate openly with other person or persons.

> "A man who doesn't trust himself can
> never really trust anyone else."
> ~ Cardinal De Retz (1613–1679),
> French Churchman and Agitator in the Fronde

3. **Make a Commitment:** Visit your biases and prejudices and take an honest view of things. See with fairness whether you are being impartial or are you also part of the problem. Many times our personal biases end up making a problem seem worse than it is. Such introspection with a rational and impartial mind can lead to a rude awakening that jolts us up and leads to a realization on how to become a more effective leader.

Once we experience such realization we then need to make a commitment to ourselves to clear our biases. You have to make a personal effort to walk out of the shell you have created around you to protect yourself. Next is to communicate to the concerned party in a respectful and win-win manner your intentions. Gaining trust of others require honesty, being candid and accepting your prejudices. One must try to bring this discussion to a closure if one finds willingness on the other side.

4. **Create a Win/Win Attitude:** Once the open communication has succeeded and both parties have agreed to move in the same direction, it is critical to maintain and build trust at every corner, align on next steps, allocate and share responsibilities and finally provide support and gain a new productive team member. Both parties must see a clear 'win' in this relationship; otherwise motivation to drive and deliver business strategies will not be effective.

> "Teamwork divides the task and multiplies the success."
> ~ Anonymous

In my mind values play the role of the 'soul of the company'. Trust is one of the five core values in P&G. In fact when I was first introduced to the P&G values concept at the time of my orientation, I observed that trust was placed at the very bottom and I viewed it as the foundation of all the values, as if it is supporting all other values. In reality all other values such as leadership, ownership, and passion for winning have no worth if trust is not present in an organization.

For any leader to be successful, the team must have a strong level of trust in them, in their abilities and in their leadership skills. To me trust is the glue that bonds people, processes and businesses together and ensures long-term success. Without trust, no leader will be able to motivate their teams, gain their commitment and deliver all the challenges they have to overcome during their professional lifetime.

> "To be trusted is a greater compliment than being loved."
> ~ George MacDonald (1824–1905),
> Scottish Author, Poet, and Christian Minister

17 A. Insights from Stephen M. R. Covey's book "Speed of Trust"

I have always been fascinated with the power that trust brings in making any organization successful and powerful. It was not until I read the book *Speed of Trust* written by Stephen M. R. Covey, who is the son of the renowned management expert Stephen Covey that I felt justice, has finally been done to this extremely important topic. The book published in 2006 is an eye-opener and a must-read book.

In this book Covey convincingly makes a case that trust is the one thing that changes everything and literally creates profit, success and prosperity. He defines it as a 'measureable accelerator of performance' and when the level of trust in any organization goes up, the cost of doing business goes down and the speed to market of initiatives goes up. Many CEO's, marketing authorities, management guru's, business owners and senior government officials consider this book practically a leadership Bible.

> "He who does not trust enough, Will not be trusted."
> ~ Lao Tzu (571–531 BC),
> Philosopher of Ancient China and a Central Figure in Taoism

Since the day it dawned on me that the presence of trust can deliver significantly better business results, I wanted to somehow prove it through data, numbers and facts. To have this proof in my hand was even more important when I started to talk to organizations that did not believe in the power of trust and hence did not invest in human resources or in the creation of a 'trust' culture. My entire argument was based on my experience and gut feelings that such an investment will pay itself many times over. I could not prove my argument until I came across two extremely competent and in-depth studies that proved without a shadow of doubt the real impact of trust on business performance as well as on the efficient functioning of an organization.

✓ Study 1: In a 2002 Human Capital Index (HCI) study by Watson Wyatt Worldwide[65], they proved that the total return to shareholders in high-trust organizations is almost three times higher than return in low-trust organizations. That is a difference of nearly 300 percent! Trust does not make just a trivial impact on business results; it totally re-invigorates the business fundamentals and acts as a catalyst for profit, growth and success.

Five Year Total Returns to Shahreholders (April 1996-April 2001)	
HCI Score	Financial Performance
Low-HCI companies	21% TRS
Medium-HCI companies	39% TRS
High-HCI companies	64% TRS

If you go to any country's stock exchange and run a survey to find the level of trust in the top hundred large organizations, tabulate the results and sort them by their trust scores, you will find that the top 1/3rd of the companies with the highest trust scores will have financial business results three times higher than the bottom 1/3rd companies in that survey. This study factually proved the point, which I have always believed in, that trust accelerates decision-making, and empowers people to deliver better and faster results.

✓ Study 2: Another study carried out by Anthony Bryk and Barbara Schneider[66] called "Trust in Schools: A Core Resource for Improvement" studied the concept of 'relational trust', which is made up of interpersonal social exchanges that take place in a school community, such as between principal to teacher, principal to parents, teacher to teacher and teacher to parent. It was evaluated on four criterions: respect, competence, personal regard for others and integrity.

This study again proves that schools with high trust had higher chances of improving test scores then schools with low trust. As a result, these schools were also more likely to demonstrate marked gains in student learning. In contrast, schools with weak trust relations' saw virtually no improvement in their reading or mathematics scores.

When I read such studies, although I have always been a staunch believer of what trust can do, I am still mesmerized and totally bowled over by their findings. What an incredible impact the presence of trust can have on a company's ability to deliver better results whether it is a business environment or an academic one. Trust helps deliver better results, which come, at a faster pace and at a lower cost.

There is a myth in many companies that trust is 'soft'; it is something that is nice to have but you really cannot define it, drive it or measure it. These people will be shocked to know that trust is in fact hard, it is real, and it is quantifiable and measurable. Trust affects speed and cost of an organization and both speed and cost can be measured and quantified. Tom Peters, a management guru in his own right, has very aptly said that he is quite surprised that nobody has ever written before on this very important topic. It's a must-read book.

> "Trust is like a mirror;
> Once it's broken you can never look at it the same again."
> ~ Anonymous

At the beginning of the book *Speed of Trust* there are many quotes from renowned people including CEO's, marketing authorities, media personalities, etc., which provide a very candid view of the power of trust and how they viewed this book. I would like to share some of their quotes with you:

"Trust reduces transaction costs, it reduces the need for litigation and speeds up commerce; it actually lubricates organizations and societies. At last, someone is articulating its true value and presenting it as a core business competency."

Marilyn Carlson Nelson,
Chairman and CEO, Carlson Companies

"Lack of trust within an organization saps its energy, fosters a climate of suspicion and second-guessing, completely devastates teamwork and replaces it with internal politics. The end result is low morale and consequently low standards of performance. This book is timely reminder for leaders about what really matters in an organization."

Koh Boon Hwee, Chairman DBS Bank Ltd,
former Chairman of Singapore Airlines

"After you turn off the projector, quit Power Point, and end your pitch, most deals come down to a simple question: Do you trust each other? This book is a valuable and timely explanation of how to trust and how to be trusted."

Guy Kawasaki, author of *The Art of the Start*;
Managing Director, Garage Technology Ventures

"Collaboration is the foundation of the standard of living we enjoy today. Trust is the glue. This is the first book that teaches the 'what's' and the 'how's' of trust. A must-read for leaders at all levels."

Ram Charan,
co-author of *Game-Changer* and *Execution*

"I know the importance of trust. Being roped together, when crossing an ice field riddled with crevasses is the ultimate trust scenario. In the mountains, my life is often in my teammates' hands and theirs in mine. Such commitment is based on enormous trust, like much of life. Stephen's book is packed with content on sustaining and building trust. It's a must-read."

Erik Weihenmayer is the blind mountaineer
who climbed the Everest;
author of Touch the Top of the World.

Reason to share so many of these quotes is two folds, firstly to urge you to read this book as it is highly recommended and reading it will help you to properly internalize the concept of trust, and secondly, they highlight the various ways in which trust impacts us, our businesses and the societies we live in.

Trust Glasses Concept: Covey shares an interesting experience where he once went with a guide for fly-fishing on a river in Montana. He says that when they got to the river the guide asked, "What do you see?" He told him that he saw a beautiful river with the sun reflecting off the surface of the water. The guide asked him "Do you see any fish?" Covey replied that he did not see any fish. Then the guide handed him a pair of polarized glasses and asked him to "Put them on."

Suddenly, Covey says everything looked dramatically different. He discovered that he could see through the water and he could see fish, a lot of fish! His excitement shot up and he could suddenly see a lot of possibility that he had not seen before. In reality, those fish were there all along, but until he put on the glasses they were hidden from his view.

The point Covey is making is that in a similar way, for most people, the impact of trust is in every relationship, in every organization, in every interaction, in every moment of our life. But we can only see this potential once we put on the trust glasses and see under the surface. Seeing and realizing presence of trust immediately impacts our ability to increase the effectiveness in every dimension of life. It disproportionally increases possibilities and opportunities.

So I urge you to put on your trust glasses and work towards nurturing and rewarding trust in your organization and always bear in mind that there is no loyalty without trust, and without loyalty, there is no true growth. In today's competitive world to come across and discover people who are loyal and trustworthy is worth its weight in gold. So trust your people, encourage and cherish them and trust me when I say that you will see a distinct difference in how success and great results will materialize out of nowhere if you pursue this route.

17 B. Emotional Bank Account

The notion of using 'Emotional Bank Account' as a metaphor to describe the 'amount of trust that's been built up in a relationship' is credited to Stephen Covey[67]. It is a concept I use every day and is one of the reasons behind my personal success. It is probably one of the most powerful ideas for the development of interpersonal relationships. Trust is needed for a relationship to thrive. Without trust, we may be able to accommodate and endure another person for a while but it will not be sustainable.

> "It is more shameful to distrust our friends
> than to be deceived by them."
> ~ Confucius (551–479 BC),
> Chinese Thinker and Social Philosopher

The concept of an emotional bank account is very similar to that of an actual bank account except that unlike a normal bank account where you deposit actual cash, in the emotional bank account you only deposit emotional units. These emotional units that Covey talks about are centered on trust. Anyone with whom we have a relationship, whether it be our co-workers, family or friends, we maintain a separate personal emotional bank account.

This like all accounts begins with a zero balance. And just as with any regular bank account, we can make regular deposits and withdrawals. Every time you do a positive interaction with someone or a favor or help someone, a transaction takes place. It could be as small as saying 'Hi' or smiling at the person; and you end up making a small deposit.

Whenever you deposit emotional units into someone's bank account, their connection, trust, and confidence in you grows. This in turns grows and develops your relationship and if we continue to have a credit balance by making regular deposits, there will be more tolerance for any mistakes that you may end up making.

> "People will forget what you said,
> people will forget what you did,
> but people will never forget how you made them feel."
> ~ Maya Angelou (1928–2014),
> American Poet, Author, Dancer, Actress and Singer

On the contrary if we make withdrawals, i.e. ask for help, not respond to their call for help or have an argument with them, we withdraw units from our emotional bank account with that person. And if we end up with a low or a negative balance the relationship worsens, bitterness and discord grows. If we are to keep our relationship on a positive keel, we must always be conscious of the balance in our emotional bank account and keep making deposits. Covey describes six important ways of making deposits into the emotional bank account:

1) Understanding the individual.
2) Clarifying expectations.
3) Attending to little things.
4) Showing personal integrity.
5) Keeping commitments.
6) Apologizing sincerely when you make a withdrawal.

And here are a few examples of typical withdrawals:

1) Being discourteous.
2) Disrespect.
3) Overreacting.
4) Betraying trust.
5) Not honoring commitments.
6) Threatening.

> **Vital Tip 39:** If you break your promise or you do not keep your commitment that constitutes as a major withdrawal from you emotional bank account and this action of yours could end up being very expensive in the long run. So if you make a commitment or a promise, make sure you fulfill it to the best of your abilities. Be very careful making any commitment that you may not be able to keep.

I have personally seen the power of having an emotional bank account during my career with P&G and Gillette. If you called a person with whom you have deposits, invariably they will quickly respond to your request for help, information, perspective or whatever you may be looking for. If the balance is empty, the chances are that he/she will take their time, as there is nothing compelling them to answer you urgently.

I have also noticed that those managers, who keep scores of such emotional bank accounts across departments and across regions, tend to be more effective at their jobs and deliver much better results. Some personal tips that I use to enhance my emotional bank account with other people include things like:

a) Always be the first to say good morning with a smile to all colleagues in office irrespective of how junior or senior they are.
b) Be prompt in answering any query, providing help or giving out information requested.
c) Remembering birthdays and anniversaries.
d) Respect every person in the company despite their level of seniority.
e) Sending them a card on Eid or Christmas.
f) If it has been a long time since you have interacted, just send an email saying "Hello, long time no see, hope everything is fine on your end" without any reason.
g) When they are not well, make sure you visit them or send flowers or a get-well card.
h) At lunchtime, on a workday, try to have lunch with different members of your teams.
i) Once you meet anyone you like, save his or her full name, designation, email address and cell number for future reference, this will help you when you need help.

Following the above-mentioned simple rules you will realize that even such simple gestures will take you a long way in strengthening your relationship and enhancing your deposits in people's emotional bank accounts and will make you more effective on your job.

Nothing is more damaging to your relationship then lack of integrity. Integrity is the foundation of your personal character and is the foundation on which trust is created with anyone. Trust, as you will agree, is not something you can gain as part of your character overnight; you have to work hard for it. You need to have soundness of moral character, consistency when it comes to handling ethical issues and transparency in your decision-making. Over years this slowly builds your character and reputation and in turn strengthens the foundation of your emotional bank account. Always remember that those relationships that will stand the test of time are built on the foundation of enduring trust.

> **Vital Tip 40:** Never take anyone for granted. Just because a person is not in an important or influential position, do not ignore him or be disrespectful. Always keep basic decorum of human dignity and interaction as you never know when things can change and at that point in time you will regret not having an emotional bank account with that person.

17 C. Push vs. Pull Strategy

Push-pull strategy is more often used in disciplines such as marketing, logistics and supply chain management. I find it to be a fascinating strategy and feel that it can be fittingly applied to the concept of trust. Let's first understand, what this push-pull strategy is?

In marketing it has to do with how the company attracts consumers to their product:

- ✓ Pull is when consumer demands the product and the company makes and supplies the product to meet their needs. In this case the consumer pull's the product.
- ✓ Push is when the consumer is not yet convinced and does not demand the product, but the company has strong faith in the product and pushes the product into the market, creates awareness through the media, promotion plans or discounts to the trade and makes the consumer want the product, although he has not shown any interest in it.

To me pull in the long run is better than push. Pull is linked to market demand and hence is driven by true requirements. Push on the other side is more artificial as it requires the company to create demand by pushing the product in the stores and on to the shelves. Push strategy could be good when you are introducing a new product, but for mature products and on a long-term basis, push is not a sustainable strategy.

For a true leader who is trying to implement his or her vision, the ideal way is for them to inspire the organization so that they get *pulled* towards their vision and goals. If you have to push your agenda and vision onto your teams, then the chances of success will be relatively low. This is because everyone will consider it as your vision, which is being pushed onto them for execution, and delivery and they will not have the passion that is needed to win in today's competitive environment.

However, if your team is inspired by your direction setting and are pulled towards your vision, they will work towards delivering it with full commitment and passion. One of the key characteristics of a manager who tends to inspire people and uses the pull strategy effectively in business matters is the one who has the highest level of trust built around their character within the organization.

So trust again plays a critical role and has to be nurtured and developed. Managers with high level of trust have people automatically pull towards them for advice, for counseling and guidance. The manager's trust is built over time through the visible display of their capabilities, leadership skills, hard work, empathy and unstoppable commitment towards the company's vision.

For such high trust managers, people will deliver projects with a passion that is much deeper and in many cases over and above the call of duty and clearly beyond regular performance levels.

Team members are attracted to such managers as they trust their leadership, they trust their vision, and know that they will never do anything to break their trust. I urge you to think about how you can effectively use trust as a pull strategy in your business to deliver results that are better and faster.

> Trust takes years to build,
> seconds to break,
> and forever to repair
> ~ Anonymous

●●●●●●●—■■—■■—■■—■■■●●●●●

Chapter 18 – Striving to be the Best

For any leader or an organization to deliver exceptional results on a sustainable basis, 'passion to be the best' must exist in their DNA. Always remember that once a person is willing to settle for second best, that person will never be able to win the race. Passion to be the best is something that should be ingrained over-time and hard-wired into every employee's motherboard in the first few years of their employment. You should be able to see this passion in whatever they do, especially in their eyes and in their demeanor. Goals and strategies should inspire employees to be their very best at everything they do and to stand out versus competition.

"Excellence is the gradual result of always striving to do better."
~ Pat Riley (b. 1945),
Basketball Coach

One sure-fire way to drive 'passion to be the best' behavior amongst your teams is to carry out benchmarking versus the 'Best in Class' (BIC) within your industry. The objective is to find out whether in reality we are ranked as the *best* and if not, then how much is the gap versus whoever is the best. This benchmarking allows us to see how we can raise our standards to be the best in the industry in whatever we do.

A prime example that comes to mind is when P&G Pakistan bought the soap plant at Hub, Baluchistan in 1994 and started manufacturing Camay and Safeguard soaps. In every plant team's agenda, one of the key items was always to drive cost saving so that we could price it right and win against competition. This concept of cost saving took a total new meaning when we started to benchmark vis-à-vis other P&G soap plants all over the world.

Results of the first benchmarking were eye opening, we established that on maintenance costs a South American plant was BIC and on manufacturing expenses an Asian Plant was significantly lower than us. As we had considerable gaps on both fronts, we immediately sent our managers to visit these two plants and acquire learning's to determine how we could reduce our cost in line with them.

> "No one remembers who came in second at the Olympics."
> ~ Anonymous

Our managers came back with major insights on how we could reduce our losses, optimize usage, and organize the system better in order to deliver breakthrough results via reducing cost of production. If this passion to be the best were not present in the spirit of the plant teams, then we would never have become so successful in Pakistan and overtaken the 'value' market leadership on toilet soaps in 2009. With an excellent marketing strategy based on some hard-core market research coupled with a BIC cost structure, P&G literally created the antibacterial segment in the Pakistan toilet soap market. Antibacterial segment was negligible in 1995 before the launch of Safeguard with Dettol as the only player, but today antibacterial segment has carved out a 50% share of the entire soap category with presence of all major competitors like Unilever with Lifebuoy, Treet Corporation with Bodyguard, and Reckitt Benckiser with Dettol. Due to P&G research and initiative the soap market pie has expanded profiting the soap companies and also benefited the customers significantly by giving them access to a new health focused category.

Food for Thought:

<u>Concept of Gold Standards</u>

You can achieve this passion to be the best by introducing what I call the "Gold Standards." Look around in the market and see who is the best in any discipline and call it the gold standard. As an example, when we launched our toilet soap brands in 1995, we had to see what targets to set for the distribution levels of our soap brands.

Looking at the Pakistan market we realized that Lux a Unilever brand, has been in the market for many decades and was the best distributed soap. We took their distribution level as the gold standard. We always benchmarked our progress with this gold standard and that drove a genuine dissatisfaction with our status quo, as we wanted to reduce the gap and become a gold standard ourselves.

"The secret of joy in work is contained in one word - excellence.
To know how to do something well is to enjoy it."
~ Pearl S. Buck (1892–1973),
Writer

18 A. Stretch Mentality

This is the culmination of a few topics I have discussed in this handbook. Topics like 'Good to Great,' 'Passion to be the Best', 'Make Current Job BIC,' etc. They all finally merge into the concept of 'stretch mentality' to help deliver superior results. Having stretch mentality or as some may call it 'Raising the Bar' is difficult but a surefire way of delivering monumental results versus incremental ones. 'Mission Dugna Tigna' is a case in point.

General Electric Corporation (GE) popularized the metaphor stretch mentality when they referred to their goals in their business plans as Stretch Goals[68]. Stretch is reaching for more then you thought possible. Stretch should be something you have never attempted before and in fact you do not know how you are going to deliver it. Stretch goals need to be fresh, radical, challenging and quite hard to accomplish. Some may even consider them to be impossible! Remember stretch goals do not materialize without someone there to lead the way and to bring a paradigm shift in the culture towards positive thinking and strong can-do attitude.

"Boundary less people, excited by speed
and inspired by stretch dreams,
have an absolutely infinite capacity to improve everything."
~ Jack Welch (b. 1935),
Management Expert, Author and ex-CEO General Electric

Significant change has to occur from the normal run-of-the-mill lifestyle for anyone to deliver stretch goals and this will only happen if someone is championing and leading the change passionately. If delivering average results satisfies you, or you are comfortable with the way business is being run, then stretch mentality is not the route to take. Stretch goals as a tool are very powerful as they force people to think differently; normal planning tools and leadership style will not work.

As I mentioned earlier, you will have to plan keeping the end in mind. Agree on the stretch goals and then work backwards to figure out how to deliver them. JFK's example of landing a man on the moon eight years before it happened is a classic case in point. The Americans had no clue how to do it; in fact they did not even have a space capsule or a booster rocket designed to reach the moon at that stage, but they worked backward from the deadline set by JFK and finally did it on July 20, 1969.

Life with stretch mentality is definitely going to be painful and the goal will not be delivered overnight. But if you can create a culture where people like setting stretch goals and being challenged, then you have created something that does not exist in majority of the companies today – best of luck and God speed with your stretch goals.

"First ask yourself: What is the worst that can happen?
Then prepare to accept it. Then proceed
to improve on the worst."
~ Dale Carnegie (1888–1955),
American Writer and Lecturer

Vital Tip 41: Remember there has to be a burning desire to do the impossible, else stretch mentality will not and cannot work. If you or your organizations are satisfied with your results and the past growth trend looks fine and if there is no dissatisfaction with status quo then stretch mentality is not your cup of tea.

---

18 B. Raising the Bar

How many times have you faced the following reactions when you have challenged your teams: "it can't be done," "no one has ever delivered growth at that level," "that is impossible" or "that is the maximum we have ever done."

Before I shatter the myth of these easygoing managers, let me ask you a question in return: What is an athletics world

Olympics High Jump Record Progression

1896	Ellery Clark, United States	5 ft 11.25 in
1900	Irving Baxter, United States	6 ft 2.75 in
1904	Samuel Jones, United States	5 ft 11 in
1906	Con Leahy, Ireland	5 ft 9.875 in
1908	Harry Porter, United States	6 ft 3 in
1912	Alma Richards, United States	6 ft 4 in
1920	Richmond Landon, United States	6 ft 4.25 in
1924	Harold Osborn, United States	6 ft 5.9375 in
1928	Robert W. King, United States	6 ft 4.375 in
1932	Duncan McNaughton, Canada	6 ft 5.625 in
1936	Cornelius Johnson, United States	6 ft 7.9375 in
1948	John Winter, Australia	6 ft 6 in
1952	Walter David, United States	6 ft 8.9375 in
1956	Charles Damas, United States	6 ft 11.25 in
1960	Robert Shavlakadze, USSR	7 ft 1 in
1964	Valeri Brumei, USSR	7 ft 1.75 in
1968	Dick Fosbury, United States	7 ft 4.25 in
1972	Yuri Tarmak, USSR	7 ft 3.75 in
1976	Jacek Wszola, Poland	7 ft 4.5 in
1980	Gerd Wessig, East Germany	7 ft 8.75 in
1984	Dietmar Mogenburg, West Germany	7 ft 8.5 in
1988	Guennadi Avdeenko, USSR	7 ft 0.5 in
1992	Javier Sotomayor, Cuba	7 ft 8.5 in
1996	Charles Austin, United States	7 ft 10 in
2000	Sergey Kliugin, Russia	7 ft 8.5 in
2004	Stefan Holm, Swedan	7 ft 8.91 in
2008	Andrey Silnov, Russia	7 ft 8.91 in
2012	Ivam Ukhov, Russia	7 ft 9.70 in

record? Answer: It is a record held by a single human being who is the best of the best in that field in the entire world, i.e. best among the 7,327,403,655 human beings living on earth on July 15, 2015 @ 23:09 hours.[69]

A world champion is the best of the best or simply the only person in this world who can do that feat at that peak level. Now look at the table, which tracks the Olympic records of high jump from 1896 through 2004. Twenty-four individuals have held the record over this 108-year period. What is remarkable is that the 2004 record is higher than 1896 by 1ft 9.7in; remarkable isn't it. At every stage I am sure that all the world's athletes felt that that was the best that anyone could do; but no, someone challenged it and did it better. The biggest gaps in breaking the records happened during the two World Wars, when Olympics did not take place for many years but beyond these long breaks the athletes kept on raising the bar and setting new Olympic world records every four years.

"Champions keep playing until they get it right."
~ Billie Jean King (b. 1943),
Former World Number 1 Tennis Champion

Food for Thought:

Stretch Mentality Champions

Every organization needs inspirational leaders to succeed, but to deliver outstanding results on a sustainable basis there is a dire need for leaders with a strong bias towards raising the bar and quashing myths that have conditioned organizations to justify mediocre results. One such leader I come across and had the honor of working with is Al Rajwani, Vice President and General Manager Arabian Peninsula and Pakistan (AP&P).

In early 2000 he took over the Arabian Peninsula business (six markets), which was steadily growing at a low single-digit for

---

decades. Having very strong market leadership shares across majority of categories made the local team content with this slow steady growth. Al Rajwani took over the AP&P leadership in 2003 and immediately started to question the mediocre growth rates. He completely changed the strategy from a 'Protect & Maintain Market' low single-digit growth rate to becoming a 'Growth Engine' for the region.

This required a paradigm shift in mind-sets and a complete culture change in the behavior and thinking of the teams he had taken over. He had a strong bias towards action, questioned every opportunity, urged that if we could not increase share, we should increase the size of the pie. He made it clear that maintaining status quo was not an option and coined the acronyms DD and DDD for different markets, which stood for Double-Digit (10% to 19% growth) and Double-Double-Digit (20% to 29% growth rates); nothing less was acceptable.

My Mission Dugna Tigna was inspired by this very thinking. He believed in these growth rates, walked the talk and made his expectations very clear in every discussion/meeting; his every email had his vision for growth as a footnote. He made everyone focus on driving executional excellence and drove a culture of deep diving and finding opportunities in distribution, customer/consumer insights and finding niches into the categories we did business in. Another area where Al excelled and provided invaluable and timely help to his teams was in breaking down barriers so the teams could single-mindedly focus on growth, growth and more growth.

His legacy in AP&P will always be remembered for coining and bringing to life the acronym BOF (Brutal Obsession with Fundamentals); which stood for fixing fundamentals, streamlining and simplifying all systems and processes and ingraining executional excellence into the very DNA of the organization. Today we BOF every activity and every initiative and its concept impacts every department and employee. In fact, we have had many international visitors from other P&G markets to review our in-market practices, and many have adopted this BOF concept. As a result of Al's super stretch mentality and positive attitude coupled with an amazing level of trust, we delivered some amazing results. The growth rates over the decade after Al took over the leadership of this region jumped six to eight times versus the earlier low single-digit growth rates.

The current high jump record is held by Javier Sotomayor from Cuba who cleared 2.45 m (8 ft ¼ inches) on July 27, 1993 at Salamanca in Spain, which is 3.6 inches higher than what was considered possible just a decade ago (I would not be surprised that by the time this book is published even that record is history). How and why did this happen? Because there was someone who challenged the world record and believed that he or she could do better. Someone researched and found a better technique, a better style or an improved physique.

A classic example came in 1968 when Dick Fosbury came up with a unique high jump style, which broke the 1964 Olympic record by a full two and half inches!! The style dramatically revolutionized the high jump, which popularly became known as the  'Fosbury Flop' (see picture). Dick's movement technique involved racing toward the bar in a curved approach, lifting off with his left foot, pivoting his right leg backwards and sailing over the bar backwards, stretching his back and flipping his legs upward. By 1980, thirteen of the sixteen Olympic high jump finalists were using the 'Fosbury Flop'.

Interestingly the current female outdoor high jump record was set in Rome some twenty six years ago (on August 30, 1987) by Stefka Kostadinova of Bulgaria when she cleared 2.09 m (6 foot 10 ¼ inches); it is one of the longest surviving athletics world record. Imagine it is twenty-eight years since any female from the roughly 3.5 billion odd women have been unable to challenge and break this record, but you can be sure if not today, tomorrow this record will be broken. That to me is a true testament of the fighting spirit and unrelenting passion to excel in the human race and if applied to the business environment it can and has delivered some very impressive results. Try working on raising the bar and pushing your comfort zone to set *stretch goals* for yourself as well as your teams.

> "In order to succeed, your desire for success
> should be greater than your fear of failure."
> ~ Bill Cosby (b. 1937),
> Actor, Author, Television Producer,
> Educator, Musician and Activist

Other impossible barriers broken in human history that everyone thought were impossible:

1) **4 Minute Mile**: Until English athlete Roger Bannister shattered this myth by running a mile in 3 minutes and 59.4 seconds on May 6, 1954, everyone, until that point in time in history, thought humans lacked the physical capacity to run a mile in less than 4 minute. Physiologists of that time believed that it would be dangerous to the athlete's health if anyone attempted to break this barrier.

After that, many others have broken the record and Hicham El Guerrouj of Morocco who ran the mile in 3 minutes and 43.13 seconds in Rome, Italy on July 7, 1999 holds the current record (to note, women have yet to break the four minute barrier, current world record is held by Svetlana Masterkova of Russia at 4:12.56).

2) **Breaking the Sound Barrier**: Again here the general public as well as the scientists of those times believed that breaking the sound barrier was just not physically possible and that there was this 'unseen' barrier that would destroy any plane that attempted to break it. Many believed that the sound barrier was in fact a solid invisible wall, which would not allow anything to pass through it.

This myth was shattered on October 14, 1947 when US Air Force Captain Chuck Yeager in an X-1 broke the barrier by flying at Mach 1.06 (807.2 mph). Current record is held by Lockheed SR71, which attained Mach 3. Space shuttle's module on re-entry attains speeds of over Mach 30.

> "The greater danger for most of us is not that
> our aim is too high and we miss it, but
> that it is too low and we reach it."
> ~ Michelangelo (1475–1564),
> Italian Renaissance Painter, Sculptor, Architect, and Poet

Get it into your mind that *nothing is impossible* and that anything can be achieved if you put your mind to it. What seemed impossible in a certain year was achieved a few years later. The unrelenting human spirit continues to motivate human beings to raise the bar and to set new levels of performance. Same concept is applicable in business environments as well. Nothing should be taken as impossible; one should continue to raise the bar; that is what we call the true spirit of stretch mentality. Next time you hear the comment that "This is not possible or that is not possible," show them the chart of the high jump world records (given earlier) and let them make up their own minds.

"To be the best you have to beat the best."
~ I saw it on an apron once ☺

18 C. Walk Out of Your Comfort Zone

What is a comfort zone? Comfort zone is a stage in your life where you are in a comfortable, risk-free and relaxed situation. It applies to individuals, teams and companies. When you are in the comfort zone you are doing things that you would normally do and feel comfortable with. You don't push your mind, your body, or your spirit into unknown territories. By remaining in your comfort zone nothing will change for you and slowly you will decay and would most probably be overcome with fear (of what is outside the comfort zone) and boredom (nothing new happening) overtime.

To succeed in life it is important to walk out of your comfort zone, right now! If you want to have an interesting existence, if you want to achieve something worthwhile in life or if you just want to mature up as a successful human being, you have to take some risks; and for that you have to leave your comfort zone.

"You'll always miss 100% of the shots you don't take."
~ Wayne Gretzky (b. 1961),
Legendary Canadian former Professional Ice Hockey Player

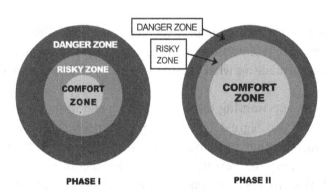

Moving out of your comfort zone is not easy! Phase I requires you to move out of your comfort zone and into the risky zone by challenging and pushing yourself (see diagram). In time you get comfortable there and learn to operate in this risky zone. After a while what was earlier your risky zone turns into your comfort zone, you are now in Phase II. You will notice that your comfort zone is now much larger you have much more opportunity and more leeway to maneuver. In Phase II, by expanding your comfort zone, your risky zone has now encroached into the earlier danger zone and the new danger zone has shrunk.

Once you have the ability of moving into the risky zone and feeling comfortable there, you have clearly overcome one of the biggest hurdles holding back your success. A larger comfort zone means a bigger area or canvas to look for business and personal growth opportunities. It will not be easy, as you will have to push yourself, you will have to do things that are different and that you have never tried before; only then will you experience adventure, create opportunities for yourself and achieve something substantial in life.

> "Anyone who has never made a mistake
> has never tried anything new."
> ~ Albert Einstein (1879–1955),
> Theoretical Physicist and father of Modern Physics

Let me share two examples from my personal life where I challenged my comfort zone and the way it changed and improved my life and made me what I am today, a happy and content person.

1. I grew up wanting to be an engineer and in its pursuit got myself two degrees, one in Systems Engineering (Automation) and the other in Computer Science Engineering from the University of Petroleum and Minerals, Dhahran, Saudi Arabia, in 1982 and 1983 respectively. The question arises, how come I have ended up as CEO of Gillette, a consumer

goods manufacturing, distribution and marketing company? This is because after completing my two degrees and working for two years as a Systems Engineer in Dhahran, I decided to walk out of my comfort zone.

At that point in time I had two options, either to continue my studies and get a Masters degree in one of the engineering disciplines (stay within my comfort zone) or to move away and get a qualification in business administration (walk out off my comfort zone). When I proceeded to the University of Michigan, Ann Arbor, USA in 1985 for my Masters in Business Administration, I had no clue what was in store for me, whether the engineering background will be helpful or whether I will enjoy this new field of study. But what I did realize was that this qualification would clearly increase the number of opportunities open to me and I went on to complete my MBA with a major in Finance.

After the MBA my life changed completely, I moved from practicing my engineering skills to a finance and accounting job in P&G based in Switzerland and the rest is history.

"If you circle your wagons to protect what you have,
you close off the path to what you desire."
~ Dr. Suzanne Zoglio (b. 1960),
Consultant and Motivational Speaker

2. A more recent example is related to my interest in humanitarian work. I have always had a very caring heart for the poor and the needy and used to help them in my own private way.

My key interests are in the area of health, education and childcare. I was also sadly aware that my private efforts were quite limited and touched only a handful of people. I wanted a force multiplier which would help me touch thousands of poverty affected people and children. I made up my mind that I had to challenge myself to take on bigger and more challenging roles and projects. Up till the middle of the 90's I had never been associated or worked with any NGO and was totally unaware of what such work entailed. I had watched from the sidelines and read the success stories of many famous NGO's in Pakistan such as Indus Hospital, TCF (The Citizens Foundation), Kidney Center, SOS Villages, etc.

One day I got a request to become a founding member of the Agha Khan Hospital Patient Welfare Committee known as 'The Annual Giving Committee', I immediately accepted the offer. I was suddenly thrown into the middle of a large scale fund raising program, met many philanthropic professionals and got involved in helping and organizing scores of large scale functions and was instrumental in collecting millions for the Agha Khan Hospital Patient Welfare Program.

 This experience opened my eyes and I wanted to do more and touch many more lives. One day I met Dr. Mobina Agboatwalla who is the founder and patron of HOPE (Health Oriented Preventive Education). I found to my surprise that although she was running a great program, her fund collection was mainly from word of mouth; she did not have a fund collection committee. I proceeded to partner with Dr. Mobina and took total ownership of founding and leading its collection committee, which we call Helper's of Hope (HOH).

Today, HOPE operates over two hundred informal schools, two formal schools and five full-fledged hospitals 24/7 as well as many vocational and maternity health centers. During natural disasters such as earthquakes and floods, HOPE is one of the first NGO's to show up in the affected areas with medical camps and flood relief assistance.

"Life loses its meaning when we get stuck up in comfort zone."
~ M.K. Soni
Academician and Researcher

In late 2009 these earlier experiences of helping the needy drove me to request the US government to donate Rs 1

The American Business Council of Pakistan

billion for the Karachi Bolton Market tragedy in which traders and wholesalers faced a tragic fate when nearly 3,000 of their shops and their life's earnings went up in smoke in a night of rioting and fire. Being an Executive Board member of the American Business Council (ABC) I was attending a previously arranged meeting with the USAID director Robert Wilson just two days after this incident. In this meeting I brought up, what I called, a 'crazy idea'. Full credit to the US government who immediately accepted this idea and within a week the US Ambassador Anne Peterson was in Karachi announcing the donation.

As it was my idea to request the funds, the then ABC President, and CEO of Citibank Arif Usmani, requested that I lead the project. I led the complex job of verification and disbursement of the fund, which included direct cash subsidy plus a structured financing via a consortium of banks to help them with working capital. It was an extremely difficult task, as we had to separate genuine from opportunistic claims. We held town-hall meetings, hired an organization to carry out due diligence, visited claimants homes, etc. These efforts significantly helped the people affected by the tragedy and also created much needed goodwill for the US amid the general business population of Karachi. Today such kind of work, where I get to touch people lives, brings me immense internal satisfaction and I am glad I challenged my comfort zone.

Today I am on the board of directors or in an advisory position of a dozen NGO's in diverse areas such as:

1) Health Care (HOPE, Agha Khan Hospital, Jinnah Hospital),
2) Education (HOPE, Teach for Pakistan, Possibilities Schools),
3) Vocational Training (Peace for Prosperity),
4) Street Kids (LettuceBee Kids),
5) Women Empowerment (Ladiesfund),
6) Mental Health (Karavan-e-Hayat),
7) Youth Leadership (AIESEC),
8) People with Disabilities (Family Education Services Foundation (FESF), Network of Organizations Working for People with Disabilities (NOWPDP), Estanara),
9) Solar Energy for villages with no electricity (EcoEnergy),
10) Energy Conservation (Knowledge Energy)
11) Micro Health Insurance (Naya Jeevan)
12) The Corporate Advisory Council (COC) @ National University of Science & Technology (NUST).
13) Society for Human Resource Management (SHRM)
14) Victims Assistance Program (VAP).

I am also the co-founder of Pakistan Innovation Foundation (to create an ecosystem for innovation), Network of Entrepreneurs Working Group (to create ecosystem for entrepreneurs) and Alamut Consultants (to drive governance and sustainability in social enterprises). I am also the President of Public Interest Law Association of Pakistan (PILAP), Chairman of South East Asia Leadership Academy (SEALA), Chairman of the Karachi Street Vendor Association and founding consortium member of I AM KARACHI. All this would not be possible if I had not challenged my comfort zone and pursued my inner passion to help others in the mid 90's.

"A man who limits his interests, limits his life."
~ Vincent Price (1911–1993),
Actor, famous for his roles in horror movies

Comfort zones can be shattered in two ways: a) self motivated or b) encouraged by someone you respect or admire. If you consider yourself to be an inspirational leader then you must help others move out of their comfort zones. Much of this grooming happens when you are a child and in my case the credit surely goes to my late father Air

Commodore (R) M. Amanullah Khan (see picture), a fighter pilot in the Pakistan Air Force who was such a protagonist in my life.

In everything I did as a child, whether it was learning sports, eating an exotic fruit, or preparing for a challenge or debate, my father made me step out of my comfort zone multiple times. When I felt scared or nervous his favorite quote was "If I had not challenged your comfort zone, you would still be drinking milk." With this spirit my father made me and my siblings learn swimming, skating, biking, roller skating, aero modeling, and various other sports and hobbies. Something I fondly remember is the number of exotic fruits (especially different types of mangoes) he would buy for us and invariably say that unless you try them you will never know what they taste like.

The point I am trying to make here is that if I had not moved out of my comfort zone and challenged myself to go into an unknown area where I lacked expertise and experience; I would never have become a CEO or gotten involved in philanthropic activities at such a grand scale. My MBA opened my eyes to management studies including finance, marketing and HR, while from my Agha Khan and HOPE experience I get huge personal satisfaction and I get to touch the lives and hearts of thousands of poor and needy people. All this continues to give me an opportunity to meet my inner desire to spread much needed education and health care among the poverty stricken population of my country as well as positively impact innovation and entrepreneurship ecosystem.

To move out of your comfort zone you will have to do things differently, things that may scare you initially, things that may have a certain risk factor built into them but the key is not to be afraid and to continue to push the boundaries. Go with your heart and do things that give you inner satisfaction, whether they are a business ventures, an adventure or a charitable endeavor. Over time by testing the limits of your comfort zone you will become comfortable in taking calculated risks, you will learn new skills and gain knowledge on what is possible. You will be surprised to know that many of the people, who are reading this right now, are stuck in some sort of a comfort zone from which they have not yet escaped. Each one is in one way or another shying away from following a passion, which to them sounds and feels too risky.

To be able to realize that you can improve your chances of success and inner satisfaction by accepting and challenging your comfort zone, you should start by taking your first baby steps out it, today. To start, you can begin by doing things differently such as driving to office using a different route every day, picking up a new hobby, going to a restaurant you have never visited before, meeting new people, visiting the local jail and helping out, learning a foreign language, reading a new foreign author, start cooking, going on a blind date, going fishing or learning how to fly a kite; start by challenging your comfort zone in small ways.

I think you get the idea; you must try to get out of your current normal daily routine. This may look risky but doing it will help you to explore and expand your comfort zone. By starting with these you will then graduate to bigger and more risky activities at work; such as, start a new business, take a dicey initiative at work, get involved in charity work, implement stretch mentality to your latest project, or drive a culture change in the organization. Moving out of your comfort zone is not easy and will require a lot of efforts and determination on your part but nothing happens until you start.

"A scholar who cherishes the love of comfort
is not fit to be deemed a scholar."
~ Lao-Tzu (571–531 BC),
Philosopher and Poet of Ancient China

If you look around, you will see many examples of individuals and companies taking a risk with their businesses and testing new ideas. To motivate you, let me share a few examples in which you will be surprised to see the paths many took to reach where they are today. Do note that without getting out of their comfort zone these companies would never have been able to achieve the current global leadership status that they enjoy today. Let me take you through a short historic journey of three such companies namely Nokia, The Virgin Group and IBM:

"If you put yourself in a position where
you have to stretch outside your comfort zone,
then you are forced to expand your consciousness."
~ Les Brown (b. 1945),
Motivational Speaker and Author

1. Nokia a company that was acquired in 2014 by Microsoft had a very interesting history. Nokia started its operation in 1865 and took the name of the town, Nokia (Finland), which originated from the river Nokianvirta that flows through the town. Nokia is a classic case of walking in and out of many comfort zones by trying a variety of diverse businesses, creating and divesting them over time. Finally they settled on the communication field and today are one of the world's leading providers of mobile phones and are admired as leaders in innovation. A short history of their diverse interests are:

   a. In 1865 Nokia was founded as a small Finnish wood pulp manufacturing company.

b. In 1898 it started manufacturing galoshes (rubber overshoes) and other rubber products.
c. In 1902 it added electricity generation to its portfolio, including generators.
d. In 1912 it added production of telephone, telegraph and electrical cables.
e. In 1960 it entered the electronic business sowing seeds of Nokia future into the current successful telecommunications business.
f. In 1988 it divested rubber products such as car and bicycle tires business.
g. In 1990 it divested the rubber footwear business.
h. In 1990's it divested its consumer electronics businesses.

> "'If you remain in your comfort zone
> you will not go any further."
> ~ Catherine Pulsifer,
> Inspirational Writer

2. Virgin Group is a branded venture capital organization, which was founded by British business tycoon Richard Branson in the 70's. Today it is worth over £5 billion and consists of over 400 companies around the world – Yes! 400 businesses in a very diverse range of sixteen different product categories (see box below).

> *Beverages, Airlines, Games, Consumer Electronics, Financial Services, Films, Internet, Cable TV, Music, Radio, Books, Cosmetics, Jewelry, Houseware, Retail and Mobile Phones.*

Virgin originally started as a music record label, which helped fuel, a lot of their diversifications and experiments and which was later spun off and sold. It's hard to imagine the number of times Branson has challenged his comfort zone. Richard Branson has led countless high-risk ventures and is known to many as a true entrepreneur and a true risk taker. Many experiments have failed but they have established a foundation of many solid businesses.

Branson is a risk taker in his personal life as well where he made several world record-breaking attempts including the 1986 fastest Atlantic Ocean crossing with the "Virgin Atlantic Challenger II" or the 1987 hot air balloon "Virgin Atlantic Flyer" in which he crossed the Atlantic. In 1991, Branson crossed the Pacific from Japan to Arctic Canada in a balloon. Between 1995 and 1998 he made many unsuccessful attempts to circumnavigate the globe by balloon. In 2004 he set a record for the fastest crossing of the English Channel in an amphibious vehicle. Branson is a true inspiration to the entire concept of walking out of your comfort zone.

"Take chances, make mistakes. That's how you grow.
Pain nourishes your courage. You have to fail
in order to practice being brave."
~ Mary Tyler Moore (b. 1936);
Actress in Sitcoms e.g. Mary Tyler Moor Show (1970-77)

3. IBM was founded in 1896 as a tabulating machine company in New York, USA and was listed on the New York Stock Exchange in 1916. In the new age with evolution of companies such as Microsoft, Apples, Dell, etc., IBM had to rethink and review its overall strategy. Lou Gerstner was brought in as CEO to halt the slide as the giant corporation lumbered towards irrelevance and oblivion. He took many deliberate and highly symbolic steps to change the company's culture and to move it out of its comfort zone.

One key change that was initiated was to turn it away from dependence on computer products and to become a leader in computer services. Today even P&G has outsourced many of its functions globally to IBM such as salary processing, portion of employee services, etc. IBM closed 2014 at $92.8 billion Revenues, $12.0 billion Net Income and spending on R&D of over $ 5.5 billion.

"Every time we've moved ahead in IBM,
it was because someone was willing to take a chance,
put his head on the block, and try something new."
~ Thomas J Watson (1874–1956),
American Entrepreneur and former CEO and Chairman of IBM

From these examples you can well imagine how these companies, moved out of their comfort zone in order to test out new ideas and opportunities. If not for the risk taking spirit of these companies and their management they may not even exist today. If not for the fact that they tested new ideas and actively stepped out of their comfort zones, they would not have been this successful and would not have found their core competencies and the businesses they are so successful in today.

It is interesting to note that many of these risk taking overtures were not successful and many of these were divested as they were in areas that were not their core competencies, e.g. for Nokia wood pulp manufacturing, rubber products, footwear; Virgin Groups venture into the music business. In my case after working for nearly 3 decades with P&G and Gillette and taking early retirement, I have 3 new start-ups namely, Big Thick Burgerz, Alamut Consulting and Vanguard Matrix, plus continuing with my extensive social and foundation work; I am having a time of my life and sleeping with a smile of my face. So I urge you to become aware of your comfort zone, challenge it, move out and you will be surprised to see the myriad of opportunities waiting for you to capture and exploit. Good luck and God speed.

"I learned that courage was not the absence
of fear, but the triumph over it.
The brave man is not he who does not feel
afraid, but he who conquers that fear."
~ Nelson Mandela (1918–2013),
Anti-apartheid Activist and Former President of South Africa

Just like companies where their leaders have taken risks, led their companies into uncharted territories and made them successful, many famous individuals have done the same. I will share with you a few examples where you will be dumbfounded if you notice their initial profession or line of work and what they were able to achieve by challenging their comfort zone.

"If we do not change our direction, we are
likely to end up where we are headed."
~ Chinese Proverb

Here is a list of 10 such incredible individuals:

Name	What were they?	What did they become?
Albert Einstein	Ordinary Patent Clerk	World Famous Scientist
Abraham Lincoln	Poor Farmer's Son	President of America
Franklin D, Rossevelt	Sick and Both Legs Paralyzed	President of America
Homer	Blind	Great Greek Writer
Golda Meir	School Teacher	Prime Minster of Israel
Helen Keller	Blind, Deaf and Mute	Renowned Writer
Demosthenes	Nervous Stammerer	Well Knowned Music Composer
Beethoven	Deaf	Renowned Music Composer
Thomas Edison	Matriculate	Greatest Inventor
M.S.Oberoi	Low Paid Billiing Clerk	Biggest Hotel Chain Owner

All information here is from Wikipedia, the free encyclopedia

"In bullfighting there is a term called querencia.
The querencia is the spot in the ring to which the bull returns.
"Each bull has a different querencia,
but as the bullfight continues, and the
animal becomes more threatened,

it returns more and more often to his spot.
As he returns to his querencia, he becomes more predictable.
And so, in the end, the matador is able to kill the bull
because instead of trying something new, the bull
returns to what is familiar - his comfort zone."
~ Carly Fiorina (b. 1954),
CEO of Hewlett-Packard Co (1999–2005)

I am not sure if you are, but I am totally convinced, that whatever the circumstances may be, no matter what the odds are, but if any person puts his mind and spirit to achieving something, then the only barrier between them and their dream is no one else but themselves.

18 D. Out-of-Box Thinking

The phrase 'Out-of-Box Thinking' is referred to as thinking creatively, for finding unconventional solutions to a problem, for coming up with new perspectives or new solutions to an old problem. It connotes creative or smart thinking. We humans have an intrinsic ability to make life more difficult than it is. We place boundaries or constraints around us that do not exist and can turn a simple problem into a crisis all by ourselves, if we are not careful.

The most classic example of humans creating self-imposed constraint is in the Quran in Chapter 2, Verses 67-71 where when calamity befell the Children of Israel, they fled the land of the merciless Egyptian Pharaoh. To a problem they faced on their way God suggested a solution and requested them to sacrifice a heifer (baby cow), on which the following dialogues took place:

> 67. And remember Moses said to his people: "(Allah) commands that ye sacrifice a heifer." They said: "Makest thou a laughing-stock of us?" He said: "(Allah) save me from being an ignorant (fool)!"

68. They said: "Beseech on our behalf Thy Lord to make plain to us what (heifer) it is!" He said; "He says: The heifer should be neither too old nor too young, but of middling age. Now do what ye are commanded!"

69. They said: "Beseech on our behalf Thy Lord to make plain to us her color." He said: "He says: A fawn-colored heifer, pure and rich in tone, the admiration of beholders!"

70. They said: "Beseech on our behalf Thy Lord to make plain to us what she is: To us are all heifers alike: We wish indeed for guidance, if Allah wills."

71. He said: "He says: A heifer not trained to till the soil or water the fields; sound and without blemish." They said: "Now hast thou brought the truth." Then they offered her in sacrifice, but not with good-will.

For a problem as simple as sacrificing a common heifer, they in their discussion with God continued to create constraints and restrictions until they were left with a near impossible option, i.e. to find a heifer which was neither young nor old, was fawn in color and which had never tilled or watered the fields.

The point is that due to our curiosity and human temperament, we make life difficult for ourselves by creating self-imposed constraints, turning a simple problem into something near to impossible.

The origin of this phrase thinking out-of-the box stems from a '9-dot Puzzle', which is designed so that the only solution is to 'think out-of-the-box'. The objective of the puzzle is to link up all the nine dots (laid out in a matrix of 3 x 3) by drawing maximum of only four straight continuous lines or less, without ever lifting the pencil from the paper. Try it!

The solution is extremely frustrating and difficult for those who live in a world of limitations and draw boundaries around themselves. The recommended solution is given at the end of Chapter 19. If you see the solution you will notice that the puzzle can be solved easily only if you are willing to draw the straight lines beyond the confines of the imaginary square area defined by the nine dots (which looks like a box); hence the phrase thinking outside-the-box.

"To me some of the most amazing people are
the ones who don't fit into boxes."
Anonymous

Many of you created an imaginary square boundary around the 9-dots, no such boundary was mentioned or stated in the preamble of the puzzle but you did it anyways. You made the puzzle much more difficult than it really was by creating self-defined constraints. Similarly in our daily life, in our business environment we do exactly the same, we create artificial boundaries which are not there and their presence makes our life, our ability to find solutions very difficult and sometime frustrating. So start to think out-of-the box and fight your inherent bias to create artificial boundaries around the problems we face.

"Innovation distinguishes between a leader and a follower."
~ Steve Jobs (1955–2011),
American Entrepreneur and Founder of Apple

Interestingly if you claim to be very creative then I challenge you to use your imagination and come up with more than the one stand-alone solution to this '9-dot Puzzle'. For this you will have to think unconventionally and use your imagination. To give you the confidence that there are potentially more solutions out there, I will share with you two possible solutions, first solution is where you solve this challenge with just one line and the second with three lines.

1. If you had a pencil whose face is like a paint brush, which is six inches wide, all you had to do is go over all the nine dots in one straight line or a single stroke. Unusual idea but it does meet the objective of the puzzle.

2. Draw one line through the top three dots and draw it to infinity, then from infinity you come back and take it through the second row of three dots to infinity again. When two lines are drawn to infinity, such a minor variation or angle is not noticeable; the two lines are nearly parallel. Next draw the line back to the puzzle from infinity and draw it through the third row of three dots. This way you have drawn three lines in parallel from infinity to infinity going through all the nine dots without picking up your pencil. Crazy but creative.

As you can see if one is willing to be unconventional and think out-of-the-box, a person can come up with many different solutions to a problem that a few minutes ago sounded quite impossible. The same is true for any problem you may face in your personal or professional life.

This concept of out-of-box thinking is used actively in the business environment and by management consultants when teaching executives to come up with novel approaches to a business problem. It is also used to drive brainstorming sessions to help come up with a variety of ideas to solve difficult problems.

"Problems cannot be solved by the same
level of thinking that created them."
~ Albert Einstein (1879–1955),
Theoretical Physicist and father of Modern Physics

How To Carry Out a Creative Brainstorming Session: In order to get the juices flowing for a session where the end result is to come up with an out-of-box or creative solution to a problem, you need to start by telling everyone to think openly, tell them not to think with constraints or boundaries, inform them that all ideas are good and during the session no one's idea is bad, stupid or crazy. To start the process you can take the marker in your hand and ask the people "How many uses can we think for this marker?" Initially people will be living in their internal paradigms and will use conventional thinking. Someone will say 'to write', which is the most obvious. Another may say 'use as a ruler' or 'use it as a back-scratcher, 'clean your ears', 'use as an arrow', 'to stir your coffee', etc. Keep writing all ideas on a flip chart.

What is happening here is that people are starting with conventional thinking but after being challenged to come up with new ideas move onto non-conventional thinking, crazy thoughts, and automatically start to think out-of-the-box. Once you see the group getting excited, wild ideas flowing freely, you ask them a new question which is a real life business problem bothering your company or department.

A Real Life Example: Let me share with you a real life example where I used out-of-box thinking to solve a real life business problem. This was when I took over Gillette and we needed to come up with a powerful product display idea for the High Frequency Stores (HFS), which constitutes small and medium sized grocery shops. Gillette products such as razors, blades, tooth brushes, batteries, etc. were to be found in different places in the shop, on different display stands, inside shelves or drawers and some even inside boxes until some customer asked for them.

The challenge Gillette faced was that its products, except for shaving foams and aftershaves, all needed to be suspended for better viewing unlike the products of our sister company P&G where all their product can be placed on shelves such as shampoos, detergents, soaps, and diapers. I placed the following question to my team, "Can you think of a different and more effective way to display Gillette products so that when a consumer walks into an HFS, he immediately sees our product?"

As the question was asked just following the crazy brainstorming session to find various uses for a marker, people immediately started to suggest new and crazy ideas. Some said "hang them from the roof', 'hang them from a string at the entrance" etc.

> "No great thing is created suddenly."
> ~ Epictetus (55–135 AD),
> Greek Philosopher Associated with the Stoics

Finally someone suggested that we remove the shelves from the wall behind the area where the shopkeeper stands in an HFS and replace it with hooks or protruding metal supports to hang our products. Eureka! We had stumbled upon a novel and creative solution. We improved on this idea, which finally came to be known as the 'Gillette Hot Spot'. A metal board was hung behind the counter right where the shopkeeper stood. When a consumer entered, he would walk to the shopkeeper to ask for his items or before leaving to pay for them and would immediately see the Gillette products hanging elegantly behind the shopkeeper.

This was the first of its kind solution of HFS stores in the Gillette world. We implemented it in 5,000 stores in just under six months with over 90% being placed right behind the counter were the shopkeeper stood. A very difficult task but well executed by the Gillette sales force; our sales in the first six-months went up by 30% in the stores with Hotspots. This was followed a year later by the second generation of Gillette Hotspots. The idea was so novel that our Vice Chairman of Global Operations Werner Geissler based in Cincinnati overlooking all countries requested the Hotspot idea to be implemented in HFS outlets across the globe!

Such is the power of brainstorming and thinking out-of-the-box; Juxtaposition of these two is a surefire approach which can help deal with finding solutions to difficult challenges and aid in changing reality for the better.

<blockquote>
"It is the mark of an educated mind
to be able to entertain a thought without accepting it."
~ Aristotle (384–322 BC),
Greek Philosopher, Student of Plato
</blockquote>

•••••-----— —-----•••••

Chapter 19 – Experience Rules

"Experience is not what happens to you;
It is what you do with what happens to you."
~ Aldous Leonard Huxley (1894–1963),
English Writer

Experience is one of the most valuable lessons that anyone can ever gain in one's life. Experience is built over time and is the process of personally observing, encountering and undergoing things that generally occur in the course of one's lifetime. You must have heard the expression 'put it down to experience' which means to capture a certain impression or insight so that if anything like that ever happens to you in the future, you have a base line to compare it with and it would help you make a better decision, on how to react.

Why don't humans like to touch fire? It is because once in their lifetime as a baby or as a young kid, driven by curiosity they got burned as they tried to touch or catch a burning flame. However, that will be the first and last time they will ever do such an act. This information gets stored in that person's brain as experience. Like a famous saying goes that a wise person learns by the experience of others, an ordinary person learns by his or her own experience while a fool learns by nobody's experience.

It is important not to let an experience go to waste and not to repeat ones mistake. Based on our life experiences we gain knowledge and wisdom, which we utilize to make balanced, calculated and mature decisions. In totality such experiences build into what we call intuition in a person's mind, heart and guts. The faculty of knowing or sensing without the use of rational process to make decisions is called intuition. Leaders' who have this enhanced ability of perception, insight or an ability of immediately recognizing the situation are a notch above conventional leaders.

"If we could sell our experiences for what
they cost us, we'd all be millionaires."
~ Pauline Phillips (1918-2013),
Advice Columnist Better Known as Dear Abby

Helen Keller once observed: "Character cannot be developed in ease and quiet. Only through experience of trial and suffering can the soul be strengthened, vision cleared, ambition inspired, and success achieved." So never take it lightly when someone says "I didn't get these white hair for nothing."

In certain situations experience can be worth its weight in gold; it is an extremely valuable asset. Experience can vary based on opportunities and circumstances in one's life. The first time you enter a business venture, you are bound to make mistakes, lose money, lose confidence or get de-motivated. However, what one must remember is that there is no alternative to learning from experience as one internalizes such experiences and the next time when you encounter a similar situation you will or you should not make the same mistake again.

Oscar Wilde explains this very aptly when he says, "Experience is simply the name we give our mistakes." Business acumen or business intuition is gained through experience. When you read about famous business leaders such as Warren Buffett or Jack Welch, you can be assured that they have had their share of mistakes during their lifetime as they gained the much needed experience and built their intuition which they, unlike many others, promptly applied in future situations and which helped them turn into great business leaders.

19 A. Habit

"Chains of habit are too light to be felt until
they are too heavy to be broken."
~ Warren Buffett (b. 1930),
American Investor, Businessman, and Philanthropist

Habit is an acquired pattern of behavior that often occurs automatically and subconsciously. Habits usually take place without directly thinking consciously of the act and it happens unnoticed by the person doing it. How are habits formed? If a person repeats a certain action with a specific reason or context, the chances of it happening naturally without actively thinking of the act increases. This incremental increase in the link between the context and the action is generally known as habit.

There are good habits as well as bad habits. It is important that one focuses on ones action so that we do not end up with bad habits, as they will start to happen unintentionally or without active control if not handled properly. Habits reside somewhere in a person's brain and when the situation demands, they act without thinking. Classic examples of habits are putting on your safety belt as soon as you get into the driving seat, brushing your teeth before going to bed, grabbing your wallet before leaving home, putting on your glasses when you get up, etc.

Food for Thought:

<u>Chains and Pegs – What is holding you back?</u>

Have you ever noticed why at a circus a giant five-ton elephant is tied up to a chain and a wooden peg in the earth and is not trying to break free? Why would this powerful creature that can uproot a tree as easily as we can pluck a rose will not make any effort to break away and remains tied to a small peg and a flimsy chain.

The reason is that since the time the elephant was a baby, the trainers used to chain it with the same flimsy chain and a peg. At that age the metal chain and peg were strong enough to hold back the baby elephant. If the baby tired to pull away, the chain tied to the leg would cut into the skin and make it bleed. This would hurt the baby and slowly over time the baby decided that it was futile to try to escape. So the baby stopped trying to escape.

Now when the elephant has grown up and is ten foot tall, it still remembers the pain it felt when it was a baby and never tries to break away although the chain and peg are not strong enough to hold him back. Similarly our self-limiting experiences or beliefs hold us back. Some failures in our childhood or teenage years act as chains and pegs and stop us from achieving our goals or even dreaming of bigger things. You must ask yourself "What is holding you back?"

Poor habits are those that have a negative behavior pattern such as nail biting, procrastination, picking your nose, smoking, sleeping late, etc. Even such softer intangible skills such as honesty, caring, and affection come through practice and become habits. It is important to note that all of these habits which we learn over time, later in life will happen without us even thinking twice about them. That is why it is so important to impart good habits to our children so that they grow up to be good human beings with good habits.

The difference between a habit and an addiction is that while a habit is a routine of behavior that is repeated regularly and tends to occur unconsciously, an addiction is when you do not have control over a negative behavior, like smoking or drinking. The difference is the capacity of having willpower over your actions. So try to build proper and positive habits, as they will help you to be more effective in your life and business.

In a business environment try to build the following habits:

- ✓ Seek to be the best in everything you do.
- ✓ Know yourself and your business inside and out.
- ✓ Always consider your client to be the ultimate boss.
- ✓ Be flexible and willingly embrace change.
- ✓ Display modesty and honesty in everything you do.
- ✓ Maintain good work life balance.
- ✓ Uphold positive thinking under all circumstances.
- ✓ Create and cultivate a strong network via emotional bank accounts.
- ✓ Grab opportunity especially in adversity.
- ✓ Believe in a mentality of continuous improvement.

"Habits are at first cobwebs, then cables."
~ Spanish Proverb

Here I would like to encourage all of you to read Stephen R. Covey's number one bestseller *The Seven Habits of Highly Effective People* that was first published in 1989 and has since sold over fifteen million copies in thirty-eight languages. Covey has very successfully presented a framework for personal effectiveness and argued that it is achieved by aligning oneself to what he calls 'The True North' principles of character ethics.

He believes these principles to be universal and timeless. Traits of character ethics are virtues like integrity, justice, courage, etc. Superimposed on the foundation of character ethics are personality ethics that help more in the short run to help solve specific problems. Personality ethics traits include things like skills, techniques, knowledge, positive thinking, etc. Covey while researching for his doctorate in the 1970's reviewed over two hundred years of literature on success and noticed that long term success was much deeper rooted and was based on the foundation of character.

Covey concluded that character ethics are primary traits for success while personality ethics are secondary. Secondary traits help us play the game and to succeed in specific situations and circumstances, but for long-term success, both are necessary.[74]

"Sow a thought, reap an act; sow an act, reap a habit; sow a habit, reap a character; sow a character, reap a destiny."
~ Anonymous

One's character is what is most visible in long-term relationships. Ralf Waldo Emerson once said, "What you are, shouts so loudly in my ears I cannot hear you say." The problem of relying too much on personality ethics may be ineffective if the basic underlying paradigms are not right; simply changing outward behavior is not the solution. It is a known fact that two people may see the same picture or the same situation with divergently different perspectives mainly as a result of past conditioning. For example if two people are sitting across from each other with the princess photo in the middle (*see picture*), one will see a princess and the other an old woman. The perspective changes everything.

Hence it is important that we base success on basic paradigms and not on how we perceive things. Character ethics are more like principles while personality ethics are like practices; practices are for specific situation whereas principles have universal applications. His book presents a unique approach on how to first change ourselves or on how to know your 'true north' where the discussion is all centered on principles and character of individuals. This approach provides a paradigm shift away from personality ethics and towards character ethics.

"Excellence is not an act but a habit.
The things you do the most are the things you will do the best."
~ Marva Collins (b. 1936),
American Educator

As Covey states, our character is a collection of habits and these habits have a very powerful impact and a role to play in our lives. Habits consist of three basic factors namely knowledge, skills and desires. Knowledge allows us to know what to do, skill gives us the ability to know how to do it, and desire is the motivation to do it. The book takes you through three stages,[70]

1. **Dependence:** the paradigm under which we are born, relying on others to take care of us.
2. **Independence:** the paradigm under which we can make our own decisions and take care of ourselves.
3. **Interdependence:** the paradigm under which we cooperate to achieve something that cannot be achieved independently.

The flow of this book has been designed in such a way that it takes you through the three stages to help you form useful habits. Today too much emphasis is placed on independence as can be seen with the obsession with liberation causes, freedom, etc. What people fail to see is that in reality we are interdependent and without effective collaboration, teamwork and cooperation we can achieve nothing.

However, in order to achieve true interdependence, one must first become independent from within, since dependent people have not yet developed the characteristics needed for interdependence. Hence, the first three habits focus on self-mastery that is what is required to move from dependence to independence. The first three habits are:

- **Habit 1:** Be Proactive: Principles of personal choice.
- **Habit 2:** Begin with the End in Mind: Principles of personal vision.
- **Habit 3:** Put First Things First: Principles of integrity and execution.

Habits four through six help addresses the transition from independence to interdependence:

- **Habit 4:** Think Win/Win: Principles of mutual benefit.
- **Habit 5:** Seek First to Understand, Then to be Understood: Principles of mutual understanding.
- **Habit 6:** Synergize: Principles of creative cooperation.

The final and **seventh habit** is all about renewal and continual improvement, i.e. of building one's personal production capability. According to Covey to be effective one must find the proper balance between actual production and in improving one's capability to produce.

- **Habit 7:** Sharpen the Saw: Principles of balanced self-renewal of body.

Covey illustrates this last habit with a famous Aesop's fable called the "The Goose that laid the golden eggs," The story goes as follows:

The Goose That Laid the Golden Eggs

A man and his wife had the good fortune to possess a goose, which laid a golden egg every day. Lucky though they were, they soon began to think that they were not getting rich fast enough, and imagining the bird must be made of solid gold inside, they decided to kill it. They thought that they would obtain a huge store of precious gold instantly; however, upon cutting the goose open, they found its innards to be like that of any other goose.

There are two lessons in this; a) One must not be greedy and thank God for what he has given us; b) One must have a balanced approach and patience when reviewing potential to increase capacity of anything, may it be abilities, capabilities, wealth, production capacity, etc. Nothing happens overnight and by pushing the limits one would invariably lose in the long run.

Let me share an example from the business world to emphasize the importance of keeping a balanced approach between actual production and production capacity. Let us assume that there is a soap plant SOAPY and it manufactures two soap brand and it is imperative that they produce it to meet market demand, and at the same time make sure that maintenance programs are active, in place and are being given due importance. Maintenance requires downtime, which hurts production capacity but is necessary for the long-term sustenance of the machinery.

Let's say that due to some successful promotion there is a sudden increase in market demand, the volume forecast suddenly goes sky high. While reviewing shipment plans the plant manager realizes that the current production capacity is not enough to meet the increased demand. In order to impress his management the manager stops carrying out scheduled maintenance work and utilizes the time saved to produce even more soap.

Management is impressed and rewards him with a promotion and improved performance ratings. However, what management is not aware of what the plant manager has done, i.e. compromised the long-term operational efficiency of the plant to deliver extra volume. Lack of maintenance will eventually catch up resulting in machinery breakdown and consequently longer downtimes in production.

Unfortunately the person who inherits this plant will get blamed when the machines break down and the plant is unable to meet the market demand. Hence it is important to find the right balance between actual production and production capacity. Covey's final and seventh chapter is focused on creating this very habit.

> "The best way to break a bad habit is to drop it."
> ~ Leo Aikman (1908–1978),
> American Columnist, Humorist and Speaker

19 B. Instincts

As talked about in the previous section, habits are formed through practice and repetition. Without practice we would be unable to learn to walk, ride a bike or drive a car or even learn to type. Instincts on the other hand are behavioral patterns that come about due to two reasons a) we do not have to learn them but they occur in finished form and are triggered whenever the need arises; b) they are built through experience and through constant practice. Instincts of the first kind occur both in humans and animals; biting your nails, a baby sucking its thumb, a cat falling and landing on its feet with no motherly training, etc.

Instincts of the second kind get built over time. As you get older many of your behaviors and experiences through constant practice, will start happening on autopilot; you do not have to scratch your head, actions happen automatically. Examples includes a pilot flying a plane, riding a bicycle, rollerblading, skiing, driving a car, staying away from dark alleys and especially in sports like a great batsmen using instincts while batting.

"Instinct is untaught ability."
~ Alexander Bain (1810–1877),
Scottish Inventor and Engineer

A classic example of instincts, which has mesmerized me since I saw it seventeen years ago, was at the Sandspit beach on the Arabian Sea coast. Pakistan's coast, especially the sandy beaches of Hawkesbay and Sandspit near Karachi are among the eleven most unique beaches around the globe where marine turtles come to lay their eggs every five years.[71] Anywhere between September and December turtles come to the beach and lays between 100 and 150 eggs in a pit, after which she covers the pit and pulls herself to the sea, leaving the eggs at the mercy of many predators. (Unfortunately these turtles face extinction as only one of 1,000 eggs survives into an adult turtle).

In 1997 I had gone with my family to the beach and our beach hut's chowkidar (security guard) showed us a few newly born turtles that he had captured and placed in a bucket of water. When my daughter Sarah, who was only six at that time, saw the baby turtles, she was so moved that she came to me and said: "Abba I am feeling very sorry for the baby turtles and want the chowkidar to let them go." I told Sarah that it was an excellent idea and that she should talk to the chowkidar herself, who on Sarah's insistence agreed to release the baby turtles. We took the bucket onto the sandy beach and took the turtles out one by one and as soon as we laid them on the sandy beach they immediately started to run towards the foamy tide and vanished into the big blue Arabian Sea.

My curiosity got the better of me while I was assisting my daughter to release the remaining few turtles. Instead of placing them with their heads pointed towards the ocean, I placed them pointing towards the land. To my utter amazement the baby turtles did not take a single step away from the sea and immediately turned and ran towards the tide. To further test the instincts of the baby turtles I took two of them in my hand and went off the beach and onto the road behind the beach hut from where the beach was not visible. Then I put them on the road facing away from the sea towards the Karachi city. I was again shocked but also pleasantly surprised to see that they immediately turned towards the coast and ran quickly through the bushes and rocks towards the sea.

This is what is called instinct and is something that is hard wired in the brain and does not need to be taught or practiced. In some cases we are born with our instincts but in majority of cases we build our instincts from experience, which helps us to survive.

Most of us believe that we are in full control of all our behaviors and can decide when to and when not to act on them. However, scientific research has shown that most of what a person does is driven by instincts and habits, behaviors that happen without effort, automatically. The key for you is to pay close attention to your instincts and habits and try to control or change those that are harmful or not beneficial to your personal well-being or business success.

It is interesting to note that instincts often help us develop a certain habit. The example of an outburst out of sheer anger is a classic example. Babies cry every time something unpleasant happens like hunger, wet diaper or when they can't sleep; that is instinct. However as we grow older the expression of anger becomes increasingly sophisticated. But it is not the instincts that become sophisticated; it is the developing habit of an angry outburst, supported by instinct, which makes it sophisticated. In the office environment or in a marriage one of the most destructive behaviors are incidences of angry outbursts, which are clearly inappropriate.

The habit of such outbursts may have been created as a valid solution in certain other situations, but they are unsuitable for other problems that trigger them automatically. This is where our intelligence plays a role and we must work to control or eliminate such destructive or ineffective habits and stop them from converting into instincts. Remember we can't change our instinct but we can find a way around them and solve the problem. To help control our instincts to shout and scream when faced with failure or bad news, one can create new habits that prevent you from losing your temper. An ideal way is to immediately disconnect from the news bearer and get time to cool down. You will be much more effective in your job, marriage and other relationships if you review your instincts and selectively find ways of controlling the bad ones.

Instincts can save lives: On July 5, 2008 a Qantas 747-438 aircraft, carrying 365 people, was flying over the South China Sea when an explosion blew a car-sized hole in the fuselage five-feet in diameter, causing a loss of cabin pressure. The plane was en route from London to Melbourne, Australia and it rapidly descended thousands of feet and flew about 300 miles to Manila, where it made a successful emergency landing. The investigation confirmed that an exploding oxygen tank below the cabin floor was the cause.[72]

There has been a lot of news coverage about where to lay the blame but very little coverage on the actions of the pilot and the crew in avoiding a potential disaster. In an interview the pilot said that he was flying on instinct and your instincts are the strongest when you train and work hard at being the best at what you do. One passenger praised the flight crew and said that they were calm, took control and helped the passengers through the unfortunate experience.

Never underestimate the hours of training and preparing for such emergencies that enabled the pilot and his team to avoid disaster and land the plane safely. The pilot's vast experience over time had turned into instincts, which helped him save the day. It is good to know that if you fly Qantas, you are in safe hands.

Compare this to a recent experience by a friend on another Asian carrier in which, due to major turbulence, the place suddenly dropped 1000's of feet in seconds, but the scariest part was watching the flight attendants running down the aisles screaming in fear.

"A moment's insight is sometimes worth a life's experience."
~ Oliver Wendell Holmes (1809–1894),
American Physician, Poet and Author

19 C. Gut Feelings

Gut reaction or gut feeling is an emotional reaction to action, situation, feelings, etc. and is most often a feeling of uneasiness. Gut feeling is not usually regulated by conscious thought but comes from within, what your brain instinctively tells you to do. You must have heard people say, "Use your gut feelings" or "I made that call based on my gut feeling"; which refers to using your built-in instincts or gut feelings to make a decision. In most cases the gut feeling is driven mainly by your common sense or perception of what is considered to be the right thing to do.

In a situation where we have to make a decision between two options and where everything looks that same, i.e. all data is giving a balanced point of view, the most likely gut feeling will be towards what is the right thing to do within the person's perception of what is right and what is wrong. Some examples of everyday gut feelings would include things like not going into a dark alley at night, helping an injured person or saving someone's life by putting your life at risk, etc. Gut feelings are all reflexive unconscious decisions and one can re-program them over a lifetime using your experiences, knowledge and your value system. Many also call it a hunch, an intuition, or a gut feeling. In general gut feelings usually do deliver the best results.

Let me share a personal story where not following my gut feeling has hurt me. I am in the habit of helping anyone who comes to me for assistance; these include people I know as well as strangers in dire need of help. Majority of requests are related to helping them finding a job, or for providing financial support or giving them medium term loans to help pay rent, or other personal expenses. Whenever, I have loaned money to someone, in majority of the cases I never saw the money again, I just knew even at the time of giving the loan that they would not return it. My gut feeling of who will return and who would not has been spot-on, but in order to keep the recipients dignity I continue to give the loan rather then calling it charity. This sense of 'just knowing' is what I call gut feeling. Gut feeling is spontaneous; we never have to ask our guts how it is feeling ☺

Summary on Experience: The key learning from this chapter on habits, instincts and gut feeling is that a person who has programmed these in ways that delivers positive behaviors further enhances their leadership skills and their chances of success. In today's competitive world where margins of victory are razor thin, such honing of conscious and subconscious skills will make the difference between winning and losing or between the success and failure of a strategy.

So the lesson is not to ignore such subtle and intangible issues such as habits, instincts and gut feelings but to actively work on them to make them work in your favor. By doing so they will help support you in gaining that extra edge to make a difference in today's competitive world and in managing today's complex interpersonal relationships.

> "My view in life is that you should go with your gut feeling
> when you have a threshold level of relevant experience."
> ~ Marc Bodnick,
> American Entrepreneur, Venture Capitalist,
> and Co-Founder of Elevation Partners.

19 D. Advice from the Masters

I genuinely believe that there is no compromise for experience; experience is sheer gold. What you learn from your personnel experiences, you can never learn from reading books or articles. Experience gets ingrained into your DNA, it turns into instinct and gut feelings and you will be able to recall it just like it happened yesterday whenever a similar situation arises. I will share advice from some masters' of their profession, one is a businessman and the other is a famous sports legend. There is so much one can learn from them, from their experiences and from their successful careers. Let's hear them talk:

A. **Warren Edward Buffett** (born 1930) is an American investor, a businessman, and a renowned philanthropist. He is one of the most successful investors in the world today and is the primary shareholder and CEO of Berkshire Hathaway. According to Forbes, Warren Buffet in 2013 was one of the top three richest people in the world with a personal wealth of $59.1 billion. In 2006 he announced that he would gradually give away 85% of his wealth to five foundations of which Bill and Melinda Gates Foundation will get the biggest chunk.[73] Although extremely rich, he is a very practical man.

Some distinct characteristics of Warren are,[74]

a. Still lives in the same small three-bedroom house in midtown Omaha that he bought after getting married some fifty years ago. Warren says why he should change it, when the home meets all his needs. Like other middle class people in the US his house does not have a fence or a wall.

b. Warren does not have a driver or security people around him and drives his own car for his daily use. He does not carry a cell phone nor has a computer on his desk in the office.

c. Although he owns a private jet company, he never travels in a private jet.

d. As a child he was very savvy and dexterous, he bought his first share at the age of eleven and still regrets starting very late. By age fourteen he had bought a small farm from the savings he made by selling newspapers in his neighborhood.

e. His company Berkshire Hathaway owns sixty-three companies. It is said that he writes just one letter each year to each of the CEOs giving them the goals for that year. He never holds meetings or calls them on a regular basis.

f.   He has given his CEO's only two basic rules. Rule 1: Do not lose any of your shareholder's money. Rule 2: Do not forget Rule 1.

His advice to young people is simple and to the point, namely: Stay away from credit cards and invest in yourself and above all remember:

- Money doesn't create man, but it is the man who created money.
- Live your life as simply as possible, as you are.
- Don't do what others say. Just listen to them, but do what makes you feel good.
- Don't go on brand names. Wear those things in which you feel comfortable.
- Don't waste your money on unnecessary things. Spend on those who are really in need.
- After all, it's your life. Why give others the chance to rule your life?

"In the business world, the rearview mirror is always clearer than the windshield."
~ Warren Buffett (b. 1930),
American Investor, Businessman, and Philanthropist

B.   **John Robert Wooden:** Coach John Wooden (1910-2010) has won the Basketball Hall of Fame in the United States both as a player (1961) and as a coach (1973); He was the first person ever enshrined in both categories. He had a very impressive record that includes ten NCAA (National Collegiate Athletic Association) Championships in a twelve year period while at UCLA (University of California, Los Angeles).[75]

"Success is peace of mind which is a direct result of self satisfaction in knowing

you made the effort to become the best
you are capable of becoming."
~ John Robert Wooden (b. 1910-2010),
Retired American Basketball Coach

His philosophies on success, leadership, and team building are so clear and yet so simple that one cannot help but marvel at this man's clarity of mind. Here are some of Coach John Wooden's pearls of wisdom taken from an interview with Mr. Harrison's in the October 2008 issue of *Toastmaster:*[76]

On Leading and Motivating Teams
In my opinion, one of the greatest motivational tools we have is a pat on the back. Another technique is listening.

Tips for New Leaders
Lead, don't drive. And give credit. Don't blame. Criticism must always be given in a gentle way, never harshly.

As a coach I had three rules:
1. Never be late.
2. You must never criticize a teammate.
3. I would not tolerate profanity from anyone, anytime.

Pursuit of Excellence
My bench never heard me mention winning. My whole emphasis was for each one of my players to try and execute the fundamentals to the best of their ability. Not to try to be better than somebody else, but to learn from others, and never cease trying to be the best they could be.

On Resolving Conflict
Unless a problem is brought to the forefront, it will just continue to fester.

On Struggle and Difficulty
Hardship brings people closer together if you share it.

On Patience
Leaders must have patience for those under their supervision. Don't expect too much too soon. Maybe it was easy for you, but that doesn't mean it's going to be easy for somebody else. And then you must believe in what you are doing, that what you're doing is the proper thing, the right thing.

It is interesting to note that although a sports giant, his advice can very well be applied to business situations and people. Indeed some tremendous insights from a true master!

.........----- ----------....

Solution to the '9-dot Puzzle' (see challenge in Section 18 D):

Objective:
Challenge of this puzzle is to link up all the 9 dots (you see them laid out in a matrix 3 x 3) by drawing four straight continuous lines or less. You need to do this WITHOUT lifting the pencil from the paper.

Biggest Hurdle:
Many of you when attempting to solve this problem create an imaginary square boundary around the 9-dots; no such boundary was mentioned or stated in the objective of this challenge but you did it anyways.

Easy Solution:
If you are willing to draw the lines beyond the confines of the square area (2 arrows) defined by the 9 dots (which looks like a box), the solution is then very easy. Hence the phrase thinking out-of-the-box was born.

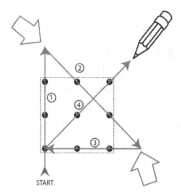

Chapter 20 – Embracing Change

Whatever we do as leaders results in change! The objective of setting a vision is to change reality, make the environment better, build a bigger business, improve processes and make things more efficient; all of these require change. Change is a way of life; it happens every day mostly in smaller doses, but sometimes in significant ways especially in relation to technological and demographic changes.

As far back as 500 BC, a pre-Socrates philosopher Heraclitus stated, "Nothing is permanent except change." A profound statement indeed as it clearly illustrates the true impact of change in yesteryears, current world and the future; only change is what will continue to occur, hence it is important that we know how to manage change, influence it, embrace it and get the maximum benefit out of it. Leadership and change are tightly interwoven.

A leader's job is to inspire and mobilize people to go forth and deliver something substantial, a new state of affairs that is different and better than reality, i.e. Change! If you look at famous leaders such as Nelson Mandela, Martin Luther King, Abraham Lincoln, Mohammad Ali Jinnah, Steve Jobs, etc., they all delivered great changes during their life time which impacted and improved the lives of millions of people.

"I cannot say whether things will get better if we change; what I can say is they must change if they are to get better."
~ Georg C. Lichtenberg (1742–1799),
German Scientist, Satirist and Anglophile

To emphasize how innocuously changes are happening around us, I will share a very impressive presentation made by Karl Fisch under the title *Shift Happens*.[77] In his presentation Fisch shares some demographic evolution that will baffle your mind, such as:

1. China will soon become number one English speaking country in the world.
2. Today nearly 25% of Chinese with the highest IQ's are greater in number than the entire population of North America.
3. India today has more honor kids than there are kids in the USA of that same age.
4. It is estimated that 40 Exabyte's (4×10^{19}) of unique new information will be generated worldwide that is more than what was generated in the last 5,000 years.

It is sometimes hard to imagine and comprehend how dynamic and constantly changing our lives are. In just the last 100 years we have seen everything from the invention of a car and airplane to landing of a spacecraft on Mars, from discovering penicillin to successfully carrying out a heart transplant and delivering test tube babies. Fisch also shares some troubling statistics on how fast technology is advancing and how quickly market dynamics are changing, such as:

1. We are currently preparing students for jobs that don't exist yet using technologies that haven't been invented in order to solve problems we don't even know are problems yet.
2. According to the US Secretary of Education Richard Riley the top ten in-demand jobs in 2010 did not exist in 2004.

3. The amount of new technical information is increasing exponentially; doubling every two years.
4. US Department of Labor estimates that today's learner will have ten to fourteen jobs by the time he is thirty-eight years old.

It is an established fact that the world is constantly changing around us; something that was true and relevant yesterday may be totally irrelevant tomorrow. The Walkman rave of the 80's today looks like a joke in front of the ever-popular iPod's. Hence it is critical that we stay abreast of the changes that are happening around us and be ready to embrace the new paradigm with full fervor else we may cease to exist as individuals, organizations or even as a race.

John Paul Kotter (b. 1947) the Konosuke Matsushita Professor of Leadership Emeritus at Harvard Business School is regarded as one of the world's foremost authority on the process of change and change leadership. In October 2001 *Business Week* magazine rated Kotter as the number one Leadership Guru in America based on 504 enterprises surveyed. He is particularly famous for his insights into how the best organizations bring about or implement change (Kotter & Cohen, 2002).

In his international bestseller *Leading Change* Kotter outlines eight essential steps, which help bring about successful change.[78] This process for implementing successful transformations is a four-stage process and has become the change bible for managers around the world. According to Kotter the stages are:

A. Set the Stage
B. Decide What to DO
C. Make it Happen
D. Make it Stick

A. SET THE STAGE

   i. Create a Sense of Urgency: Help others see the need for change and the importance of acting immediately.

   ii. Create a Powerful, Guiding Coalition: Make sure there is a powerful group guiding the change, one with leadership skills, bias for action, credibility, communications ability, authority, and analytical skills.

B. DECIDE WHAT TO DO

   iii. Develop the Change Vision and Strategy: Clarify how the future will be different from the past, and how you can make that future a reality.

C. MAKE IT HAPPEN

   iv. Communicate the Change Strategy: Make sure as many people as possible understand and accept the vision and the strategy.

   v. Empower Broad-based Action: Remove as many barriers as possible so that those who want to make the vision a reality can do so.

   vi. Celebrate Short-Term Wins: Create some visible, unambiguous successes as soon as possible.

   vii. Continuously Reinvigorate the Initiative with new Projects and Participants: Press harder and faster after the first successes. Be relentless with instituting change after change until the vision becomes a reality.

D. MAKE IT STICK

   viii. Anchor the Change in the Corporate Culture: Hold on to the new ways of behaving, and make sure they succeed, until they become a part of the very culture of the group.

These eight steps help lead successful changes and are a result of extensive research carried out by Kotter to verify his hypothesis across various companies, governments, and large institutions.

He found that of the change programs these organizations are implementing, nearly 70% of the change efforts either did not stick or did not go down or the results were simply disappointing. Kotter then focused on the top 10% and later on the top 5% of successful change programs and that is where he found a pattern, which drove successful change and from which the eight steps were identified.

> "A bend in the road is not the end of the road …
> unless you fail to make the turn."
> ~ Anonymous

According to Kotter of all the eight steps, *urgency* is the most important guiding force especially at the outset of a change initiative. Without a deep-rooted urgency for change, nothing will happen. Kotter goes on to highlight two key pitfalls related to the first step which he calls having a 'Sense for Urgency,' they are:

1) People often think they have a sense of urgency when they in fact do not.
2) Even if people recognize that there is a need for change, they still do not know how to go about doing it.

One of the key learning's from his research into the top 5% of companies who had successfully implemented change into their organization was the 'difference in the thinking level' which drove the change. It was clear that it was not just the sense of urgency that drove them to success; it was also a very deeply rooted belief on data-based facts and awareness of the core benefits that would be realized once the change took place.

Sense of urgency is clear when you hear from the leaders on how important or how urgent it is to bring change. If you hear a leader say "I am going to initiate a major change in the next six months," to Kotter that is just not urgent enough. Leaders ideally should be saying, "I am going to make the change happen today"; there has to be a strong bias towards change, a clear urgency to challenge the status quo and an urge to bring change yesterday!

The biggest threat to change is having a false sense of urgency. Kotter captures this very well when he states:

> "False urgency is the killer, because it gets mistaken constantly for real urgency, which creates a huge problem; that's the sort of headless chicken behavior. But what causes it and what can we do about it? False urgency tends to be driven by anxiety, fear, and sometimes anger. It is usually produced by pressure being put on people. And in terms of behavior, it's just franticness; it's this running in circles; it's the meeting, meeting, meeting, task force, task force, task force, report, report, report sort of behavior. But it's activity not productivity. It's not being driven by this determination to do something now; it's being driven by anxieties and angers. But because it's energetic, people from a distance will mistake it for urgency."[82]

To bring real and lasting change, one must fully believe and buy into the need for change as well as the benefits that will be realized by this change. Each and every member of the team needs to embrace this change and drive it. Having team members who do not buy into the change will be detrimental to this effort, they should be worked upon, convinced and if still not converted replaced. You cannot have critics within while you are trying to drive change. You need ambassadors or as we call them 'Champions of Change', to drive this change across all levels as well as in every function and department.

Only then will change take place, which is lasting and will eventually deliver the expected benefits. I have seen many examples in P&G as well as in several other companies where when there is no definite buy-in by the team yet the change program is continued and pursued, only to be re-visited and re-implemented with significant costs and time delays to the company and to individuals.

"If you don't like something, change it.
If you can't change it, change your attitude.
Don't complain."
~ Maya Angelou (1928–2014),
American Author Poet, Dancer, Actress and Singer

20 A. Boiling Frog Story

The boiling frog story is a well-known anecdote to help understand the negative impact of change. What happens when you, your team or your company refuses to accept or notice the signs of changes that are taking place around you? The premise of the story is that if you take a frog and put it in a pot of boiling water it would immediately jump out, however if it is placed in a pot of cold water that is slowly being heated, it will not perceive the danger and will slowly get boiled until it is cooked to death. The expression 'boiling frog syndrome' is sometimes used as shorthand for this metaphor.

This story is often used to help describe the inability of peoples in reacting or in recognizing changes that are gradually happening around them. We as humans are adverse to change; we get very comfortable with status quo (i.e. comfort zones) and sometime find it very hard to see or agree to embrace change; Change will happen whether we like it or not. And if the change is forced upon us especially when we least expect it, we will lose out in a very big way. Many classic examples exist about companies that have lost everything because they resisted change and just would not budge from their comfort zones'.

In the book *Good to Great* when Jim Collins compared companies that were considered great but failed, one of the key reasons was their inability to recognize change that was taking place in the market place. They were unable to read the change happening in the demographics or in people's habits and preferences, due to which they lost out to competition, which did recognize the impending changes and embraced them wholeheartedly. This ability to embrace change willingly does eventually lead to companies being more successful and in beating competition on a sustainable basis.

> **Vital Tip 42**: Always keep your finger on the pulse; stay updated and in-touch with changes happening around you. Like the frog that ignored the sensation of heat increasing gradually around it, and ended up being dead, don't let the same thing happen to you. If you have an edge in technology or in a demographic segment, keep a close tab on any gradual changes that may be impacting it and be brave enough to face the truth, rather than allowing it to hit you unprepared.

20 B. Insights from "Who Moved My Cheese?"

In 1998 Spencer Johnson wrote a very motivational book, which helped explain in an amazing way on how to deal with change in your work and in your life (I strongly recommend buying and reading this book). The book is called *Who Moved My Cheese?* and is written in a fable or tale style format. The story revolves around two mice and two little people and their quest for cheese (cheese connotes their goal in life). The concept and insights of this book are used by many consulting companies to help organizations learn how to identify change, how to manage it and how to embrace it.

The book remained on the New York Business Bestseller List for almost five years and spent over 200 weeks on Publishers Weekly's hardcover nonfiction list. To date more than 26 million copies have been sold worldwide in 37 languages and remains one of the best-selling business books.[79]

The story revolves around four characters, namely Sniff and Scurry (two mice) and Hem and Haw (two little people) who live in a maze. Maze is a metaphor for the environment we live in and can be correlated with the companies or organizations we work in or the communities we live in. Their food source is cheese, which is correlated to success and is located somewhere in the maze, which they visit daily to get nourishment.

One day to their surprise the cheese is gone and the rest of the story revolves around how the two mice and the two little people react to this change. As they go through their various experiences to find a new source of cheese, they note down their experiences that helps define the concept of how to react or adapt to change.

The story sends a very solid message by the way each of the four characters handle this change. Their reactions can be summarized as follows:

- ✓ When calamity hits the maze Sniff and Scurry are not surprised as they have been mentally prepared for such a day and are ready to go look for a new source of cheese. They immediately start to hunt for new sources.
- ✓ The reaction of Hem and Haw is diametrically different as the very thought that the cheese would finish never crossed their minds. They are very upset and annoyed and demand to know "Who moved my cheese?"
- ✓ Due to Sniff and Scurry's quick acceptance of the change and the fact that they immediately go off looking for new cheese, they are quickly able to find a new source (adapt to the change). Meanwhile Hem and Haw continue to disbelieve their predicament and blame each other for this dire situation (refuse to accept the change).

✓ Reaction between Hem and Haw is also very interesting to note.
  ○ Hem throughout the story feels victimized and very frustrated with the change. Until the very end he refuses to accept reality and the story ends not knowing if he ever changes.
  ○ Haw on the other hand, who was initially devastated, but soon starts to accept reality and suggests that they go searching for new cheese but Hem refuses. Haw finally goes searching for the cheese on his own.
✓ Some of the key concerns of Hem and Haw are that they are afraid of the unknown. Haw goes through different phases, worrying about the unknown, brushing aside his fears, and finally handling this immense change. Haw finally smiles and realizes that "When you move beyond your fears, you feel free."

"Don't fear change - embrace it."
~ Anthony J. D'Angelo (b. 1972),
Personal Development Guru

The seven key learning's from this story as per Spenser Johnson the author are given below. Note that these are exactly the type of steps one must go through to accept change in our personal and professional life. Never allow change to hit you on your blind side.

1. **Change happens** →The cheese will keep on moving.
2. **Anticipate Change** →Get ready for the cheese to move.
3. **Monitor Change** →Smell and check the quantity of cheese often so you know when it is getting old or running out.
4. **Adapt to Change quickly** →The quicker you let go of old cheese, the sooner you can enjoy new cheese.
5. **Change** →Move with the cheese.
6. **Enjoy Change!** →Savor the adventure and enjoy the taste of new cheese!

7. **Be ready to Change quickly and enjoy it again & again**
→They keep moving the cheese.

So who are you, Scurry, Sniff, Hem or Haw? Can you deal with change? Do you react immediately to change? Do you believe change will ever happen to you? How many of you are afraid of change? One thing you must remember is that change happens to all of us so be confident that change will definitely happen to you. Always be ready to look for the new cheese when it happens.

"Change alone is eternal, perpetual, immortal."
~ Arthur Schopenhauer (1788–1860),
German Philosopher

Once at the P&G year-end meeting in Cincinnati, the CISCO chief who was invited as a guest speaker asked the following question to the P&G senior management in the audience: "At what stage should one think of changing one's strategy?" CISCO chief's answer to his own query was very profound and highlighted the importance of anticipating change, he replied, "When you are most successful."

Why would anyone want to change when they are on top, in fact that is the time to relax, rest on your laurels and savor the moment? The reason is that according to the products life-cycle theory you reach peak performance when you are most successful and if you continue to do things the same way, your performance will drop as competition or even customers will become more knowledgeable and demanding.

Hence, the best time to change your strategy is when your idea has reached its peak. In the case of Hem and Haw, when they were enjoying the cheese, they should have started to look for new sources keeping in view that it would not last forever; which they did not do and hence were shocked to find it gone.

I find this story to be very insightful and close to how some of us are living our lives. Many of us are terrified and scared to let go of our comfort zones, just like Hem. Haw had the courage to move out of the comfort zone, but did so gradually. Sniff and Scurry are what we all need to be, agile, willing to accept change on face value and find new solutions. People who are like Hem, i.e. who even after knowing that change has taken place continue to fight the change, they hurt no one but themselves and eventually don't survive.

If you are a leader then the implication of such a denial on the organization or the company will be far reaching and can cause permanent and everlasting damage. The world and our environment continues to constantly evolve and you can be assured that competition will not wait for you to react and if one is late in accepting the approaching change, you and your company will be left far behind and will eventually become obsolete and fail.

> "Everyone thinks of changing the world, but
> no one thinks of changing himself."
> ~ Leo Tolstoy (1828–1910),
> Russian Writer, One of the Greatest Novelists

20 C. Embracing Change: Case Studies

I will share with you examples of how four well known companies have reacted to change which their respective industrial sectors were faced with. Each of the stories reflects the character of one of the individuals in *Who Moved My Cheese?* and each example gives a different and an indepth illustration of how organizations react to change.

A) A Scurry Story - INTEL

The Intel story starts in 1968 when Robert Noyce and Gordon Moore incorporate NM Electronics, which was later, renamed as Intel Corporation (from the two words Integrated Electronics). Noyce and Moore's business plan was to start development and large-scale manufacturing of memory chips, i.e. DRAM (Dynamic Random Access Memory).

Memory chips were an integral part of the computer revolution and everyone related to the large-scale integrated (LSI) semiconductor industry wanted to cash in on this golden opportunity. For perspective, before LSI technology was developed, memory was stored on transistor flip-flops or vacuum tube flip-flops and their prices were exorbitant; a 1 MB memory ranged in prices from as high as $400 million in 1957 dropping by more than 80% to $68 million by 1959, in just two years, due to technological advancement.[80]

As LSI memory's global demand grew exponentially, every country with a high-tech industrial base joined the fray, especially countries like South Korea, Malaysia and Taiwan. Prices plummeted as new approaches, mass production techniques and economies of scale kicked in.

DECADES	MAX ($/Mbyte)	MIN ($/Mbyte)	AVG ($/Mbyte)	Cost Price Reduction
1957-60	411,041,792	5,242,880	161,410,799	-
1961-70	2,642,412	734,003	1,688,208	99%
1971-80	399,360	8,616	136,250	92%
1981-90	6,480	78	1,963	99%
1991-00	44	1.0	20	99%
2001-10	0.30	0.01	0.13	99%

If you look at the table you will be astonished! Nothing like this has ever happened in the history of mankind. Every decade starting from 1950 to today, memory prices have continued to plummet by an average of 99% per decade. For example, from

~ $9,000 price of a single 1 MB chip in 1979, in just a matter of three decades, it was selling for just over one cent in 2009.[80]

With this background, Intel had very ambitiously entered the memory chip business in 1968 knowing well the immense potential as well as the attractive payout behind this investment in memory manufacturing; in 1968 the 1 MB memory chip was selling for $1 million dollars. But then Intel made a fundamental and life-saving change in their strategy. This change in strategy was not instigated by something real but more by: a) their ability to forecast the future as well as by tracking memory price trends; b) having their finger on the pulse of the industry and its underlying evolving trends.

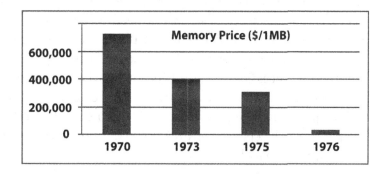

To give full credit to Intel's senior management although they were pioneers in the business of memory chip manufacturing and design, they were not complacent and kept their eyes and ears open to the potential change that was about to hit the memory chip industry. In-line with their forecast, memory prices would plummet by as much as 95% between 1970 ($234,000/1MByte) and 1976 ($36,000/1MByte) (see bar chart in US$).

Another sign of this impending doom was apparent merely by watching how aggressively the Asian Tiger countries were joining the fray and investing billions of dollars in

LSI production capacity. One day Intel decided, against all wisdom, to pull out of memory manufacturing (their main line of business) when it was at its peak and focus on a breakthrough idea that they had stumbled upon; a central processing unit (CPU) on one chip.

> "Change will not come if we wait for some
> other person or some other time.
> We are the ones we've been waiting for.
> We are the change that we seek."
> ~ Barack Obama (b. 1961),
> 44th President of the United States

The CPU came about as a byproduct of a request made by a Japanese calculator manufacturer, Busicom, who needed a design for a cost-effective chip for a series of calculators. During their research for such a design, Intel engineer Ted Hoff conceived a plan for the first ever central processing unit (CPU), the Intel 4004 microprocessor. Intel 4004 was crammed with 2,300 transistors on a $1/8^{th}$ by $1/16^{th}$ inch chip and had the power of the old 3,000-cubic-foot ENIAC computer, which depended on over 38,000 vacuum tubes. History was clearly in the making.

Although the microprocessor had started as a computer enhancement, very soon Intel realized its true potential as it could be used for everything from calculators to cash registers and traffic signals. They soon followed the Intel 4004 with the Intel 8008, the first 8-bit microprocessor. Intel then placed significant resources and investment behind designing and developing the next generation of microprocessors, leaving the memory chips market as their prices continued to plummet.

Intel introduced the first truly general microprocessor in 1974, the Intel 8080. For just $360 Intel was selling a whole computer on one chip and soon Intel 8080 became an industry standard, which set the basis for their eventual domination of microprocessor market with the 16-bit Intel 8086 in 1978. The Intel 80486 introduced in 1989 contained 1.2 million transistors and the first built-in math coprocessor and was fifty times faster than the Intel 4004, the first microprocessor.

In 1993 Intel released its fifth generation Pentium processor, a chip capable of executing over 100 million instructions per second (MIPS) and supporting real-time video communication. The Pentium processor, with its 3.1 million transistors, was up to five times more powerful than the 33-megahertz Intel 486DX microprocessor and 1,500 times the speed of their first processor, the Intel 4004.

Why Intel is Scurry? Just like Scurry who was the first to react to the change and without a second thought had ran into the maze to look for new cheese, Intel also, due to their ability to recognize the winds of change that were fanning the computer industry modified their strategy when everyone and their grandmothers were getting into large scale memory chip manufacturing. They showed immense flexibility, a can-do attitude and openly challenged their comfort zone. Due to this, Intel's revenues were $5.9 billion, with a net income of $11.7 billion (financial year 2014).

This is a classic case of 'changing your strategy when you are most successful', i.e. you make a move right before your company starts to move down the classic product life cycle curve. That in fact is a step ahead of Scurry and is rarely seen in any industry. To me that was the beauty of Intel's strategy that they moved to a new and powerful direction, minutes before a head-on collision was about to take place. And due to Intel's ability to embrace and anticipate change, Intel continues to dominate the CPU market worldwide ever since.

Food for Thought:

Moore's Law[81]

Gordon E. Moore, one of the co-founders of Intel is an exceptional visionary. As far back as 1965, three years before even NM Electronics (later renamed Intel) was founded, he suggested a principle, which is famously known as the Moore's Law. The law states: "Number of transistors on a chip will double about every two years." Later it was discovered that this law was also strongly linked with capabilities of many other digital devices such as processing speed, memory capacity and even the number and size of pixels in digital cameras. All of these are improving roughly at the exponential rates Moore predicted.

This law has since been used in the semiconductor industry to help guide long term planning and setting targets for research and development. According to experts this trend has continued for more than half a century and is not expected to stop until 2015 or later. Intel has kept pace with this prediction for nearly forty years. It has helped drive technological and social change in the late 20th and early 21st century.

B) A Sniffy Story – CATERPILLAR

This story is centered on how Caterpillar Inc. came into being back in 1925 in Peoria, Illinois USA. This classic tale starts back in late 19th century when the steam engine was the ultimate power source and was the key moving force behind the industrial revolution. Steam power was dominating every aspect of life with widespread use in railways locomotives, ships and road vehicles. The only place where it was not being utilized was over rough terrains and open un-even fields.

This is what caught the eye of two smart individuals who are the key characters of this story, namely Daniel Best an adventurer-cum-inventor-cum-entrepreneur and Benjamin Holt an inventor. They both in their own right were leading the steam revolution by designing and selling steam tractors and similar vehicles and dominated the logging and farming industries on the West Coast. What they were unable to do was go off track into the wild due to the inability of the heavy steam tractor to grapple with rough and rutted terrain.

They 'Sniffed' this void as a key opportunity and pursued it until they were able to develop the first practical continuous tracks to be used on rough and un-even terrain. This utilization of steam power in the field of agriculture led to a significant increase in land available for cultivation and thus meeting the ever-increasing feeding needs of the world population.

They both left their mark on history by leaving a legacy of designing the first commercial continuous tracks for use on tractors; the continuous tracks help to spread the weight of the vehicle and its load over a large area thus preventing the vehicle from sinking into the soft ground, as well as allowing it to travel easily over rough and uneven terrain. By 1904, steam-powered tractors were being actively used for plowing the land in California. Unfortunately these vehicles would occasionally get bogged down in the soft soil, especially during the rainy season. And once stuck in the mire, they were difficult to pull free even with a team of horses. One possible solution, when faced with such a challenge, was to lay temporary planks on the terrain ahead of the steam tractor, but this was extremely time consuming and expensive and impacted the operation significantly. That is when Holt thought of 'carrying the road with the vehicle'.

On November 24, 1904 Holt added wooden block-linked treads around the idlers on his test steam tractor Holt No.77. The results were impressive, and the modern Caterpillar track was born. The idea was very unique and its application was so wide that their company continued to grow right through the 1930's, which is more aptly remembered as the decade of the Great Depression.[82]

Why Caterpillar is Sniffy? Sniffy was the little mouse that was eager to embrace change but needed to sniff out the opportunity first. Both the Holt Manufacturing Company as well as the C. L. Best Gas Traction Company which later merged and gave birth to Caterpillar Inc. were well entrenched and doing well in their respective lines of business. The fact that they were able to 'sniff-out' an unmet need shows that they were open to new ideas, for taking appropriate risks to win and were able to successfully come up with a unique competitive advantage.

Today based on this advantage they have built a very successful and also the world's largest manufacturing company for construction and mining equipment. They have impacted the building of the world's infrastructure from highways to dams, and have helped drive positive and sustainable change on every continent. Today Caterpillar turnover exceeds $55 billion and net income is $3.7 billion (fiscal year 2014 data).

> "It is impossible for a man to learn what
> he thinks he already knows."
> ~ Epictetus (55 AD–155 AD),
> A Greek Stoic Philosopher

C) A Haw Story – IBM

IBM, also nicknamed the Big Blue (for its official corporate colors) dates back to the early 1880's, decades before the development of electronic computing age. Thomas Watson the first general manager of International Business Machines (renamed IBM in 1924) grew the company from $9 million to $900 million in his extraorinary forty-four year career (double digit top line growth for over four decades; ~11%).

Despite its exceptional success over the century of its existence, it faced some major challenges in the early 1990's when it failed to grasp the changes taking place in its industry and had a near disasterous experience. This experience is the point of this dicussion and it was instigated by the introduction of Personal Computers (PC).

Intriguingly it was no other than IBM which designed and launched the first proper PC under the name IBM PC on August 12, 1981 at a base price of US$ 1,565 (Apple had launched a personal computer kit in 1977 under the name 'Apple I' but was far from being a complete PC and was meant only for computer enthusiasts. Their big breakthrough by Apple was Macintosh which was launched in 1984). The relatively low pricing of the IBM PC made it affordable for small and medium sized businesses and allowed IBM to finally have a presence in the consumer marketplace rather than only at corporate levels.

IBM unfortunately lost is first movers advantage due to its unprecedented decision to contract out PC components (both software and hardware) to third parties such as Microsoft and Intel. This was totally against its history of being vertically integrated but was done in an attempt to quickly gain a chunk of the PC market; hence IBM chose not to build proprietary operating systems and microprocessors although they had both the resources and technical know how.

Ironically it was this fateful decision which marked the end of IBM's monopoly of the computer industry and paved the way for the creation of billions of dollars of market value outside IBM; in companies such as Microsoft, Intel, Compac, Dell and many others. IBM led the change but embraced this change only half-heartedly which later resulted in billions of dollars of business losses.

> "Progress is impossible without change,
> and those who cannot change their minds
> cannot change anything."
> ~ George Bernard Shaw (1856–1950),
> Irish playwright and a co-founder of the
> London School of Economics

By the end of the 80's decade IBM was clearly in trouble. The explosive expansion and acceptance of PC's had dramatically undermined IBM's core mainframe business. PC revolution placed computers directly in the hands of millions of users and IBM's problem were further compounded with the development of client/server applications which linked many PC's together as well as with larger computers where data and applications resided.

IBM Cummulative Annual Growth Rate

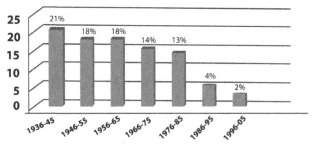

This totally trans-formed how customers viewed, used and bought computer tech-nology and it shook IBM to its core. IBM earnings took a hard hit; their earnings which had surpassed $5 billion in the early 1980's would drop by more than a third to only $3 billion in 1989. Its revenues which had been growing in double digits for nearly five decades (see bar chart) flattened to low single digit growth rates in the decades following 1985.[83]

What happened here? IBM clearly failed to see the change happening around it and when they did finally realize it, it was too late. A major paradigm shift was taking place in the computer industry which was to forever change the way computers were designed and used. IBM having missed the boat could not stop the bleeding, as competition and innovations in the computer industry developed along segmented lines versus the past vertically integrated ones (which was IBM's core competency); companies such as HP (printers), Compaq (PC's), Dell (PC's), Novell (networking), Seagate (diskdrives), etc. evolved and prospered.

After losing over $1 billion dollars in two consecutive years, IBM on January 19, 1993 announced the largest single-year corporate loss in US history, $8.10 billion in the **RED** in 1992 year-end results. Hundreds and thousands of IBM employees lost their jobs including their CEO as the company struggled to restructure and to survive.

Why IBM is Haw? IBM's top management had clearly not seen the signs as the market changed and the demographics of electronic computer users moved from corporates to individuals, from one company solution to specialized-segmented company solutions; a major pardigm shift had taken place right under their very noses. IBM finally did change but not without losing time, money and people.

Just like Haw who took some time to realize that change was taking place and that the change, was permanent. Companies that have the ability to read and anticipate such gradual changes happening in the market dynamics, will remain and continue to lead the pack.

"Don't reinvent the wheel, just realign it."
~ Anthony J. D'Angelo (b. 1972),
Personal Development Guru

D) A Hem Story – FIRESTONE

This is a story of three companies over three continents making the same product, all three being flagship brands of three recognized countries; one hurts the other, another fails and the third gobbles it up. The industry I am talking about is the Tire Industry and companies involved are Michelin from France, Firestone Tire & Rubber Company from the US and the Bridgestone Corporation from Japan. All stalwarts in their own rights, three of the world's most reliable tire and rubber manufacturers operating since 1888, 1900 and 1931 respectively.

Michelin is the oldest of the three companies and it started its operation in 1888 as a rubber factory in Clermont-Ferrand, France by two brothers Andre and Edouard Michelin. Their first encounter with a tire was when someone brought a pneumatic bicycle tire to their shop for repairs. At that time the tire was attached to the rim of the bicycle. In 1891 Michelin got their first patent for a removable pneumatic bicycle tire that could easily be removed and attached to the rim.

For the next century Michelin was established as one of the most innovative companies in the tire business. Over the years Michelin gained a strong reputation as one of the world's most reliable tire manufacturer. In fact they were the first tire company to design the famous radial tire, a major innovation as far back as the 1940's. On global revenues, Bridgestone leads with $29.3 billion, followed by Michelin at $24.4 billion, Goodyear third with $17.8 billion and Continental fourth with $12.9 billion in FY 2014.[84]

Shojiro Ishibashi founded the second company in this story, Bridgestone, in 1931 in the city of Kurume, Fakuako, Japan. I always felt the name Bridgestone was unusual for a Japanese brand until I found the meaning of its founder's name Ishibashi means Stonebridge, i.e. 'Ishi' is stone and 'Bashi' is bridge in Japanese. Bridgestone is currently ranked as the number one tire manufacturer in the global tire market with over 141 production facilities spread over twenty-four nations of the world.

Harvey Firestone founded the Firestone Tire and Rubber Company in 1900 to supply pneumatic tires for wagons, buggies and other forms of wheeled transportation common in that era. With the advent of automobiles, starting with the Ford Model-T in 1906, Henry Ford chose the Firestone brand for his automobile and hence they became the original equipment manufacturer (OEM) for the Ford Motor Company. This close relationship continued for six decades as Firestone remained their most preferred supplier accounting for roughly 50% share of Ford tires as late as the 1960's.

Firestone pioneered mass production of tires and owned huge rubber plantations in Liberia covering more than 4,000 square kilometers of land. For five decades Firestone led the US market. What happened next has become the topic of numerous case studies and has delivered key insights into how best to manage change.

"Technological progress is like an axe in the
hands of a pathological criminal."
~ Albert Einstein (1879–1955),
Theoretical Physicist and father of Modern Physics

Story of Firestone Tire and Rubber Company is a classic story of riches to rags, of someone showing the classic Hem characteristics. Firestone was a recognized leader in the tire industry but it failed to respond appropriately to the threat of new technology and foreign competition. Before I share the story of their demise, it is important to acquaint you with the company's character, corporate culture as well as their performance track record.

The irony in the story I am about to tell you is that Firestone did respond to the external and technological threat but only by accelerating the activities that had contributed to its past successes; which in this case were the very reason for their eventual demise. They did not grasp the true implication of the changes happening around them; failed to embrace this change and disappointingly went under.

For perspective, by the 1930's the US tires industry was dominated by five large established US firms namely Goodyear, Firestone, Uniroyal, B. F. Goodrich and General Tires. These five companies continued to dominate the domestic market for nearly half a century. The key irritant to shake things up for them was an initiative by the French tire manufacturer Michelin when they introduced radial tires in the US market in the late 60's. In their fight to close the technology gap, the US tire manufacturers suffered significant financial losses and lost a huge chunk of the US market share to foreign competition.

In 1966 Michelin stuck a deal with Sears to manufacture radial tires under the Allstate label and within four years were selling one million units per year. To put salt into the US tire makers wounds, Michelin in 1970 inaugurated a large radial tire plant in Canada and Bridgestone compounded this by significantly expanding their radial tires exports to the US. By 1988 Firestone had been acquired by the Japanese competitor Bridgestone, and only Goodyear, of the five largest US tire firms, remained independent.

> "The greatest danger in times of
> turbulence is not the turbulence;
> it is to act with yesterday's logic."
> ~ Peter Drucker (1909–2005),
> Writer and Management Consultant

What happened here? Firestone Tire and Rubber Company were considered as one of the best managed US tire companies during the decades prior to the introduction of radial tires in the US market. Failure of such magnitude with a historical par excellence performance made Firestone a paradox for the industry analysts.

Why had the industry's best-managed company turned in such a poor performance when it was most needed? Harvard's professor Donald Sull has done extensive research in this case and states in his article that "In the years immediately following World War II, Firestone had honed a competitive formula that focused attention on its domestic rivals and large customers, refined processes to design and make tires, forged a dense set of relationships with customers and employees that secured their continued loyalty, and reinforced a strong set of corporate values. While this competitive formula enabled Firestone to succeed in the booming tire market of the 1960s, it constrained the company's ability to respond to the changes brought about by the advent of the radial tire."[85]

Closer analysis reveals that Firestone failed, not despite but because of its historical success. It is important to review Firestone's performance on three facets in order to comprehend the true reason for its demise. These three facets as per Donald Sull are:

1. Operational Systems and Processes
2. Relationships with key Customers
3. Set of Corporate Values

1. **Operational Systems and Processes:**
   Firestones success was no accident. They had a very positive and committed corporate culture. Firestone's management carried out detailed analysis of their competition, did frequent reviews of all their strategic initiatives and tactical moves. They kept track of their competitor's patents and technical innovations, new product innovations, market innovations, pricing and even customer purchases were tracked. Firestone's strategic competitive tracking was reinforced by management information systems that provided a laser-like focus on the core tire business and the company's traditional rivals.[86]

Firestone management best practices were so first-rate in the 60's that Peters and Waterman exemplified the company in their book *In Search of Excellence*. During the 60's as major take-over waves hit the tire industry, Firestone remained unscathed and totally focused on running their business efficiently. Peter and Waterman further noted that the best companies are not only focused on studying their competitors, but have a distinct bias-for-action which they called "a preference for doing something-anything, rather than sending a question through cycles and cycles of analyses and committee reports."

Firestone had exactly the same kind of bias towards rapid action in their approval processes for designing new products, new manufacturing processes and capital spending programs. A classic example to support this claim is when Goodyear first introduced 'belted bias' tires in November 1967; Firestone reacted quickly with its version in just a matter of months.

In addition they had a unique demand driven capital spending approval process initiated by the front line marketing and sales manager, which in most cases was accepted on face value. Their Executive Committee rejected or reduced less than 10% of proposals forwarded to them. Between1960-69 Firestone built five new plants accounting for 25% of all tire plants built in the US during this period; all based on aggressive forecast made by their sales and marketing executives.[87]

> "Everybody gets so much information all day long
> that they lose their common sense."
> ~ Gertrude Stein (1874–1946),
> American Writer

2. **Relationships with key Customers and Suppliers**
   Of all the leading tire companies, Firestone exemplified the principle of staying close to your customers. Even after six decades Firestone continued to be a disproportional supplier for Ford; they made up roughly half of the Ford's yearly tire requirement. This relationship took an interesting turn when Harvey's granddaughter married Henry Ford's grandson who was also the largest shareholder of Ford Motors. In addition Firestone's close relationship with their largest dealers was well known. This involved a number of services ranging from shared advertising to technical assistance to even helping in financing, when their loyal dealers fell into financial difficulties.

"The art of progress is to preserve order amid change
and to preserve change amid order."
~ Alfred North Whitehead (1861–1947),
English Mathematician and Philosopher

3. **Corporate Values**

Majority of their past successes since their inception in 1900 was a result of their core values. Firestone management placed a great deal of emphasis on these core values, which were used to unite and inspire their organization. Harvey Firestone was committed to the corporate values that bind the company as a family. In line with their values, Firestone constructed the Firestone Park as well as 1,000 low-cost residential units for their employees in 1916. The same year Harvey introduced an eight-hour workday for all employees.[85]

During the Great Depression, which was characterized by widespread labor strife, Firestone treated their workers paternalistically and had very few layoffs. When the going got tough with the Michelin invasion of the US market, over half of the existing US tire plants closed down but Firestone managers did not put their weight in closing their plants; Firestone accounted for 24% of US tire plants but closed only one.[86] Unfortunately these money-losing plants continued to pile up losses for Firestone but due to their family values they resisted investor and board pressure to close plants solely to shield the affected employees and communities. At best a counterproductive strategy.

To counter the growing foreign competition and to close the technological gap, Firestone decided to manufacture radials using modified bias tire equipment rather than setting up radial tire factories from scratch. To achieve this they spent nearly $150 million in capital investment just in the first year. And subsequently in the next seven years Firestone would invest on average $60 million in capital. This allowed Firestone to rapidly build radial production capacity and narrow the gap with other tire makers, especially Michelin. Within two years of introduction, the company flagship 'Firestone 500 Steel Belt' became the most recognized brand in the industry.

It is pertinent to note that the immense size of investment was driven by their strong relationships with established customers like Ford and General Motors. The return for Firestone on this investment was around 6.5%, which fell way below the cost of capital of 8% and significantly below the 28% average return on investments the company enjoyed outside its North American tire business.[85]

"If you have always done it that way, it is probably wrong."
~ Charles Kettering (1876–1958),
American Inventor, Engineer and Businessman

Later Firestone was to realize to that their decision to revamp existing manufacturing processes rather than creating new ones would seriously contribute to quality problems with the tire's steel cords as they failed to adhere to the tire properly. Although all tire manufacturers were faced with quality issues, Firestone's problems were much more severe. In 1978 under heavy pressure from consumer groups and the National Highway Safety Administration, Firestone voluntarily recalled 8.7 million Firestone 500 tires. This cost them nearly $150 million after tax, the largest consumer recall action till that date in US history. All these issues compounded its problems and finally in 1988 Firestone agreed to be bought out by Japan's Bridgestone for $2.6 billion.[88]

Key Learning's: Although there was a great culture existing at Firestone, but a deeper analysis unfortunately reveals some obvious symptoms. Like they say hindsight is 20/20, so from our vantage point, Donald Sull reviewed their failure and identified the following key reasons and shortcoming, namely:

a. Stringent processes and set systems are not suitable in a very dynamic and constantly changing environment, one needs to be flexible;
b. Strong and binding relationships with customers on one hand can be very beneficial but on the other hand can be obstructive and restrict your maneuverability to react effectively;
c. Set of values if taken blindly can mislead management to make decisions not in the interest of the company.

These shortcomings locked Firestone into a set trajectory, which did not allow the managers to change when the environment around them changed. One must remember that commitments are not your destiny and maintaining status quo on behaviors is not the solution; transforming commitment with shifting competitive environment while protecting your core values, in essence, is the true recipe for success. In this example not requesting Ford or General Motors, the true beneficiaries, to partner in the major investment in view of their deep relationships as well as delaying plant closures to save jobs eventually led to a much bigger and permanent hit to the employees as Firestone ultimately ceased to exist as a company.

Firestone's management's blind reliance on certain values proved counterproductive in the constantly changing and dynamic competitive environment.

"When we blindly adopt a religion, a
political system, a literary dogma,
we become automatons. We cease to grow."
~ Anais Nin (1903–1977),
French Author

In the article *Why Good Companies Go Bad*, Professor Donald N. Sull introduces a new term: 'Active Inertia'; the tendency of an organization to follow established patterns of behavior even in response to dramatic environmental shifts. In his research Sull states that many companies' continue to follow the models and behaviors that had brought them past successes.

In fact in some cases it was observed that they in fact accelerated their tried-and-tested activities to turnaround the businesses only to dig themselves deeper and to make the problem more complex and difficult. Sull's extensive analysis on companies such as Firestone, Xerox, Apple, Polaroid, etc. led him to identify four traits of active inertia namely:

1 - Strategic frames become Blinders
2 - Relationships become Shackles
3 - Processes harden into Routines
4 - Values harden into Dogmas

The key insight is that one must look deeper into the assumptions of any strategy or tactic at that point in time and take into account latest changes in the economic, demographic and technological environment. Just because something worked a decade ago does not mean that the same tactic holds true today; the world is constantly changing.

Static Action

Embracing change is not just about reacting but reacting in the right manner with the right strategies and the right focus areas; all customized to be in sync with the latest economic, competitive and technological environment. In line with Sull's learning's I have also coined a word which describes Firestone's action to save their company, what I call 'Static Action'; an oxymoron. Static is for copying past behaviors and processes, making no changes thus keeping the act static. Action is for doing something or taking action.

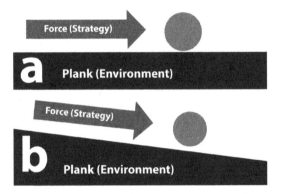

Let me explain this using a simple example. Look at the diagram and assume that force is strategy, plank is the environment and the ball is your business. As the environment changes so should the forces (or your strategy). Let us now assume for simplicity sake that for the last six decades the environment has been plank 'a' (diagram above) in which you used a certain force (or strategy) very successfully. In option 'a' as the environment (plank) is flat, so the strategy (force) needed to drive your business forward is uniform and gentle.

Now image that over time the environment changes significantly. Option 'b' now depicts the new environment where the plank has a downhill slope tilting at an angle of 15°. By imparting the same strategy (or force) in the new environment, you will not get the same business results; in fact the earlier strategy (force) which successfully led business growth in the plank 'a' environment, will backfire and totally destroy the business in the new environment shown by plank 'b'.

In the new environment you have to totally change the strategy and push the ball (business) upward to stop it from rolling down. Hence the concept of 'Static Action', where you act in a fixed manner without modifying your strategy, taking into account any changes in the environment, or else your business will roll down into oblivion.

Hence, having a bias-for-action may indeed be a great virtue, but knowing on 'how to act?' and 'what to act upon?' is what finally makes the difference between winners and losers. Firestone's example underscores the fact that merely taking action can sometimes be a drawback, even if the action is based on successful past behaviors. One must gain a clearer view of the circumstances, the ground realities and look more deeply at the latest underlying assumptions and environment; only then take action that will surely lead to success.

"All change is not growth, as all movement is not forward."
~ Ellen Glasgow (1873–1945),
Pulitzer Prize Winning American Novelist

Why Firestone is Hem? Firestone was very much like Hem, maybe a tad better. Hem refused to act at all to the change it was faced with while on the other hand Firestone acted but without changing or modifying their strategy according to the changing environment, hence they also failed.

When one drives up to a certain destination in ones car, that does not guarantee that the same route will still work years and decades later; roadwork, changes in landscape and many such modifications can render past behaviors impractical. When Firestone was hit with technological transformation and a rapidly changing competitive landscape, they continued to drive as nothing has changed and sadly fell of a cliff; in hindsight they did not react in the right manner.

Just like Hem, they wanted their old cheese back, they reacted as if nothing had changed and that they're past strategies and tactics will still work; they failed miserably. They believed that the tire industry was still the same tire industry in which they had ruled for six decades. You must change with the environment, you must embrace what is happening around you, or otherwise you will be destined to the same fate as Firestone.

> "The first problem for all of us, men and
> women, is not to learn, but to unlearn."
> ~ Gloria Steinem (b. 1934),
> American Feminist, Journalist and Social and Political Activist

...........— —— ———————....

Chapter 21 – Roadmap to Drive Organizational Excellence

Organization excellence acts as a catalyst and facilitates to deliver executional excellence at every level of direction setting, winning in the market place and against competition

- ✓ **To achieve Organizational Excellence, focus on having an Organizational Culture where:**
  - People are considered as the <u>real assets</u> of the company.
  - Company polices are <u>equally balanced</u> for both the company and its employees.
  - <u>Dissatisfaction with status quo</u> is hard wired into everyone's genes.
- ✓ **Check out the 'Smell of the Place'**
  - Does management inculcate a <u>winning</u> and <u>can-do</u> attitude?
  - Are the senior management <u>approachable</u> and an <u>integral part</u> of the teams?
  - Is <u>positive thinking</u> a way of life in the company?
- ✓ **Make sure each and every manager displays strong Leadership qualities.**
  - Builds enduring greatness through a unique blend of <u>personal humility</u> and <u>professional will</u>.
  - Every senior manager is a <u>role model</u> for their department and others.

- Tutors the organization to champion the 5 E's of the Leadership Model.
- Makes winning contagious.
✓ **Make sure each employee understands what it takes to get Top Ratings.**
  - Must deliver on four factors on a sustainable basis: 1) Beyond the scope; 2) Ahead of the deadline; 3) Impeccable in quality and 4) With minimum supervision.
✓ **Ingrain in every employee's DNA the passion to strive for Greatness.**
  - Make current job best-in-class (BIC).
  - Become a great people's manager.
  - Succession planning should be paramount.
  - Efficient manager of both time and energy.
  - Display passionate ownership behavior.
  - Fully utilize the power of brainstorming and out-of-the-box thinking.
✓ **Become aware of your Comfort Zone, challenge it & move out. Take calculated risks.**
✓ **Build Trust as the foundation for every act and every decision in the company.**
  - Make everyone aware of the concept of an emotional bank account and use it.
  - Ensure everyone endeavors to use trust to pull people towards their vision.
✓ **Nurture a culture where Striving for Excellence is a way of life and should include:**
  - Passion to be the best in everything we do.
  - Mind-set where everyone focuses on breaking down barriers as and when needed.
  - Willingness to raise the bar and drive stretch mentality on all projects.
✓ **Enable the organization to Embrace Change and be a Champion of Change.**

✓ **Build Positive Habits, as they will help you to be more effective in everything you do.**

- Do not use multitasking as a way of doing your work, use chunking.

Recommended Reading

1. *"The 7 Habits of Highly Effective People"*, by Stephen R. Covey
2. *"Put Your Dreams to the Test"*, by John C. Maxwell
3. *"The Richest Man Who Ever Lived - King Solomon's Secret of Success, Wealth and Happiness"*, by Steven K. Scott
4. *"Built to Last"*, by Jim Collins
5. *"The Game-Changer"*, by A. G. Lafley and Ram Charan
6. *"Good to Great"*, by Jim Collins
7. *"The Balanced Scorecard"*, by David P. Norton and Robert S. Kaplan
8. *"Strategy-Focused Organization"*, by David P. Norton and Robert S. Kaplan
9. *"Built to Last"*, by Jim Collins
10. *"How the Mighty Fall"*, by Jim Collins
11. *"In Love and War"*, by Jim Stockdale and Sybil Stockdale
12. *"Execution-The Discipline of Getting Things Done"*, by Ram Charan and Larry Bossidy
13. *"The Secret"*, by Rhonda Byrne
14. *"The Power of Full Engagement"*, by Dr. Jim Loehr and Tony Schwartz
15. *"The Game-Changer"*, by A. G. Lafley and Ram Charan
16. *"Speed of Trust"*, by Stephen M. R. Covey
17. *"Who Moved My Cheese?"*, by Spencer Johnson
18. *" In Search of Excellence"*, by Tom Peters and Robert H. Waterman
19. *"Revival of the Fittest"*, by Donald Sull
20. *"The Dynamics of Standing Still: Firestone Tire & Rubber and the Radial Revolution"* by Donald Sull

References for
"It's Business, It's Personal"

[1]   *Wikipedia*, s.v. "Martin Luther King Jr.," last modified April 9, 2015, *http://en.wikipedia.org/wiki/Martin_Luther_King,_Jr.*

[2]   John F. Kennedy, "Special Message to the Congress on Urgent National Needs," May 25, 1961, transcript, last modified June 4, 2013, Wikisource.org: *http://en.wikisource.org/wiki/Special_Message_to_the_Congress_on_Urgent_National_Needs.*

[3]   John F. Kennedy, "Address at Rice University on the Nation's Space Effort," September 12, 1962, transcript and Realmedia video, *Rice Webcast Archive*, Rice University: http://webcast.rice.edu/speeches/19620912kennedy.html (September 20, 2007).

[4]   "Cost of US Piloted Program" by Claude Lafleur, (Monday, March 8, 2010) *http://www.thespacereview.com/article/1579/1*

[5]   *Wikipedia*, s.v. "John F. Kennedy," last modified April 9, 2015: http://en.wikipedia.org/wiki/John_F._Kennedy.

[6]   "Sir Muhammad Iqbal's 1930 Presidential Address": Speeches, Writings, and Statements of Iqbal; *http://www.columbia.edu/itc/mealac/pritchett/00islamlinks/txt_iqbal_1930.html.* Retrieved 2006-12-19.

[7]   "Iqbal and Pakistan Movement", *http://www.allamaiqbal.com/person/movement/move_main.htm*

[8]   "Allama Iqbal Biography", "Allama Iqbal - Biography - Iqbal and Politics" (PHP). 26 May 2006.

[9]   "Iqbal and Pakistan Movement", http://www.allamaiqbal.com/person/movement/move_main.htm

[10]   Museum of Science; http://www.mos.org/sln/Leonardo/LeosMysteriousmachinery.html (1997)

[11] P&G Investors / Shareholder Relations: Purpose & People – The Power of Purpose, http://www.pg.com/company/who_we_are/ppv.shtml

[12] Gillette site; http://www.gillette.com/en-GB/#/international/

[13] Center for Business Planning; http://www.businessplans.org/Mission.html

[14] Google, About Google; http://www.google.com/about/

[15] WhatIs.com; http://whatis.techtarget.com/definition/googol-and-googolplex

[16] Center for Business Planning; http://www.businessplans.org/Mission.html

[17] MBA Tutorials; http://www.mba-tutorials.com/strategy/303-top-10-mission-statements.html

[18] Sony Mission Statement; http://www.sony.net/SonyInfo/

[19] Boeing Speeches; http://retailindustry.about.com/od/retailbestpractices/ig/Company-Mission-Statements/Boeing-Mission-Statement---Vision.htm; http://humanresources.about.com/cs/strategicplanning1/a/strategicplan_2.htm

[20] Walmart: Our Story; http://corporate.walmart.com/our-story/

[21] About.com: Human Resources; http://humanresources.about.com/cs/strategicplanning1/a/strategicplan_2.htm

[22] P&G Global Operations; http://www.pg.com/company/who_we_are/ppv.shtml

[23] Harvard University, "Harvard at a glance", http://www.harvard.edu/about/glance.php

[24] The Richest Man Who Ever Lived – King Solomon's Secret of Success, Wealth and Happiness by Steven K. Scott

[25] M&A Professor; http://maprofessor.blogspot.com/2009/09/disneymarvelp.html

[26] Book: *Put Your Dreams to the Test;* John C. Maxwell, page 26;

[27] Silicon India Blog: C K Prahalad: Distinguished Thinker and Visionary Passes Away; http://blogs.siliconindia.com/indianspices/Business/C-K-Prahalad-Distinguished-Thinker-and-Visionary-Passes-Away-bid-5VJ01D3p20092261.html

[28] *Wikipedia*, s.v. "Think and Grow Rich", last modified on 29 May 2015, http://en.wikipedia.org/wiki/Think_and_Grow_Rich

[29] *Wikipedia*, s.v. "Goal Setting", last modified on 8 June 2015, https://en.wikipedia.org/wiki/Goal_setting

[30] Goal Setting Guide, "SMART Goal Setting: A Surefire Way To Achieve Your Goals by Arina Nikitina", http://www.goal-setting-guide.com/smart-goal-setting-a-surefire-way-to-achieve-your-goals/

[31] My Article Archives, "Why People Fail to Achieve Their Goals" by Douglas Vermeeren, http://www.myarticlearchive.com/articles/7/189.htm

[32] *Wikipedia*, s.v. "Big Hairy Audacious Goals", last modified on 9 July 2015, http://en.wikipedia.org/wiki/Big_Hairy_Audacious_Goal

[33] *Wikipedia*, s.v. "Strategy", last modified on 18 May 2015, http://en.wikipedia.org/wiki/Strategy

[34] Harvard Business Review, "The Core Competence of the Corporation" by C.K. Prahalad and Gary Hamel, May/June 1990, https://hbr.org/1990/05/the-core-competence-of-the-corporation

[35] Dictionary.com, "Dictionary", 2015, http://dictionary.reference.com/browse/tactics?db=luna

[36] SlideShare, Strategy Versus Tactics Presentation by Jeremiah Josey, http://www.slideshare.net/jeremiahjosey/Strategy-versus-Tactics-Presentation-20081029

[37] *Wikipedia*, s.v. "Balanced Scorecard", last modified on 8 July 2015, http://en.wikipedia.org/wiki/Balanced_scorecard

[38] "CEO Swap: The $79 billion Plan", Last Updated: November 20, 2009, http://archive.fortune.com/2009/11/19/news/companies/procter_gamble_lafley.fortune/index.htm

[39] "Building Your Company's Vision" in Sep-Oct 1996 issue of Harvard Business Review; www.tecker.com/downloads/buildingvision.pdf

[40] F1Technical, "Formula One Engines" by Steven De Groote, last updated on 18 Jul 2009, http://www.f1technical.net/articles/4

[41] Leadership in the New World series, "Leadership in (Permanent) Crisis" (page 64) by Ronald Heifetz, Alexander Grashow, and Marty Linsky; Harvard Business Review Jul/Aug 09 Issue

[42] The Stockdale Paradox; Book *'Good to Great'* by *Jim Collins*; pages 83-85, First Edition, HarperCollins, 2001

[43] Point Lookout an email newsletter, "The Paradox of Confidence" by Rick Brenner, Last Modified on 08-Jul-2015, http://www.chacocanyon.com/pointlookout/090107.shtml

[44] Dictionary.com, "Virtuous Cycle", http://dictionary.reference.com/browse/virtuous%20circle

[45] BusinessDictionary.com, "Virtuous Cycle", http://www. businessdictionary.com/definition/virtuous-circle.html

[46] "Inside Procter & Gamble's New Values-Based Strategy" by Rosabeth Moss Kanter Sept 14, 2009, Harvard Business Review, http://blogs.hbr.org/kanter/2009/09/fall-like-a-lehman-rise-like-a.html

[47] P&G Investors / Shareholder Relations: Global Structure & Governance, Corporate Governance, http://www.pg.com/en_US/company/global_structure_operations/governance/index.shtml

[48] Harvard Business Review, Productivity, "Positive Intelligence" by Shawn Achor, January/February 2012 issue, http://hbr.org/2012/01/positive-intelligence/ar/1

[49] Harvard Business Review, Communication, "Good Communication That Blocks Learning" by Chris Argyris, July/August 1994 issue, https://hbr.org/1994/07/good-communication-that-blocks-learning

[50] Harvard Business Review, Leadership and Managing People, "Why should Anyone be Led by You?" by Robert Goffee and Gareth Jones, July/August 1994, https://hbr.org/2000/09/why-should-anyone-be-led-by-you

[51] Encyclopedia.com, "William Cooper Procter", Encyclopedia of World Biography 2004, http://www.encyclopedia.com/topic/William_Cooper_Procter.aspx

[52] P&G Investors / Shareholder Relations: Leadership Brands and Purpose & People; http://www.pg.com/en_US/brands/index.shtml?category=hair

[53] "Merck; Be Well", About Us, http://www.merck.com/about/home.html

[54] All About Science, "Darwin's Theory of Evolution – A Theory in Crisis"; http://www.darwins-theory-of-evolution.com/

[55] "Nelson Mandela", HISTORY, http://www.history.com/topics/nelson-mandela

[56] www.chinaview.cn, Business, "Interview: P&G Leaders See Opportunity in Crisis", June 23, 2009, http://news.xinhuanet.com/english/2009-02/23/content_10871635.htm

[57] Maver Management Group, Lessons from Procter and Gamble: Leaders, Nov 29, 2011 http://mavermanagement.blogspot.com/2011/11/lessons-from-procter-gamble-leaders.html

[58] Our Values and Principles, Procter and Gamble, http://www.pg.com/images/company/who_we_are/pdf/values_and_policies907.pdf

[59] Entrepreneur, "Should you Always Promote from within your Company?", Dec 20, 2014, http://www.entrepreneur.com/article/240486

[60] HR Marketer, "CEO or CHRO? Procter and Gamble's Top Brass Gets Human Resources", December 8, 2008, http://hrmarketer.blogspot.com/2009/12/ceo-or-chro-procter-and-gambles-top.html

[61] P&G.com, Value-Based Leadership, Bob McDonald, http://www.pg.com/en_US/downloads/company/executive_team/Bob_McDonald_Values-Based_Leadership.pdf

[62] "90/10 Principle", http://msa.medicine.iu.edu/files/2713/3236/9537/90-10Principle.pdf

[63] Scripting news, "Al Pacino's Inch By Inch speech from Any Given Sunday", http://essaysfromexodus.scripting.com/stories/storyReader$1492,

[64] Harvard Business Review, Social Responsibility, "Inside Procter & Gamble's New Values-Based Strategy", http://blogs.hbr.org/kanter/2009/09/fall-like-a-lehman-rise-like-a.html

[65] Human Capital Index®: Human Capital As a Lead Indicator of Shareholder Value, Watson Wyatt-2002, http://www.oswego.edu/~friedman/human_cap_index.pdf

[66] Russell Sage Foundation, "Trust in Schools: A Core Resource for Improvement" by Anthony S. Bryk and Barbara Schneider; https://www.russellsage.org/publications/trust-schools

[67] Stephen R Covey home, Posts tagged 'Emotional Bank Account', http://www.stephencovey.com/blog/?tag=emotional-bank-account

[68] Future of Human Resource Management, "From Business Partners to Driving Business Success: The Next Step in the Evolution of HR Management", (Chapter 12) by Wayne F. Cascio.

[69] World Population WORLDOMETER; http://www.worldometers.info/world-population/

[70] QuickMBA Knowledge to Power your Business, "The 7 Habits of Highly Effective People", http://www.quickmba.com/mgmt/7hab/

[71] Turtles of Karachi are protected, but what of their habitat? by Farhan Anwar, July 21, 2014, Tribune.

com.pk, http://tribune.com.pk/story/738490/
turtles-of-karachi-are-protected-but-what-of-their-habitat/

[72] Australian Transport Safety Bureau, "Oxygen cylinder failure and depressurisation - Boeing 747-438, VH-OJK, 475 km north-west of Manila, Philippines", 25 July 2008, http://www.atsb.gov.au/publications/investigation_reports/2008/aair/ao-2008-053.aspx

[73] *Wikipedia*, s.v. "Warren Buffett", last modified on 1 July 2015, http://en.wikipedia.org/wiki/Warren_Buffett

[74] "11 Interesting Facts About Warren Buffet", January 18, 2012, http://nedhardy.com/2012/01/18/11-interesting-facts-about-warren-buffet/

[75] *Wikipedia*, s.v. "John Wooden", last modified on 10 July 2015; http://en.wikipedia.org/wiki/John_Wooden

[76] members.toastmaster.org, "A Legendary Coach offers lessons in leadership: The Wooden Way", http://www.toastmasters.org/~/media/19FFD274E9594264AC48E98D47E67226.ashx

[77] slideshare.net, "Shift Happens" presentation by Karl Fisch; http://www.slideshare.net/jbrenman/shift-happens-33834

[78] Kotter International, "The 8-Step Process for Leading Change", http://www.kotterinternational.com/the-8-step-process-for-leading-change/

[79] Who Moved My Cheese, "An Amazing Way to Deal with Change in Your Work and in Your Life", by Dr. Spencer Johnson, http://classes.sdc.wsu.edu/classes/cstm301/readings/who%20moved%20my%20cheese.pd

[80] Memory Prices (1957–2015) by John C. MacCallum; http://www.jcmit.com/memoryprice.htm

[81] Moore's Law, Wikipedia; http://en.wikipedia.org/wiki/Moore's_law

[82] *Wikipedia*, s.v. "Caterpillar Inc.", https://en.wikipedia.org/wiki/Caterpillar_Inc.

[83] *Wikipedia*, s.v. "History of IBM", http://en.wikipedia.org/wiki/History_of_IBM

[84] The world's largest tire producers in FY 2014. http://www.statista.com/statistics/225677/revenue-of-the-leading-tire-producers-worldwide/

[85] Harvard Business Review, Research and Ideas, "The Dynamics of Standing Still: Firestone Tire & Rubber and the Radial Revolution"

by Donald Sull, November 27, 2000, http://hbswk.hbs.edu/item/1832.html

[86] Harvard Business Review, Organizational Culture, "Why Good Companies Go Bad" by Donald Sull, July/August 1999, https://hbr.org/1999/07/why-good-companies-go-bad

[87] Book "Revival of the Fittest" by Donald Sull, https://books.google.com.pk/books?id=_qKvUOZM5pYC&pg=PA14&lpg=PA14&dq=values+firestone+sull&source=bl&ots=zpF_D6 6KDy&sig=GZdCcCMEukyrpPgIxnh3BkbmW-4&hl=en&ei=n COOS63ZGMfs-#v=onepage&q=values%20firestone%20sull&f=false

[88] Tire Business, "Bridgestone marks 25th anniversary of Firestone 'merger'", Nov 9, 2013 http://www.tirebusiness.com/article/20130911/NEWS/130919974/section/crain-brands

Saad Amanullah Khan: Biography

Saad served as the Chief Executive Officer of Gillette Pakistan from 2007 to 2014 and has also worked with Procter & Gamble (P&G) for twenty years with assignments in Europe, Middle East and Pakistan. He has an MBA in Finance from The University of Michigan and two engineering degrees; Systems  Engineering (Automation) and Computer Science Engineering.

Saad has twice been elected President of the American Business Council (ABC), the largest single country business chamber. He conceptualized and led the first two ABC Economic Summits in 2011 and 2012 to help debate and discuss Pakistan's most troubling economic issues. He has also served twice on the Executive Committee of the Overseas Investors Chamber of Commerce and Industry (OICCI), the largest foreign chamber and has held positions of Chairman of Intellectual Property (IP), Corporate Social Responsibility (CSR) & Taxation Committees in both chambers.

He is currently the Chairman of the Board for the South East Asia Leadership Academy (SEALA), board member of State Life Insurance Company of Pakistan, and ZIL Corporation.

Saad strongly supports entrepreneurship and innovation. He is the founding Chairman and Board Member of Pakistan Innovation Foundation (PIF), a private sector entity to promote science based innovation culture in Pakistan as well as Vice President and founder of the National Entrepreneurship Working Group (NEW-G), with an aim to map Pakistan entrepreneurship ecosystem, formulating a national entrepreneurship strategy and to act as a national platform dedicated to promoting entrepreneurship. Saad is also the President of Public Interest Law Association of Pakistan (PILAP).

Saad is also very active on the social responsibility front with board or advisory roles in the following social enterprises:

1. Founding Member of the Agha Khan Hospital's Patient Welfare Committee as well as President and Founder of Helper's of HOPE, a committee to collect funds for the NGO, Health Oriented Preventive Education (HOPE), which runs hospitals, schools, maternity and welfare centers.
2. Executive Committee member of Patient Aid Foundation (PAF), a private group of volunteers who help the largest government hospital in the region Jinnah Post Graduate Medical Center (JPMC) as well as Victims Assistance Program (VAP).
3. Board member of the following: Naya Jeevan (micro insurance for the poor); LettuceBee Kids (enable street kids to reach their full potential); Ladiesfund (focused on women empowerment); EcoEnergy (providing solar solution in places without electricity); AIESEC (youth leadership development)
4. Advisor and supporter of: Family Education Service Foundation (deaf education); Possibilities Schools; Network of Organizations Working for People with Disabilities; Teach for Pakistan; Peace through Prosperity (grassroots skill building)); Kashif Iqbal Thalassemia Care Center, Sub-e-Nau (spinal cord injury).

Saad is an active speaker at different forums in Pakistan and abroad. He focuses on topics related to Leadership, Vision, Social Entrepreneurship, Governance, and Pakistan economic issues. Saad has also founded three companies, Alamut Consulting (sustainability and governance of Social Enterprises), Vanguard Matrix (software development house) and Big Thick Burgerz (fast food).

This is Saad's first formally published book. In addition, he has published research papers on diverse topics such as *Why Some Democracies Don't Survive?*, *Quran for Inquisitive Minds*, *Pakistan an Economic Powerhouse*. He is also an active contributor in local newspapers and magazines with articles focused on economic growth, democracy and other leadership related topics.

··········—————— ——————··········

Printed in the United States
By Bookmasters